More Praise for Thom Hartmann

"Thom is a national treasure. Read him, embrace him, learn from .... ullow him as we all work for social change."

—**Robert Greenwald, political activist and founder and president of Brave New Films**

"Right through the worst of the Bush years and into the present, Thom Hartmann has been one of the very few voices constantly willing to tell the truth. Rank him up there with Jon Stewart, Bill Moyers, and Paul Krugman for having the sheer persistent courage of his convictions."

—**Bill McKibben, author of *Eaarth***

"With the ever-growing influence of corporate CEOs and their right-wing allies in all aspects of American life, Hartmann's work is more relevant than ever. Throughout his career, Hartmann has spoken compellingly about the value of people-centered democracy and the challenges that millions of ordinary Americans face today as a result of a dogma dedicated to putting profit above all else. This collection is a rousing call for Americans to work together and put people first again."

—**Richard Trumka, President, AFL-CIO**

"Through compelling personal stories, Hartmann presents a dramatic and deeply disturbing picture of humans as a profoundly troubled species. Hope lies in his inspiring vision of our enormous unrealized potential and his description of the path to its realization."

—**David Korten, author of *Agenda for a New Economy*, *The Great Turning*, and *When Corporations Rule the World***

"Thom Hartmann is a creative thinker and committed small-d democrat. He has dealt with a wide range of topics throughout his life, and this book provides an excellent cross section. *The Thom Hartmann Reader* will make people both angry and motivated to act."

—**Dean Baker, economist and author of *Plunder and Blunder*, *False Profits*, and *Taking Economics Seriously***

"In an age rife with media-inspired confusion and political cowardice, we yearn for a decent, caring, deeply human soul whose grasp of the problems confronting us provides a light by which we can make our way through the quagmire of lies, distortions, pandering, and hollow self-puffery that strips the American Dream of its promise. How lucky we are, then, to have access to the wit, wisdom, and willingness of Thom Hartmann, who shares with us here that very light, grown out of his own life experience."

—**Mike Farrell, actor, political activist, and author of *Just Call Me Mike* and *Of Mule and Man***

The
Thom
Hartmann
Reader

The
Thom
Hartmann
Reader

Thom Hartmann

Edited by Tai Moses

BK

Berrett–Koehler Publishers, Inc.
San Francisco
a BK Currents book

The editor and the publisher are grateful to include the following copyrighted material in this collection.

"The Edison Gene," "How to Raise a Fully Human Child" from *The Edison Gene* by Thom Hartmann, copyright © 2003 by Thom Hartmann, published by Inner Traditions International, www.innertraditions.com.

"Older and Younger Cultures," "Life in a Tipi," "Starting Salem in New Hampshire," "Uganda Sojourn," "Russia: A New Seed Planted among Thorns" from *The Prophet's Way* by Thom Hartmann, copyright © 1997, 2004 by Thom Hartmann, published by Inner Traditions International, www.innertraditions.com.

"Walking the Blues Away" from *Walking Your Blues Away* by Thom Hartmann, copyright © 2006 by Thom Hartmann, published by Inner Traditions International, www.innertraditions.com.

"Younger-Culture Drugs of Control," "The Secret of 'Enough,'" "The Death of the Trees," "Something Will Save Us" from *The Last Hours of Ancient Sunlight* by Thom Hartmann, copyright © 1998, 1999, 2004 by Mythical Research, Inc. Used by permission of Harmony Books, a division of Random House, Inc.

"Democracy Is Inevitable" from *What Would Jefferson Do?: A Return to Democracy* by Thom Hartmann, copyright © 2004 by Mythical Research, Inc. Used by permission of Harmony Books, a division of Random House, Inc.

"The Atmosphere," "Caral, Peru: A Thousand Years of Peace," "Sociopathic Paychecks" from *Threshold: The Crisis of Western Culture* by Thom Hartmann, copyright © 2009 by Thom Hartmann. Used by permission of Viking Penguin, a division of Penguin Group (USA) Inc. For on-line information about other Penguin Group (USA) books and authors, see the Internet website at http://www.penguin.com

"After the Crash" reprinted from *Imagine,* edited by Marianne Williamson. Copyright © 2000 by Global Renaissance Alliance. Permission granted by Rodale, Inc., Emmaus, PA 18098.

Berrett-Koehler Publishers, Inc.
235 Montgomery Street, Suite 650
San Francisco, CA 94104-2916
Tel: (415) 288-0260   Fax: (415) 362-2512   Orders: (800) 929-2929.
www.bkconnection.com

Berrett-Koehler and the BK logo are registered trademarks of Berrett-Koehler Publishers, Inc.

Distributed to the book trade in the United States by Ingram Publisher Services.

Printed in the United States of America

Library of Congress Cataloging-in-Publication Data
Hartmann, Thom, 1951-
    The Thom Hartmann reader / Thom Hartmann ; edited by Tai Moses. — 1st ed.
        p. cm.
    Includes bibliographical references and index.
    ISBN 978-1-57675-761-1 (pbk. : alk. paper)
1. United States—Politics and government—1989- 2. United States—Social conditions—1980-
3. Political culture—United States. 4. Social problems—United States. 5. United States—Economic conditions. 6. Ecology. 7. Climatic changes. 8. Hartmann, Thom, 1951-—Travel. I. Moses, Tai.
II. Title
    E839.5.H378 2011
    973.927—dc23

                                                                                          2011027608

16   15   14   13   12   11   10   9   8   7   6   5   4   3   2   1

Cover photo by Kindra Scanlon. Cover design by Richard Wilson.
Interior design and composition by Gary Palmatier, Ideas to Images.
Elizabeth von Radics, copyeditor; Mike Mollett, proofreader; Medea Minnich, indexer.

To Louise, forever

Contents

Editor's Note

THE CHAPTERS, ESSAYS, AND ARTICLES IN THIS VOLUME REPRE-
sent the best, most revealing, and accessible examples of Thom
Hartmann's writing. I don't pretend neutrality; my first criterion for
shaping the book was to select the chapters I loved the most, the ones
I returned to again and again while reading Hartmann's work. They
are also the pieces I believe most relevant to people's lives today, pieces
that will make you think and feel, that you may want to discuss and
share. The subject matter is various, the ideas provocative, the opinions spirited. Taken all at once, it's a heady brew, so this is a book to
savor, to dip in and out of at will.

The *Reader* is arranged thematically, divided into six sections
inspired by Hartmann's chief preoccupations. The brief essays that
introduce each section provide some context and background for
what follows. Some pieces have been edited for clarity and flow and
to enhance the reading experience. In some cases slight excisions have
been made, and some chapters appear in a shorter form than in the
original source material.

Those who are familiar with Thom Hartmann will find some
surprises here. For those just discovering him, this sampler will be the
ideal introduction. One of Hartmann's gifts is that he makes his readers and listeners feel that they are a part of the conversation. This book
is a conversation in progress—we invite you to join in.

Tai Moses

Introduction:
The Stories of Our Times

MY WIFE, LOUISE, AND I CAME OF AGE IN A WORLD THAT WAS fundamentally different from the world in which today's young people are growing up. We both left home around the age of 16, with no support, inheritance, or stipend, and yet we were still able to make it in the world.

We raised three children, our greatest legacy, and started a series of successful businesses, either from scratch or with money I borrowed first from a credit card and later, when we had a bit of a track record, from local, community banks. Most of those businesses still exist; we long ago sold our shares and moved on, taking our retirement "in installments," in the model of John D. MacDonald's Travis McGee (we lived at slip 18 in a houseboat community in Portland, Oregon).

Louise and I were fortunate to have come of age in the 1960s in America. We had a quarter-century of incredible opportunity before the ideologies and the policies of political and economic predators began dismantling the American Dream for all but those Thomas Jefferson referred to as "the well born and the well bred."

Our parents remembered World War II (Louise's dad was in the US Navy, mine in the US Army), and both her dad and mine used the GI Bill and the Federal Housing Administration and other "big government" programs to leverage themselves into the middle class. Her father went through law school on the GI Bill and ended up an assistant attorney general for the state of Michigan, after coming from a home of poverty in Detroit. My father's story is told in this book. Our parents also remembered the Republican Great Depression of the 1930s, albeit as children, and our grandparents told us both many stories of life in those days and the lessons they learned from it.

Just 40 years ago, Louise worked her way through college as a waitress at a Howard Johnson's and I as a minimum-wage DJ (neither of us graduated, but that's another story unrelated to economics). I picked apples in White Cloud, Michigan, with migrant workers one summer; worked in a gas station; and washed dishes at Bob's Big Boy while I was spinning records at WITL and WVIC. That was enough to cover the cost of higher education in the late sixties. My friends who moved to pre-Reagan California were able to attend the University of California system—one of the world's best—for free.

Student debt? The idea was alien to Americans for most of our history, until the predators got into the system, for-profit colleges began to proliferate (their students are about twice as likely to default as students of nonprofit and state institutions), and banksters decided to get into the education business. Last year student loan debt in America exceeded credit card debt for the first time in history—more than $1 trillion. It's creating a generation of serfs for the multinational corporations—kids so afraid to challenge or leave their employers that they are little better off than the indentured workers who came here in the nineteenth century from Europe and lived lives of near-poverty and insecurity.

When Louise and I began our family, we were debt-free—broke, but debt-free. Today the system's rigged so that young people can't even imagine such a thing, and banksters are making billions on student loans.

* * *

I remember sitting with Louise and our son almost two decades ago, as a psychologist ticked off the symptoms of attention-deficit disorder (ADD). With each one I thought, *That's me, too!* And then he told my son, who was just hitting his teenage years, that ADD was such a serious mental problem—a "disorder" and a "deficiency"—that instead of pursuing his passion, a career in science, he should consider car mechanics.

"Be sure to work on foreign-made, high-end cars," the well-meaning doc said. "That's where the money is. You wouldn't believe how much they charge to fix my Mercedes!"

My son was in tears, and I was outraged.

This experience led to several years of intense research. I took with me the background of having been executive director for five years of a residential treatment facility for emotionally disturbed and abused children, most of whom had some sort of "hyperactive" or ADD-like diagnosis. I developed the firm conviction and gathered some solid evidence suggesting that ADD wasn't a disorder at all—a hypothesis that has now been well corroborated. It led to my writing seven books on ADD, most about kids but one—*Focus Your Energy: Hunting for Success in Business with Attention Deficit Disorder*—specifically about how adults with ADD could be more successful than their "nonafflicted" peers.

As for our son, he recently graduated with a master's degree in the biological sciences.

Realizing the power that came from simply reframing a story, I moved my attention to the stories we all tell ourselves about the world and our relationship to it. That led to my book *The Last Hours of Ancient Sunlight: Waking Up to Personal and Global Transformation,* in which I come to the conclusion that it's not our behavior that's killing us and so much life on the planet; it's not our technology or even our wasteful ways of living. All of these are just symptoms that derive from our stories, which over the millennia have become, in many cases, highly dysfunctional. Only by changing our stories—our understanding of our relationship to everyone and everything else—can we stop the destruction and begin the process of healing our planet and ourselves.

The biggest collection of controlling stories, of course, comes from religion and politics. The former has been a lifelong fascination that led to my writing *The Prophet's Way: A Guide to Living in the Now,* a book chiefly about my spiritual mentor, Gottfried Müller, who passed away a few years ago at the age of 93, leaving behind the international Salem work.

I'd largely ignored the political stories for most of my adult life, outside of my Students for a Democratic Society years in the sixties and lengthy discussions/debates with my Republican father. But after Louise and I sold our last business in Atlanta and moved to rural Vermont, we drove to Michigan to visit family for Thanksgiving. All the way there, we searched the radio dial for an intelligent conversation to listen to, but city after city all we found was Sean Hannity at a Habitat for Humanity site (he called it "Hannity for Humanity"), telling us that no "liberal" was ever going to live in the house they were helping build.

It was a bizarre experience. Having worked in radio back in the sixties and seventies, I wrote an article, "Talking Back to Talk Radio," about how liberal talk radio might succeed, if done right. Sheldon and Anita Drobney read my article online, and as Sheldon noted in his book *The Road to Air America: Breaking the Right Wing Stranglehold on Our Nation's Airwaves* (in which he reprints the article), it became the first template for a business plan for that ultimately ill-fated network.

But rather than wait the almost two years it took the Drobneys to launch Air America, Louise and I, with the help of a local radio guy and friend, Rama Schneider, looked around the state and found a station in Burlington, Vermont, that was willing to put us on the air. The slot was Saturday mornings at 10 a.m., right after the swap-and-shop, so many of our callers, instead of discussing politics, wanted to know, "Is that John Deere still available?"

Ed Asner was kind enough to come on as a guest, helping us make a tape that caught the interest of the i.e. America Radio Network run out of Detroit by the United Auto Workers. Suddenly, broadcasting from our living room in Montpelier, Vermont, with a studio I'd thrown together mostly from parts bought on eBay, we were on the air nationally, including Sirius, taking on Rush Limbaugh (and beating him in some markets) in the noon–to–3 p.m. slot ever since.

When we bought our house in Montpelier, we found in the attic a 20-volume set of the collected writings of Thomas Jefferson, published in 1909 and badly water damaged but still quite readable. I spent almost two years immersed in that incredible man's brain, from his autobiography to his letters to his work as president. Inspired, I wrote two books: *What Would Jefferson Do?: A Return to Democracy* and *Unequal Protection: How Corporations Became "People"—and How You Can Fight Back.*

Applying the lessons of nearly a decade spent in the whirlwind of national and international politics, I wrote *Rebooting the American Dream: 11 Ways to Rebuild Our Country,* one of my favorite books. In 11 chapters *Rebooting* follows a model Alexander Hamilton first used to set forth 11 steps we could take to restore and rebuild this once-great nation. Combining my experience and training in psychology and neuro-linguistic programming (NLP), I wrote *Cracking the Code: How to Win Hearts, Change Minds, and Restore America's Original Vision,* a book on political messaging and strategy. And I've been watching how the first few years of the Obama administration have not produced the core true changes necessary in our trade, industrial, and fiscal structures. I'm so convinced we're staring down the barrel of another disastrous Great Depression that I'm working on a book about that right now.

I once read that wisdom is the result of knowledge tempered and shaped by experience. This year is my sixtieth on this planet, and while I'm loath to call myself wise, over the past decade I've begun to understand the concept in a way I never could have when I was younger. Wisdom requires that an arc of history be both superimposed on knowledge and lived. I mention this not so much in my own context but as a universal. The stories you're about to read cover, roughly, the span of time from 1968 to 2005. While they're our stories, they're also stories of our times. They cover the arc of what was, what is, and what could be—much of it as I've lived through it or learned directly from those who did, including a great deal of wisdom I found in those older than me. May it be your wisdom now, too.

Thom Hartmann
Washington, DC, May 2011

PART I
We the People

I T'S HARD TO PIGEONHOLE THOM HARTMANN. HE HAS A UNIQUE synthesis of qualities not often found in one person: a scholar's love of history, a scientist's zeal for facts, a visionary's seeking after truth, an explorer's appetite for adventure and novelty. While he advocates a return to simpler, egalitarian values of community, he is no dreamy idealist. He is a fierce critic of the powerful corporate interests that have taken over our culture and corrupted our politics. He is a merciless dissector of our government's hypocrisies, no matter which party occupies the White House. His dreams for this country are the same ones that Thomas Jefferson had two and a quarter centuries ago, dreams that Hartmann describes here in "The Radical Middle." In an eloquent, articulate voice, he writes in the hopes of guiding the reader toward increased responsibility and consciousness. He is interested in changing not just our behavior and actions but the thoughts and the attitudes that are at the root of widespread social problems. What he offers us is a radically different way of thinking.

While I was reading through the books, essays, and articles that make up Thom Hartmann's published body of work, I began to distinguish several threads that run throughout the work, weaving in and out, and illuminating Hartmann's unique vision. All of these threads are represented in the pieces that make up this collection, but the most vivid of them, the one that unites and defines all the others, is this: *democracy is the natural state of nature and of mankind.*

The study of democracy is one of the pillars of Hartmann's life. He spent years immersed in the writings and the correspondence of Jefferson and the other Founders, researching the family tree of the American democratic experiment. He has studied ancient democracies all over the world, including the Iroquois Confederacy, which inspired Jefferson. Going back further he read the histories recorded by the first-century Roman senator Tacitus. He has spent time with indigenous and aboriginal peoples, the remnants of what he calls "older cultures," and observed that they tend to live in egalitarian societies. He has examined how and why democracies fail; he understands the components of peace and the causes of war.

Investigating the biology of democracy, he has delved into animal studies showing that cooperation, not dominance, is the natural tendency of many species. In his book *What Would Jefferson Do?*, from which "Democracy Is Inevitable" is drawn, he exploded many of the most entrenched myths about American democracy, making short work of the neocons' beloved notion that dominance is the natural way of the world, by showing that over time democratic systems will always push out despots and authoritarian governments.

He is a passionate advocate of the democratic way of life, of cooperation, person to person, on an individual level because democracy is, after all, personal. It supports and nurtures us, and we in turn support and nurture it. Democracy is our most cherished bond, and it is the most cherished of Thom Hartmann's themes. Not for nothing does the highest law of our land, the US Constitution, begin with the words *We the People*. But We the People are in trouble today. Our economy no longer works for middle- and working-class Americans. As Hartmann describes in "The Story of Carl," the "cons" have damaged our democracy and weakened our country's once-vibrant middle class with the policies of Reaganomics: financial deregulation, tax cuts for the richest Americans, the destruction of our manufacturing sector, freezing the minimum wage, and undermining labor laws.

The media is also in trouble. In Hartmann's trenchant analysis of the state of our media, "An Informed and Educated Electorate," he analyzes how the corporate news media has abandoned its vital public-service mission and caters only to what people want, not what they need. After Ronald Reagan revoked the Fairness Doctrine, we saw the rise of right-wing shock jocks on conservative talk radio and the rapid erosion of the national conversation about politics into screaming matches, name-calling, and flat-out lying. Hartmann further chips away at the Reagan myth by showing how the great communicator was opposed to public education and subverted Jefferson's intention that every American should have a decent education, free of cost.

In "Whatever Happened to Cannery Row?" Hartmann uses John Steinbeck's classic novel as a vehicle to visit the recent past, America before Reagan, "a time of challenge and a time of opportunity." While the piece is a paean to Hartmann's parents and a lost era, it also drives home his deeper point: our country has gone off course, drifted off in a "dream-fog of consumerism"; and in 30 short years, America has become unrecognizable, our uniqueness replaced by a vast corporate footprint of chain stores and shopping malls. To find out who we are, we don't need to completely reinvent ourselves—we just need to wake up and look to the past, salvage what was most precious, and bring it back home.

The Radical Middle

From ThomHartmann.com

THE FOUNDERS OF THIS NATION REPRESENTED THE FIRST RADI-cal Middle. Back then they called it "being liberal." As George Washington said, "As Mankind becomes more liberal, they will be more apt to allow that all those who conduct themselves as worthy members of the community are equally entitled to the protections of civil government. I hope ever to see America among the foremost nations of justice and liberality."

They didn't want King George or his military or corporate agents snooping in their houses, mails, or private matters; preventing them from organizing together and speaking out in public in protest of government actions; imprisoning them without access to attorneys, due process, or trials by juries of their peers; or reserving rights to himself that they felt should rest with the people or their elected representatives. (They ultimately wrote all of these in the Bill of Rights in our Constitution.)

They also didn't want giant transnational corporations dominating their lives or their local economies. The Radical Middle has always believed in fairness and democracy and understood that completely unrestrained business activity and massive accumulations of wealth into a very few hands can endanger democratic institutions.

As James Madison said, "There is an evil which ought to be guarded against in the indefinite accumulation of property from the capacity of holding it in perpetuity by . . . corporations. The power of all corporations ought to be limited in this respect. The growing wealth acquired by them never fails to be a source of abuses."

Similarly, John Adams wrote that when "economic power became concentrated in a few hands, then political power flowed to those possessors and away from the citizens, ultimately resulting in an oligarchy or tyranny."

Thomas Paine, among others, wrote at length about the dangers to a free people of the massive accumulation of wealth, and following the excesses of the Gilded Age—which led to massive corruption of the American government by corporate and wealth-based interests— laws were put into place limiting the size and the behavior of corporations and taxing inheritance of the most massive of family estates so that a new hereditary aristocracy wouldn't emerge in the nation that had thrown off the economic and political oppressions of the hereditary aristocracy of England.

The Radical Middle always believed in the idea of a commons— the things that we all own collectively and administer the way we want through our elected representatives. The commons includes our parks, roads, police, fire, schools, and our government itself; our ability to vote in fair and transparent elections; our military and defense; our systems for protecting our air, water, food, and pharmaceuticals; our ability to retire in safety if we've worked hard and played the game by the rules; and the security of knowing that an illness won't financially wipe us out.

Regardless of electoral politics (since both of the major political parties often overlook these values, and both have become corrupted by wealth and corporate influence), poll after poll shows that the vast majority of Americans embrace the values of the Radical Middle.

In recent years America has been hijacked by the Radical Right. Corporations now write most of our legislation. Our elected representatives cater to the interests of wealth rather than what is best for the commons we collectively own or what will sustain that bulwark of democracy known as the middle class. They have, in large part, seized control of our media, wiped out our family farms, and wiped out small, middle-class-owned businesses from our towns and cities. They seek a "merger of corporate and state interests"—a definition Benito Mussolini used for what he called "fascism."

The Radical Right has even gone so far as to use sophisticated psychological programming tools, like Newt Gingrich's infamous "word list," to paint the Radical Middle as some sort of insidious anti-Americanism.

We in the Radical Middle are calling for nothing less than a restoration of democracy, of government of, by, and for We the People, in a world that works for all.

The Story of Carl

From *Screwed: The Undeclared War against the Middle Class*

ARL LOVED BOOKS AND HE LOVED HISTORY. AFTER SPENDING two years in the army as part of the American occupation forces in Japan immediately after World War II, Carl was hoping to graduate from college and teach history—perhaps even at the university level—if he could hang on to the GI Bill and his day job long enough to get his PhD. But in 1950, when he'd been married just a few months, the surprise came that forced him to drop out of college: his wife was pregnant with their first child.

This was an era when husbands worked, wives tended the home, and being a good father and provider was one of the highest callings to which a man could aspire. Carl dropped out of school, kept his 9-to-5 job at a camera shop, and got a second job at a metal fabricating plant, working with molten metal from 7:00 p.m. to 4:00 a.m. For much of his wife's pregnancy and his newborn son's first year, he slept three hours a night and caught up on the weekends, but in the process he earned enough to get them an apartment and prepare for the costs of raising a family. Over the next 45 years, he continued to work in the steel and machine industry, in the later years as a bookkeeper/manager for a Michigan tool-and-die company as three more sons were born.

Carl knew he was doing the right thing when he took that job in the factory, and he did it enthusiastically. Because the auto industry was unionized, he found he was able to support his entire family—all four sons—on one paycheck. He had fully funded health insurance, an annual vacation, and a good pension waiting for him when he retired. Carl had become a member of the middle class. He may not have achieved his personal dream of teaching history, but he had achieved the American Dream. He was self-sufficient and free.

Working with molten metal could be dangerous, but the dangers were apparent, and Carl took every precaution to protect himself so that he could return home safe to his family. What he didn't realize, however, was that the asbestos used at the casting operation was an insidious poison. He didn't realize that the asbestos industry had known for decades that the stuff could kill but would continue to profitably market it for another 20 years while actively using its financial muscle to keep the general public in the dark and prevent the government from interfering.

A couple of years ago, Carl tripped on the stairs and ended up in the hospital with a compression fracture of his spine. He figured that fall also caused the terrible pain he'd been experiencing in his abdomen. The doctors, however, discovered that his lungs were filled with mesothelioma, a rare form of lung cancer that is almost always caused by exposure to asbestos. Mesothelioma is terminal, and its victims die by slow and painful suffocation.

Just because some corporation put profit before people, Carl got screwed.

I was Carl's first child.

An Undeclared Way

My dad faced a painful death, but at least his job in a union shop left him with health care after retirement. Most Americans don't even have that reassurance anymore. More than 45 million Americans don't have health insurance to cover expenses for a serious illness, and 5 million lost their health insurance between 2001 and 2005. And it's not just illness that worries most Americans today. Americans are working more and making less. It's getting harder and harder to just get by.

There's a reason for the pain Americans are suffering.

The America my dad grew up in put people before profits. The America he lives in now puts profits before people.

In my dad's America, 35 percent of working people were union members who got a living wage, health insurance, and defined-benefits pensions. These union benefits lifted all boats because they set the floor for employment; for every union job, there was typically a non-union job with similar pay and benefits (meaning roughly 70 percent of the American workforce back then could raise a family on a single paycheck). People who were disabled and couldn't work could live on Social Security payments, and the elderly knew they would have a safe retirement, paid for by pensions, Social Security, and Medicare. The gap between the richest and the poorest shrunk rather than widened.

That America is disappearing fast. The minimum wage is not a living wage. Workers are now expected to pay for their own health insurance and their own retirement. Pension plans are disappearing—30,000 General Motors employees lost theirs in 2005—and there's continued talk of privatizing Social Security. The safety net is ripping apart, and the results are that the middle class is shrinking. The rich are once again getting richer, and the poor are getting poorer:

■ The inflation-adjusted average annual pay of a CEO went up from $7,773,000 to $9,600,000 from 2002 to 2004. Meanwhile, from 2000 to 2004, the inflation-adjusted median annual household income went down from $46,058 to $44,389. In other words, ordinary people's income went *down* by $1,669 while CEO pay went up by $1,827,000.[1]

■ From 2001 to 2005, America has lost 2,818,000 manufacturing jobs. If you don't count jobs produced by the military-industrial complex, the number of private-sector jobs created since 2001 has *decreased* by 1,160,000.[2]

■ Although 67 percent of large employers (more than 500 employees) offer a traditional pension, that is down from 91 percent two decades ago, and it's dropping fast as more companies freeze pensions and turn instead to 401(k)s.[3] Only 6 percent of Americans working in the private sector can rely on a defined pension,[4] and 76 percent of Baby Boomers say they don't think they are very prepared to meet their retirement expenses.[5]

You don't need the numbers because you probably already know someone who has been forced out of the middle class. Roger, for instance, who once was a vice president of research and development for a software engineering company, lost his job during the dot-com bust and never got it back. After being unemployed for seven years, he's thinking of getting a job as a "landscape engineer"—that's a gardener—at a tenth of his former salary.

Or there's the case of Bob, a college graduate who has been holding three jobs for the past five years, one full-time as a bookstore clerk, two part-time. Even though he works 60 hours a week, he doesn't make enough money to rent his own apartment (he rents a room in a shared flat) and he can't afford health insurance. He hopes his allergies don't turn into asthma because he can't afford the medication he would need for that.

Too many Americans are just holding on. Consider Amy: Divorced from her alcoholic husband, she has gone back to school full-time to become a teacher; she earns a living by catering on the weekends. A single mother, she and her daughter share a studio apartment. Amy has neither health insurance nor child care and no nearby relatives—she relies on neighbors to take care of her daughter. One major illness and Amy would be homeless.

And then there are most of the rest of us, who have good jobs but still don't feel secure about the future. Ralph and Sally both get health insurance through their jobs, but their mortgage eats up more than 60 percent of their income, and the clothes and the necessities they buy for their two kids consume whatever might be left after groceries and utilities. They have health insurance but no pension. Their retirement is based on the few thousand dollars a year they can put into their IRAs. They wonder how they will be able to send their kids to college and afford to retire.

Today a man like my dad couldn't support a family of six on one paycheck. The middle class my dad belonged to is on its deathbed. Meanwhile, sitting around the pool, waiting for the dividend checks to roll in (while paying a maximum 15 percent income tax), the corporate class grows even wealthier.

How can this be?

How is it that companies could sell asbestos when they knew it would kill people? Why do people go hungry in America, the world's wealthiest nation? Why is it that people like you and me who work long, full days cannot afford to get sick, cannot buy houses, and cannot send their kids to college? What's happened to the middle class?

These questions are about our economy, but the answer is about who we are as a country.

Democracy and the Middle Class

The most ancient form of democracy is found among virtually all indigenous peoples of the world. It's the way humans have lived for more than 150,000 years. There are no rich and no poor among most tribal people—everybody is "middle class." There is also little hierarchy. The concept of "chief" is one that Europeans brought with them to America—which in large part is what produced so much confusion in the 1600s and 1700s in America as most Native American tribes would never delegate absolute authority to any one person to sign a treaty. Instead decisions were made by consensus in these most ancient cauldrons of democracy.

The Founders of this nation, and the Framers of our Constitution, were heavily influenced and inspired by the democracy they saw all around them. Much of the US Constitution is based on the Iroquois Confederacy—the five (later six) tribes who occupied territories from New England to the edge of the Midwest. It was a democracy with elected representatives, an upper and lower house, and a supreme court (made up entirely of women, who held final say in five of the six tribes).

As Benjamin Franklin noted to his contemporaries at the Constitutional Convention: "It would be a very strange thing if Six Nations of Ignorant Savages should be capable of forming a Scheme for such an Union and be able to execute it in such a manner, as that it has subsisted Ages, and appears indissoluble, and yet a like union should be impracticable for ten or a dozen English colonies."

The Framers modeled the oldest democracies, and the oldest forms of the middle class, and thus helped create the truly widespread and strong first middle class in the history of modern civilization.

Back in Europe, however, the sort of democracy the Framers were borrowing and inventing, and even the existence of a middle class itself, was considered unnatural. For most of the 7,000 years of recorded human history, what we call a middle class is virtually unheard of—as was democracy. Throughout most of the history of what we call civilization, an unrestrained economy and the idea of hierarchical social organization has always produced a small ruling elite and a large number of nearly impoverished workers.

Up until the founding of America, the middle class was considered unnatural by many political philosophers. Thomas Hobbes wrote in his 1651 magnum opus *Leviathan* that the world was better off with the rule of the few over the many, even if that meant that the many were impoverished. Without a strong and iron-fisted ruler, Hobbes wrote, there would be "no place for industry . . . no arts, no letters, no society." Because Hobbes believed that ordinary people couldn't govern themselves, he believed that most people would be happy to exchange personal freedom and economic opportunity for the ability to live in safety and security. For the working class to have both freedom *and* security, Hobbes suggested, was impossible.

Our nation's Founders disagreed. They believed in the rights of ordinary people to self-determination, so they created a form of government where We the People rule. They declared that all people, and not just the elite, have the right to "life, liberty, and the pursuit of happiness." (In that declaration, Thomas Jefferson replaced John Locke's famous "life, liberty, and property" with "life, liberty, and *happiness*"— the first time the word had ever appeared in the founding document of any nation.) They believed that We the People could create a country founded on personal freedom and economic opportunity for all. The

Founders believed in the power of a middle class; and in defiance of Hobbes and the conventional wisdom of Europe, they believed that democracy and a middle class were the "natural state of man."

As John Quincy Adams argued before the Supreme Court in 1841 on behalf of freeing rebelling slaves in the *Amistad* case, he stood before the justices and pointed to a copy of the Declaration of Independence:

> That DECLARATION says that every man is "endowed by his Creator with certain inalienable rights," and that "among these are life, liberty, and the pursuit of happiness." . . . I will not here discuss the right or the rights of slavery, but I say that the doctrine of Hobbes, that War is the natural state of man, has for ages been exploded, as equally disclaimed and rejected by the philosopher and the Christian. That it is utterly incompatible with any theory of human rights, and especially with the rights which the Declaration of Independence proclaims as self-evident truths.

It turns out that the Founders knew something Hobbes didn't know: political democracy and an economic middle class is the natural state of humankind. Indeed, it's the natural state of the entire animal kingdom.

For example, biologists used to think that animal societies were ruled by alpha males. Recent studies, however, have found that while it's true that alpha males (and females, in some species) have the advantage in courtship rituals, that's where their power ends. Biologists Tim Roper and L. Conradt discovered that animals don't follow a leader but instead move together.[6]

James Randerson did a follow-up study with red deer to prove the point.[7] How does a herd of deer decide it's time to stop grazing and go toward the watering hole? As they're grazing, various deer point their bodies in seemingly random directions, until it comes time to go drink. Then individuals begin to graze while facing one of several watering holes. When a majority of deer are pointing toward one particular watering hole, they all move in that direction. Randerson saw instances where the alpha deer was actually one of the last to move toward the hole rather than one of the first.

When I interviewed Tim Roper about his research at the University of Sussex in the United Kingdom, he told me that when his findings were first published, scientists from all over the world called to tell him that they were seeing the same thing with their research subjects. Birds flying in flocks aren't following a leader but monitoring the motions of those around them for variations in the flight path; when more than 50 percent have moved in a particular direction—even if it's only a quarter-inch in one direction or another—the entire flock "suddenly" veers off that way. It's the same with fish and even with swarms of gnats. Roper said that his colleagues were telling him that from ants to gorillas, democracy is the norm among animals. Just like with indigenous human societies—which have had hundreds of thousands of years of trial and error to work out the best ways to live—democracy is the norm among animals, and (other than for the Darwinian purpose of finding the best mate) hierarchy/kingdom is the rarity.

Thus, we discover, this close relationship between the middle class and democracy is burned into our DNA—along with that of the entire animal kingdom (an ironic term, given this new information). In a democracy there may be an elite (like the alpha male deer), but they don't rule the others. Instead the group is ruled by the vast middle—what in economic terms we would call a middle class.

A true democracy both produces a middle class and requires a middle class for survival. Like the twin strands of DNA, democracy and the middle class are inextricably intertwined, and to break either is to destroy the viability of both.

In human society as well, to have a democracy we must have a middle class. And to have a true middle class, a majority of the people in a nation must be educated and economically secure and must have full and easy access to real news so that they can make informed decisions. Democracy requires that its citizens be able to afford to take care of themselves and their families when they get sick, to afford a decent place to live, to find meaningful and well-paying work, and to anticipate—and enjoy—a secure retirement.

This is the American Dream. It's the America my dad grew up in and the America I grew up in. It's the America that is quickly slipping away from us under the burden of crony capitalism and a political system corrupted by it.

When there is no American Dream, when there is no middle class, there cannot be real democracy. That's why when elections are brought to nations that are in crisis or that don't have a broad, stable, well-educated middle class—such as Egypt, Iraq, Iran, and the Palestinian territories—the result is aristocrats, "strongmen," or theocrats exploiting those elections as a way of gaining decidedly undemocratic power.

America's Founders understood the relationship between the middle class—what Thomas Jefferson called the *yeomanry*—and democracy. Jefferson's greatest fear for the young American nation was not a new king but a new economic aristocracy. He worried that if a small group of citizens became too wealthy—if America became polarized between the very rich and the very poor—democracy would vanish.

Our democracy depends on our ability to play referee to the game of business and to protect labor and the public good. It is both our right and our responsibility, Jefferson insisted, to control "overgrown wealth" from becoming "dangerous to the state"—which is, so long as we are a democratic republic, We the People.

When wealth is concentrated in the hands of the few and the middle class shrinks to the point where it's no longer a politically potent force, democracy becomes a feudal aristocracy—the rule of the elite. As Franklin D. Roosevelt pointed out in 1936, the rule of the many requires that We the People have a degree of economic as well as political freedom. When We the People are given the opportunity to educate ourselves, earn a living wage, own our own homes, and feel confident that we have good child care, health care, and care in our old age—in short, when America has a thriving middle class—America also has a thriving democracy.

Without this strong and vibrant middle class, democracy cannot exist; instead it becomes a caricature of itself. There are leaders and elections and all the forms, but they're only for show; the game is now rigged.

Democrats versus the Cons

There's a battle waging today in America that will decide the future of the middle class. On the one side are those like Thomas Jefferson who believe that a free people can govern themselves and have the right to organize their government to create a strong middle class—which will, in turn, keep the government democratic. On the other side are those like Thomas Hobbes who believe that only a small elite can and should govern and that the people should be willing to pay the price of poverty in exchange for security.

Those who don't want democracy understand that a middle class will always work to create democracy, which is why they are so opposed to middle-class-creating government policies like free public education, limits on the concentration of ownership of the media, and social safety nets like universal health care and Social Security. They understand that such policies have, and always will, bring about a strong and vibrant middle class that will, in turn, both demand and create a more democratic society.

Who are these people who want to undermine the middle class? They often call themselves "conservatives" or "neo-conservatives," but these people are not true conservatives. They don't want to "conserve" or protect the America the Founders gave us. I call them "cons" because they are conning America.

My dad was a staunch Republican all his life, but he didn't believe that a small elite should rule America. He was glad the government provided safety nets like Social Security and Medicare and made unionization possible. My dad, and most of the other *real* conservatives I have known, believed in the middle class and believed in democracy.

The battle we face in America today is not between liberal and conservative, nor is it between big-*D* Democrat and Republican. The battle we face today is between those of us who want to protect our democratic heritage and the cons who want to create an America that benefits only a small elite organized around corporate power and inherited wealth.

The Con Game

Two types of cons have worked together to screw the middle class. Call them the *predator cons* and the *true believer cons.*

Predator Cons

Predator cons are simply greedy. They use politics and/or philosophy as a cover for their theft of our common resources and as a rationalization for their growing wealth in the face of growing societal poverty. They are not conservatives in any true sense—they are not interested in conserving American values or even in keeping American wealth in America. They're the ones who ship jobs overseas, lobby for tax breaks from Congress, fight against the inheritance tax, and reincorporate their companies offshore to avoid paying US corporate taxes.

The predator cons' rationalization for their obscene pileup of wealth is that they're simply playing the game by the existing rules; and that's true to a large extent—except that they're also the ones who bought and paid for the politicians who set up the rules for them. They have conned America into believing that they care about the American economy when all they care about is making money for themselves.

A great example of a predatory con is NAFTA, the North American Free Trade Agreement. Free-trade agreements lower wages for American workers—they do not create well-paying jobs in America. They create record trade deficits. Cons don't even try to argue that free-trade agreements are good for America anymore. Agreements like these—such as the Central American Free Trade Agreement (CAFTA)—are passed now (by a single vote in the Senate in 2005) only because corporate America needs them to reap tremendous profits from the low wages they extract in nonunionized, nondemocratic, and socially disorganized countries; predator cons succeed in passing these agreements by threatening to withhold campaign funds from anyone who dares to oppose them.

It's an old game that the robber barons of the nineteenth century knew well how to play.

True Believer Cons

The second type of con is perhaps even more dangerous than the predators. They're the true believers.

Just as true believers in communism brought about the death of tens of millions in Russia from the time of the Bolshevik Revolution until the fall of the Berlin Wall, so too the true believers in laissez-faire capitalism believe that if only government would go away, everything would be just fine. Employers would become benevolent, employees would be enthusiastic, and bureaucratic inefficiencies would vanish.

These so-called free marketeers aren't bothered by the consolidation of companies or the loss of competition that happens when markets are unregulated. Like Thomas Hobbes, the true believers assume that society will run best when run by the small elite that comes out on top. They believe in *corporatocracy*—the view that an economic aristocracy benefits the working class because wealth will "trickle down" from above to below.

Ronald Reagan was a true believer. He didn't understand economics, and the simple notions of self-sufficiency and a pioneering spirit appealed to him. He asked, in essence: "Why would somebody want to regulate a business? Wouldn't it eventually always do what was best without regulation?"

What Reagan and his followers failed to understand was that business will *not* always do what's best for society. In fact, the fundamental goal of business—to maximize assets and profits while externalizing costs and liabilities—is often *destructive* to the public good. This becomes particularly obvious when business owners do not live or otherwise participate in the same society and culture as their customers. A small-business owner can't run sewage out his door or pay his workers below a living wage because he has to face his next-door neighbor and his next-door neighbor's kid, who may want to work in his shop.

The same is not true, however, for multinational corporations. Executives of large corporations don't live in the same society as the people who work for them and who live next to their factories. As a result, the legacy of unregulated big business and the concentration of wealth in the hands of the few is pollution, worker exploitation, cuts to worker safety, and the bestowing of profits to the company's elite while cutting benefits to the company's rank and file.

The true believer cons would just be wrong, and not dangerous, if they didn't try to hide their corporatocratic, market-before-people agenda. They have discovered, however, that most people don't agree with them that a government ruled by a small elite is the most stable form of government and that stability and predictability are more important than democracy. Saying this sort of thing out loud loses elections, so these conservatives have learned to con the public by hiding their agenda behind euphemisms and double-speak.

The Bush Jr. administration perfected the true believer con. Letting a corporate elite control, profit from, and make decisions about our air, water, and sewage systems was called the Clear Skies Initiative and the Clean Water Initiative; or, when they were feeling a bit more open, "privatization." Letting a corporate elite count our votes in secret on their privately owned machines and telling us how we voted was called the Help America Vote Act. Cutting holes in our social safety net programs like Social Security and Medicare was called "strengthening" these programs through increased "consumer-driven choice" and "personal accounts."

Cons suggest that when consumers pool their risk with a private, for-profit corporation to protect personal property, it is called "insurance" and it's a good thing; but when citizens pool their risk with the government to guarantee health care, retirement, and a social safety net, that is "socialism" and should be "privatized." Translated, the cons' policies mean only one thing: you and I get screwed.

Fighting Back

When cons took over the United States during Reconstruction after the Civil War and held power until the Republican Great Depression, the damage they did was tremendous. Our nation was wracked by the classic scourges of poverty—epidemics of disease, crime, and riots—and the average working person was little more than a serf. The concepts of owning a home, having health or job security, and enjoying old age were unthinkable for all but the mercantile class and the rich. America seemed to be run for the robber barons and not for the thousands who worked for them. Democracy in America was at its lowest ebb; our nation more resembled the Victorian England that Charles Dickens wrote of than the egalitarian and middle-class-driven democracy that Alexis de Tocqueville saw here in 1836.

All that changed in the 1930s, when Franklin D. Roosevelt's New Deal brought back the middle class. His economic stimulus programs put money in people's pockets, and the safety nets he created—like Social Security—ensured that no one would fall out of the middle class once they had gotten there. His programs worked, creating what has been called the Golden Age of the middle class. During these years, from the 1940s until Reagan took power, democracy in America resurged along with the middle class.

But after 40 years of prosperity, in the 1980s Americans began drinking the cons' Kool-Aid with startling rapidity. Three "conservative" Republican presidents and one "conservative" Democrat have crushed the middle class and brought our nation to the brink of a second Great Depression.

In 2005 the US trade deficit hit an all-time high at a whopping $725.8 billion. Over the past five years, the US economy has experienced the slowest job creation since the 1930s, with fewer private-sector hours worked in 2005 than in 2001. For the first time since the Great Depression, in 2005 American consumers spent more than they earned, and the government budget deficit was larger than all business savings combined.[8] We are financing today's consumption with tomorrow's bills, and sooner or later the chits will come in and the middle class will be the big losers—putting democracy itself at risk again.

The way out of this mess isn't difficult to understand—we've done it before. Remember that businesses are run like kingdoms, with CEO kings, executive princes, and worker serfs, so they're essentially anti-democratic. Avoiding the cons' scenario simply requires us to remember that a middle class won't emerge when business has more influence in the halls of government than do We the People. Without democracy there can be no middle class; and without a middle class, democracy will wither and die.

Whether our economy benefits billionaires or the rest of us is determined by how we handle economic policy. It depends especially on a fundamental grasp of two concepts: classical economics and an internal government-spending stimulus.

Classical Economics

For more than 200 years—until Ronald Reagan became president—economics was not hard to understand. Everyone could figure out that when working people have money, they spend most of it. When extremely wealthy people have money, they save most of it. It's the spending of money by working people that creates consumer demand. Consumer demand in turn creates business opportunities, and that creates jobs.

In 1981 Reagan introduced America to *trickle-down economics*, also called (by George H. W. Bush, who understood classical economics even though he later had to placate the con base) "voodoo economics." Reagan's concept, in a nutshell, was that if we reorganized society so that the wealth of the rich grew suddenly and quickly, they'd use that money to build factories and hire more people, thus allowing their wealth to "trickle down" to the workers.

This assertion of Reagan's was new—it had never before happened in the history of the world. Certainly, small groups of political and/or economic elites had concentrated wealth at the expense of society generally, but none had ever before said they were doing it because *economics* justified it. Kings throughout history had simply claimed the divine right of kings.

Even though voodoo economics had never been tried, Reagan was able to convince average Americans that it would work, and got it pushed through Congress. (Members of Congress saw it for what it was, but so did their wealthy contributors who would benefit from it, so Republicans and a few sellout "conservative" Democrats in Congress went along.) To institute his voodoo economics, Reagan slashed top marginal income tax rates on millionaires and billionaires from 70 percent to 50 percent in 1981 and all the way down to 28 percent by 1988.[9]

The result wasn't at all what Reagan expected. Rather than create income, the Reagan tax cuts dropped the United States into the greatest debt in the history of the world. Reagan turned to his conservative friend Alan Greenspan, who suggested that Reagan could hide part of the debt by borrowing a few hundred billion dollars a year from the Social Security Trust Fund.[10] Reagan followed Greenspan's advice, which is why we have a Social Security crisis today: the government borrowed all the money in the fund from 1982 to today to help cover the voodoo economics budget deficit; and now, to pay back Social Security, income taxes—which hit millionaires and billionaires (unlike Social Security FICA taxes, which are taken only on the first $90,000 of income from working people)—rose substantially.

Additionally, as would be expected, the rich got fabulously richer under Reagan. From 1980 to 1990, the income of the wealthiest 5 percent of Americans rose by 25 percent while the income of the bottom 40 percent stayed absolutely flat.[11] This is why the wealthiest in America didn't use their money to build factories—after all, there wasn't a significant increase in demand, so why manufacture things that people can't afford? Instead this nation's rich loaned some of their money to the US government so it could pay the bills Reagan was running up, getting it back over the ensuing 20 years with a healthy dose of interest, paid for by future taxpayers.

Although trickle-down economics did produce millions of jobs, they were almost all outside of the United States, while at the same time good US manufacturing jobs vanished. The only accomplishment of trickle-down economics was to produce a nation of peons.

The alternative is to return to classical economics. When working people have money to spend, they create a demand for goods and services, which allows entrepreneurs to start businesses to meet that demand. The entrepreneurs employ more working people, who then have more money to spend. The middle class grows.

Think about it. What would you do if someone gave you an extra $20,000? Maybe you would take a vacation or buy a new car, new clothes, or new appliances. Even if you used the money to pay off old bills, you would then have more to spend in the future because you wouldn't have interest payments. And when you buy more, you create demand, which means more people can be put to work—and the economy grows.

Now think about what Bill Gates would do if someone gave him an extra $20,000—or an extra $20 million or more, as George W. Bush's first tax cuts did. Would he even notice? He'd probably just send it along to his accountant and forget all about it. The only thing that's going to grow is Bill Gates's bank account. That's the difference between giving money to the rich and giving money to you and me.

This economic truth is just common sense. When people in the lower and middle economic layers of society have increased income, all of society eventually gets richer because working people's spending most of their incomes is the engine that creates economic demand for goods and services.

To bring back the middle class, we must reinstitute common-sense classical economics: we must pay a living wage to working people, protect US industries, and reinstate progressive taxation so the very wealthy pay a share of their income that reflects their heavier use of the commons and their increased access to the engines of wealth generation.

For more than 200 years, America was the wealthiest and most powerful nation in the world. Today—after nearly three decades of the cons' economics and insane "free-trade" policies—we're the most indebted nation in the history of the world.

We've gone from being—pre-Reagan—the world's largest exporter of finished goods and the world's largest importer of raw materials to being—just over the past decade—the exact opposite. We used to import iron ore, make steel, make cars, and export them all around the world. Now Canadian and Mexican and German companies mine raw materials from mines they own in the United States, ship the ore to their nations or to China, manufacture the finished goods, and sell those goods back to us—with dollars we give them in exchange for another few hundred billion dollars' worth of America every year.

There's no reason to let the cons screw us over. We must not stand by while our democracy becomes a corporatocracy, serving an elite group of billionaire CEOs. There is another way—and we've done it before. Thomas Jefferson knew how to build a middle class. Franklin Roosevelt knew how. We can do it, too. We can re-create the America that built the middle class my dad entered, the middle class in which he raised me.

From *Screwed: The Undeclared War against the Middle Class*
by Thom Hartmann, © 2006, published by Berrett-Koehler.

Democracy Is Inevitable

From *What Would Jefferson Do?: A Return to Democracy*

I F DEMOCRACY IS THE NATURAL STATE OF ALL MAMMALS, INCLUD-ing humans, it must be something purely temporary that has prevented it for so much of the "civilized" period of the past few millennia (even though it has continued to exist throughout this time among tribal people). The force that slowed its inevitable emergence was a dysfunctional story in our culture, which led to thousands of years of the sanctioning of slavery, the oppression of women and minorities, and the deaths of hundreds of millions. It was the story that our essential nature is sinful.

The Fundamental Issue of Sin and Punishment

Thomas Hobbes and others have assumed that we'd need a time machine to know how bad life really was 20,000 or 50,000 years ago. But there are still humans living essentially the same way that your ancestors and mine did, and if we look at their lives we find, by and large, that Hobbes was mistaken.

I remember vividly the first time I experienced this. I was sitting around a campfire with half a dozen or so men who were members of a southwestern Native American tribe. We'd just done a sweat, and after some of the heavy talk and ritual associated with that sacred ceremony the conversation gradually turned to "guy talk": telling stories, making each other laugh, and poking fun.

They were making jokes mostly about another tribe, which lived about 600 miles away. Not cutting or hurting comments but jokes that pointed out—with a humor born of respect—the historic and cultural differences between the two tribes. Because I'd never interacted with the other tribe, I made a comment typical of modern American culture: a put-down joke, with the man sitting opposite me around the fire as its butt. It was the kind of remark you'll hear within five minutes of turning on any sitcom on American television.

The group fell silent, and everybody looked down or into the fire. I realized I'd had breached some protocol. And I didn't know how to make it right or how they'd punish me for my sin.

After a long and, for me, uncomfortable silence, the oldest man in the circle roused himself, as if he knew that his age gave him the obligation to speak first.

"I remember a time when I was young," he said, "and, well, I won't say, 'stupid,' but let's say, 'not so wise.' Not that I'm all that wise now," he added with a small laugh,

> but I've learned a few things over the years. Anyhow, I remember when I was young and I was sitting with some friends, and I said something hurtful about one of the men who was there with us. I remember how badly I felt, immediately knowing that I had put a pain on his heart. I remember how confused I felt, not sure what I should do to restore balance to the circle. And I remember one of the men telling a story of a time when he'd hurt somebody's feelings, and how he'd made it right by acknowledging that, and retracting the comment, and asking the rest of the group to help him bring back balance and harmony.

The man spoke for several minutes, and my version of it is from memory so probably not exact, but it captures the essence of his comments. He was teaching me—without ever once mentioning my name—how to remedy what I had done.

Then the man next to him cleared his throat and said, "I too remember a time I said something impulsive that hurt my friend." And he went on to tell the story of what he did to make it right. His story was followed by one from the man I'd made the joke about, and this continued all the way around the circle until it got to me.

By then I knew how each person felt and had learned how I could make it right with each individual or rebalance the situation in the group. It took a few minutes, but I did it, and the oldest man gently interrupted me by hand-rolling tobacco into a corn shuck, lighting it, and passing it around the circle. It was as if something heavy had been lifted from the group. We were soon again laughing and telling tall tales.

What's important in this story is that nobody had called me a sinner. Nobody implied that I was doing what was normal or natural. Everybody accepted that I'd made a mistake, I hadn't known better, and each man had done his best to politely tell me how I could restore harmony.

This is one aspect of how a society can live without police and prisons.

This is how humans, for the most part, lived for the past 40,000 years and longer.

This is beyond the imagining of Thomas Hobbes and the people of his day who were struggling in a largely anti-democratic kingdom with the issue of whether those who rule over others—restraining sinful impulses and punishing those who err—should be appointed by gods or men (but never women).

When society agrees with the story that people are fundamentally flawed and evil, it creates repositories for those evil people or puts them to death. It assigns to some of its members the job of human trash collector who performs therapy, provides drugs, or restrains them. If they acted badly enough, they're put into a prison, where it's assumed that others of equal evil and lacking restraint of their human nature will bully, beat, and even rape the newcomer.

On the other hand, when a society agrees with the democracy-grounded story that people are fundamentally good, born in balance with the world and one another, something quite different happens when a person acts badly. It becomes the responsibility of the entire community to bring that person back into balance. The bad behavior is seen either as an indication that the person has not yet learned something or matured or that the person is suffering from a form of spiritual sickness. The solemn responsibility and work of every person in the community becomes that of teaching or healing the individual. Usually, once harmony is restored, a small ceremony is performed to acknowledge the return of the person and the community to its natural state.

Some would argue that this way of life may work well for small tribes where everybody knows everybody else but isn't viable in a city-state society where it's possible for predators and sociopaths to prey on innocent people if unrestrained by the force of law and threat or reality of imprisonment. There's considerable truth to this argument: Hobbes was writing from the midst of the British Empire in the seventeenth century, the belly of the beast of one of history's mightiest and most bloodthirsty anti-democratic cultures to rule the earth.

And yet we do have this simple metric today: generally, the more democratic a nation is, the fewer people it will have in prison.

Democracy Is Resilient, Always Rising from the Human Spirit

Most scientists who have examined the relationship between democracy and biology have concluded that democracy is so resilient an idea, so biologically ingrained an imperative, that it will continue to grow and prosper around the world even if the Texas oil barons and the New York corporations do succeed in turning America back into a Dickensian world consistent with the vision of dictators, pseudo-conservatives, and those who don't understand democracy.

Professor Rudolph Rummel made the following points in an e-mail discussion we had in November 2003:

- Freedom is a basic human right recognized by the United Nations and international treaties and is the heart of social justice.

- Freedom—free speech and the economic and social free market—is an engine of economic and human development and scientific and technological advancement.

- Freedom ameliorates the problem of mass poverty.

- Free people do not suffer from and never have had famines and, by theory, should not. Freedom is therefore a solution to hunger and famine.

- Free people have the least internal violence, turmoil, and political instability.

- Free people have virtually no government genocide and mass murder and for good theoretical reasons. Freedom is therefore a solution to genocide and mass murder, the only practical means of making sure that "Never again!"

- Free people do not make war on one another, and the greater the freedom within two nations, the less violence between them. While they may declare war on autocratic regimes that threaten them, people in a democracy never vote to attack other democracies.

- Freedom is a method of nonviolence—the most peaceful nations are those whose people are free.

As Per Ahlmark, former deputy prime minister of Sweden, said in his remarks to the European Parliament on April 8, 1999: "In a democracy it is impossible, or at least extremely difficult, to get enough support from the people to initiate a military confrontation with another democracy. Such people know each other too well. They trust each other too much. For democratic governments it is usually too easy and natural to talk and negotiate with one another—it would look and feel ridiculous or totally irresponsible to start shooting at a nation which is governed in the same way as your own country."[1]

On his website Dr. Rummel has a "Peace Clock" that shows that in 1900 only 8 percent of the world's people lived in nations that were democratic.[2] By 1950 the number had increased to 31 percent, and, Dr. Rummel says, "Now is the dawning of a new world," as by the year 2000 fully 58.2 percent of the world's people lived in democratic nations.

Rummel also coined the word *democide* in his book *Death by Government* to describe the deliberate murder (or allowing the deaths) of a state's own citizens.[3] Rummel points out that the world was shocked when the Chinese Communists slaughtered people in Tiananmen Square but should not have been shocked: the Chinese state had killed more than 35 million of its own citizens prior to that time and continues to kill them to this day.

As awful as that number is, the Soviets hold the world record, having killed an estimated 54 million to 61 million human beings, according to Rummel. Although we all know about the wars incited by Nazi Germany and Imperial Japan, what most people miss is that in the twentieth century up to four times as many people died at the hands of their own governments as in all the wars combined. The cause? According to Rummel and many other experts on the topic, it's a lack of democracy.

In his book *Breaking the Real Axis of Evil: How to Oust the World's Last Dictators by 2025,* former US ambassador to Hungary Mark Palmer says that there are only 45 dictators left in the world and that with thoughtful and nonviolent effort we may be able to end all of their reigns before the year 2025.[4] The worldwide trend, Palmer says, is solidly toward peace. In a November 2003 interview, he told me, "If you could foresee a world which was 100 percent democratic, there would be no war." There would be competition, Palmer notes, but not war, and the result would be an increased standard of living among people all across the planet.

And the trend is good. Palmer is vice chairman of the board of directors of Freedom House, which produces an annual report on democracy around the world.[5] "In 2002, the last year that we covered," he told me, "we saw roughly 26 countries moving in the right direction [toward democracy] and only about 11 doing some reversal."

We may be standing on the edge of a new era of peace because democracies have a built-in mechanism (the will of the people) to prevent aggressive wars. So long as our democratic institutions can resist being taken over by a new version of warlords, aristocrats, and kings in the form of multinational corporations (particularly those in the defense industry), we could see the prospect of the biblical "thousand years of peace"—following the brutality of the past century—in our or our children's lifetime.

Reinventing Democracy

Democracy doesn't just appear, fully formed. In every part of the world, over and over, it has to be refigured out, developed, put together piece by piece. This is why it can appear so different in different parts of the world yet always share the same set of basic values.

Democratic indigenous cultures almost always have their own laws, appropriate to their time and place, to ensure stability and peace. The Australian Aborigines, for example, have carried for as long as 80,000 years the belief that if they engage in intensive (single-crop, tilled-soil) agriculture, the gods will punish them with terrible famines.

So how do people find their way from a violent warlord, theocrat, or feudal culture into a peaceful and stable democratic culture?

- The people have learned that they must live in a sustainable fashion in balance and harmony with their environment.

- They've agreed that they're no longer willing to live in a violent society characterized by extremes of wealth and power.

- They've agreed that power must be locally held and locally exercised.

Eventually, enough people re-remember the basic tenets of democratic life and figure out how to apply them to their own particular time and place. When enough people wake up to the possibility of living in a democracy, the nondemocratic culture dissolves and a newly formed and unique democracy emerges, as we see in examples from New Caledonia to the Iroquois to the American Revolution, to the dramatic shift around the world toward democracy in the past century.

Today, all across the world, people are creating fledgling democracies with the hope that they can successfully transit them into multigenerational, long-term democratic nations.

An Informed and Educated Electorate

From *Rebooting the American Dream: 11 Ways to Rebuild Our Country*

> If a nation expects to be ignorant and free, in a state
> of civilization, it expects what never was and never
> will be. . . . Whenever the people are well-informed,
> they can be trusted with their own government; that,
> whenever things get so far wrong as to attract their
> notice, they may be relied on to set them right.
>
> —THOMAS JEFFERSON

TALK RADIO NEWS SERVICE, BASED IN WASHINGTON, DC, IS owned and run by my dear friend Ellen Ratner. Ellen is an experienced and accomplished journalist, and a large number of interns and young journalism school graduates get their feet wet in reporting by working with her.

In March 2010 I was in Washington for a meeting with a group of senators, and I needed a studio from which to do my radio and TV show. Ellen was gracious enough to offer me hers. I arrived as three of her interns were producing a panel-discussion type of TV show for web distribution at www.talkradionews.com in which they were discussing for their viewing audience their recent experiences on Capitol Hill.

One intern panelist related that a White House correspondent for one of the Big Three TV networks (ABC, CBS, and NBC) had told her that the network registered a huge amount of interest in the "hot story" that week of a congressman's sexual indiscretions. Far less popular were stories about the debates on health care, the conflicts in the Middle East, and even the Americans who had died recently in Iraq or Afghanistan.

"So that's the story they have to run with on the news," the intern said, relating the substance of the network correspondent's thoughts, "because that's what the American people want to see. If the network doesn't give people what they want to see, viewers will tune away and the network won't have any viewers, ratings, or revenues."

The two other interns commiserated with the first about what a shame it was that Americans wanted the titillating stories instead of the substantive ones, but they accepted without question that the network was therefore *obliged* to "give people what they want."

When they finished their panel discussion, I asked these college students if they knew that there was a time in America when radio and TV stations and networks broadcast the actual news—instead of infotainment—because the law required them to do so. None of them had any idea what I was talking about.

The Devolution of Broadcast News

But the reality is that from the 1920s, when radio really started to go big in the United States, until Reagan rolled it back in 1987, federal communications law required a certain amount of "public service" programming from radio and television stations as a condition of retaining their broadcast licenses.

The agreement was basic and simple: in exchange for the media owners' being granted a license from the Federal Communications Commission (FCC) to use the airwaves—owned by the public—they had to serve the public interest first, and only then could they go about the business of making money. If they didn't do so, when it came time to renew their license, public groups and individuals could show up at public hearings on the license renewal and argue for the license's being denied.

One small way that stations lived up to their public-service mandate was by airing public-service announcements for local non-profit groups, community calendars, and other charitable causes. They also had to abide by something called the Fairness Doctrine, which required them to air diverse viewpoints on controversial issues.

Separately, during election campaigns, broadcasters had to abide by the Equal Time Rule, which required them to provide equal airtime to rival candidates in an election.

But the biggest way they proved they were providing a public service and meeting the requirements of the Fairness Doctrine was by broadcasting the news. Real news. Actual news. Local, national, and international news produced by professional, old-school journalists.

Because the news didn't draw huge ratings like entertainment shows—although tens of millions of Americans did watch it every night on TV and listened to it at the top of every hour on radio from coast to coast—and because *real* news was expensive to produce, with bureaus and correspondents all over the world, news was a money-loser for all of the Big Three TV networks and for most local radio and TV stations.

But it was such a sacred thing—this was, after all, the keystone that held together the station's license to broadcast and thus to do business—it didn't matter if it lost money. It made all the other money-making things possible.

Through much of the early 1970s, I worked in the newsroom of a radio station in Lansing, Michigan. It had been started and was then run by three local guys: an engineer, a salesman, and a radio broadcaster. They split up the responsibilities like you'd expect, and all were around the building most days and would hang out from time to time with the on-air crew—all except the sales guy. I was forbidden from talking with him because I worked in *news*. There could be no hint—ever, anywhere—that our radio station had violated the FCC's programming-in-the-public-interest mandate by, for example, my going easy on an advertiser in a news story or promoting another advertiser in a different story. News had to be news, separate from profits and revenue—and if it wasn't, I'd be fired on the spot.

News, in other words, wasn't part of the "free market." It was part of our nation's intellectual commons and thus the price of the station's license.

After Reagan blew up the Fairness Doctrine in 1987, two very interesting things happened. The first was the rise of right-wing hate-speech talk radio, starting with Rush Limbaugh that very year. The second, which really stepped up fast after President Bill Clinton signed the Telecommunications Act of 1996, which further deregulated the broadcast industry, was that the money-losing news divisions of the Big Three TV networks were taken under the wings of their entertainment divisions—and wrung dry. Foreign bureaus were closed. Reporters were fired. Stories that promoted the wonders of advertisers or other companies (like movie production houses) owned by the same mega-corporations that owned the networks began to appear. And investigative journalism that cast a bright light on corporate malfeasance vanished.

And because newscasts had ads, and those ads were sold based on viewership, the overall arc and content of the news began to be dictated by what the public *wanted* to know rather than by what they *needed* to know to function in a democratic society.

The interns were aghast. "Reagan did that?!" one said, incredulous. I said yes and that Clinton then helped the process along to its current sorry state by signing the Telecommunications Act, leading to the creation of the Fox "News" Channel in October 1996 and its now-legal ability to call itself a *news* operation while baldly promoting what it knows to be falsehoods or distortions.

Now here we are in 2010, and the news media is an abject failure when it comes to reporting the *real* news—news that citizens in a democracy need to know. Even Ted Koppel, no flaming liberal by any means, said in an April 2010 interview with the British Broadcasting Corporation that he thought the state of the news industry was "a disaster."[1] He went on:

> I think we are living through the final stages of what I would call the Age of Entitlement. We fight two wars without raising a single nickel to support them. We feel entitled to mortgages whether we have jobs or not. We feel entitled to make $10 million, $50 million, or $100 million even though the enterprise we headed up is a total failure. And

we now feel entitled not to have the news that we *need* but the news that we *want*. We want to listen to news that comes from those who already sympathize with our particular point of view. We don't want the facts anymore.

Koppel was also well aware of the influence of profit-making on the news organizations, which he believed was driving the degradation of news so that it appealed to our baser instincts:

> I think it's the producer [of the particular news show] who is at fault, who desperately needs the consumer. . . . In the good old days, when you only had three networks—ABC, NBC, and CBS—there was competition, but the competition still permitted us to do what was in the public interest. These days all the networks have to fight with the dozens of cable outlets that are out there, the Internet that is out there, and they are all competing for the almighty dollar, and the way to get there is to head down to the lowest common denominator.

When we talk about news that people "need," we are really talking about the intellectual and informational nutrition that is essential for the health and the well-being of our democracy. We need an educated and informed citizenry to participate in our democratic institutions and elections, and we're not going to get that if we keep dumbing down the news and giving people what they want and not what they and society need.

Breaking Up the Media Monopolies

The Studio System

Back in the 1930s and 1940s, the eight biggest movie studios owned the majority of movie theaters in America. A Paramount theater, for example, would show only movies produced by Paramount's movie studios, which featured only people under contract to Paramount. The result was that the studios could make (or break) any movie star and control what people could see in their local community. It was very profitable to the studios, but it was stifling to competition and creativity and therefore a disservice to the moviegoing audience.

So through that era, in a series of actions that lasted almost a decade and which were capped by the big studios' signing a major consent decree with the feds, the federal government tried to force the big theaters to open up the business to competition. The big theaters said that they would, even agreeing to the 1940 Paramount Decree, but they continued with business as usual.

The issue came to a head when it was argued in an antitrust case before the US Supreme Court in 1948. The Court, in a 7-to-1 decision, ruled against the movie giants, saying that they could no longer have total control of the vertically integrated system—from contracting with actors to making movies to showing them in their own theaters across the country. They had to choose: operate in either the movie *making* business or the movie *showing* business. They couldn't do both.

The result was the beginning of the end of the "kingmaker" movie studio monopoly and a boon for independent filmmakers. It also led to a proliferation of new theaters, from ones in urban areas (many retrofitting old opera or burlesque houses) to the new fad of drive-in movie theaters. The industry today is infinitely more diverse and creative as a result of that breakup.

Television and the Prime Time Access Rule

In the late 1960s, television was going through a similar vertical integration, with the Big Three TV networks dominating the content of local television stations they either owned or had as affiliates. In response the FCC promulgated the Prime Time Access Rule in 1970, which dictated that at least one hour out of the four "prime time" hours on every local TV station in the nation would have to come from some source other than the network.

This opened the door to independent TV production companies, like MTM Enterprises, which produced several sitcoms derived from the work of Mary Tyler Moore, and competition from the new television divisions of old-line movie houses, such as Twentieth Century Fox's producing a TV version of *M*A*S*H* and Paramount's producing *Happy Days*.[2]

Although the rules against vertical theater integration are no longer enforced, and the Prime Time Access Rule was blown up in 1996, both the movie and TV industries are broadly more diverse in their programming than they would have been without these "market interventions" that increased competition and decreased monopoly. Which brings us to radio.

The Vicious Circle of Conservative Talk Radio

Many people wonder why the big 50,000-watt AM stations (and even many of the big 25,000- and 10,000-watt stations) across the country carry exclusively conservative programming, particularly programs featuring Rush Limbaugh, Sean Hannity, and Glenn Beck. In most cases, it's a simple matter of the economics of monopoly.

One of the largest owners of the biggest (full-power) radio stations in the country is a mega-corporation that also owns the largest talk-radio syndication service in the nation. When the corporation's stations carry shows that its syndication service owns, it makes money both from the local station ownership and from the ownership of the syndication service. When the stations carry shows from other syndicators or independent shows, the corporation loses the syndication revenue and the local station (which it also owns) loses typically five minutes of advertising inventory per hour that it must barter with the syndicated show for in exchange for the right to air the show.

Thus, so long as the radio industry is allowed to run like the movie studio system in the 1940s, the "studio"—in this case the giant corporation that owns radio stations as well as the nation's largest talk-radio syndication service—will have an outsized influence on what shows up on the very biggest stations in the largest markets across the country. Because of the huge, booming voice of those stations, those shows will have a significant edge in "finding" listeners (and vice versa), making those shows "successful" and thus creating demand for them from the independent stations. It becomes a self-fulfilling prophecy.

Some progressives have suggested that radio needs a "fairness doctrine" where a government panel will determine how much "liberal" or "conservative" programming each station carries and then force the stations to "balance" out any disequilibrium. But who decides what is "liberal" or "conservative"? Is there a checklist of political positions that a government watchdog would have to go through—immigration, taxes, protecting the commons, gay rights, abortion, gun control, foreign policy? It would be a mess, particularly since many of those issues don't lend themselves to easy pigeonholing.

A much easier way to balance the playing field is simply to bring into the marketplace real competition by separating syndication companies from local radio stations so that the stations will no longer have an incentive to carry programming because "it's in the family" and instead will look for shows that can attract and hold an audience.

Programming in the Public Interest

We need to return to the notion of "programming in the public interest," making news back into news. We also need to start enforcing the Sherman Antitrust Act of 1890 and use it to break up the large media monopolies that have re-formed since the Reagan and Clinton eras, thus effectively rolling back media deregulation.

And this isn't limited to radio and TV. Consumer-friendly regulation almost always has a similar effect in breaking up monopolies when it's designed to help people get around the monopoly.

For example, the company that owns the copper wires, cable, G3 or G4 wireless, or fiber-optic cabling going into your house also owns the exclusive right to carry the content that goes over that infrastructure. If you have a cable company supplying your home, it's probably competing only with the local phone company for your business. Because those two companies (and maybe a mobile provider) are the only ones "competing" for your business, they can easily keep prices—and profits—very high.

In most other developed countries, however, regardless of who owns and maintains the wires, cable, or fiber, *anybody* can offer content over it. The rationale for this is that infrastructure of physical wires and the wireless frequencies constitutes a "natural monopoly" that heavily uses public spaces (cables and phone lines go through and along public streets and rights-of-way); and so while a company can make a small profit on that part of its business, the wires and the wireless frequencies are really a part of the commons that can be regulated.

On the other hand, these developed countries believe that the content *delivery* should be competitive. After all, this is where most of the innovation comes from: it's not a matter of the newest, coolest copper wires; it's the *content* that draws customers.

The result of this is that the average citizen in France, for example, pays about $33 per month for what the *New York Times* described as "Internet service twice as fast as what you get from Verizon or Comcast, bundled with digital high-definition television, unlimited long distance and international calling to 70 countries and wireless Internet connectivity for your laptop or smartphone throughout most of the country."[3]

And that's all from private companies, with no government subsidies. Why? Because small and new companies are *allowed* to compete by the government's *requiring* whichever company carries the signal (wire, cable, fiber, wireless) to make that signal path available to *any* company that wants to offer content to consumers.

Competition—mandated by the French government—has driven the price down and innovation up. The average French citizen is not only paying one-fifth of what the average American pays for such services but is also getting better quality, more variety, and much faster Internet access.

Breaking up the media monopolies and fostering more competition, innovation, and creativity in the media world clearly has public benefits, especially in ensuring that people have access to information they need to participate in our democracy. An informed and educated electorate would be one major result of such government regulation.

The same result can also be helped by making higher education more accessible to the average American.

Access to Higher Education

Jefferson's Tombstone

Thomas Jefferson's tombstone contains an epitaph he wrote before his death with a directive that not a single word be changed. He had been the president of the United States for two terms and the vice president for one, was a member of the Virginia legislature, and was a famous inventor and architect as well as the author of nearly a million words in various letters, diaries, notebooks, books, pamphlets, and rants. But he chose not to mention any of that on his gravestone.

Besides the dates of his birth and death, he chose to be remembered for three things that he did in his 83 years of life on earth:

HERE WAS BURIED THOMAS JEFFERSON
AUTHOR OF THE DECLARATION OF AMERICAN INDEPENDENCE
OF THE STATUTE OF VIRGINIA FOR RELIGIOUS FREEDOM
AND FATHER OF THE UNIVERSITY OF VIRGINIA

Writing the Declaration of Independence was an obvious choice, and declaring forever his opposition to integrating church and state also made sense (although it got him demoted in 2010 in schoolbooks in the state of Texas). But "Father of the University of Virginia" being more important than "President of the United States of America"?

Jefferson, it turns out, had this wacky idea. He actually believed that young people should be able to go to college regardless of their ability to pay, their station in life, and how rich or poor their parents were. He thought that an educated populace was the best defense of liberty and democracy in the new nation he'd helped birth.

So the University of Virginia that he started was *free.*

Reagan's Legacy

Ronald Reagan certainly thought that that was a wacky idea, and he was diametrically opposed to the Jeffersonian ideal. When he took office as governor of California in 1967, he quickly called for an end to free tuition at the University of California and an across-the-board

20 percent cut in state funding for higher education.[4] He then argued for a cut in spending on construction for higher education in the state and set up the firing of the popular president of the university, Clark Kerr, whom he deemed "too liberal."

When asked why he was doing away with free college in California, Reagan said that the role of the state "should not be to subsidize intellectual curiosity."

Reagan further referred to college students who nationwide were protesting the Vietnam War as "brats," "cowardly fascists," and "freaks." Adding that if the only way to "restore order" on the nation's campuses was violence, that was fine with him. Just a few days before the Kent State shootings, he famously said, "If it takes a bloodbath, let's get it over with. No more appeasement!"[5]

The trend that Reagan began with the UC system continues to this day. During Republican governor Arnold Schwarzenegger's tenure, state funding for education saw drastic cuts and tuition for undergraduate students rose by more than 90 percent.[6]

Reagan set a tone as governor of California that metastasized across the nation through the 1970s and became federal policy when he was elected president in 1980. By the time he left office in 1988, federal funding for education in the United States had declined from 12 percent of total national educational spending in 1980 to just 6 percent.[7]

Interestingly, to find most of this information you have to dive into recent biographies of the former president or read old newspaper archives that are usually not available online. Not a word of Reagan's role in slashing the UC funding exists, for example, on the Wikipedia pages for either the University of California or Reagan himself. Conservative foundations have poured millions of dollars into campaigns to scrub the Internet clean when it comes to Reagan's past (and that of most other right-wingers).

Yet the reality is that before the Reagan presidency, it was possible for any American student with academic competence to attend college and graduate without debt.

Even in Michigan in the late 1960s, where education was not free but was highly subsidized by the state, my wife paid her way through college by working part-time as a waitress at a Howard Johnson's. To the extent that I went to college (I completed less than a year altogether), I paid my own way by working as a DJ for $2.35 per hour, running my own TV repair business, pumping gas, and working as a cook at a Bob's Big Boy restaurant on weekends.

Such a scenario is unthinkable today. Instead public higher education has become a big business and is often totally corporate, costs are through the roof, and if you're not from a very wealthy family, odds are you'll graduate college with a debt that can take decades to repay. As a result, the United States is slipping in virtually every measurement of innovation, income, and competitiveness. A highly educated workforce is good for innovation and entrepreneurialism: every one of the top 20 innovative countries in the world—except the USA—offers free or very inexpensive college to qualified students.

Ireland took a cue from the pre-Reagan University of California and began offering free college tuition to all Irish citizens and a flat-rate registration fee of 900 euros per year for all European Union citizens. The result, decades later, is that Ireland has gone from having a backwater economy that was largely based on agriculture and tourism to becoming one of the high-tech and innovation capitals of the world.

Ironically, Ireland's vision—and California's pre-Reagan vision—of education was at the core of Thomas Jefferson's hopes for the country he helped found.

Jefferson's Vision

On June 14, 1898, more than 70 years after Jefferson's death, a new building (then called the Academic Building, now called Cabell Hall) was inaugurated at the University of Virginia. One of the nation's most prominent attorneys at the time, James C. Carter of New York City, gave the dedication speech.[8] Carter noted that when Jefferson retired from public office, he was only 66 years old and still energetic and enthusiastic to do something for his country. That something was founding the University of Virginia.

Carter noted that Jefferson had laid out, in numerous letters and discussions throughout his life, a broad overview of how education should be conducted in the United States. Jefferson envisioned the division of states into districts and wards with primary schools and the establishment of colleges and universities where deserving students "might acquire, *gratis,* a further and higher education."

Jefferson envisioned the goal of free public education—from childhood through university—to be straightforward. In a report he prepared for a state commission in Virginia, Jefferson laid out the six purposes of education:[9]

1. To give to every citizen the information he needs for the transaction of his own business.

2. To enable him to calculate for himself, and to express and preserve his ideas, his contracts and accounts in writing.

3. To improve, by reading, his morals and faculties.

4. To understand his duties to his neighbors and country, and to discharge with competence the functions confided to him by either.

5. To know his rights; to exercise with order and justice those he retains; to choose with discretion the fiduciary of those he delegates; and to notice their conduct with diligence, with candor and judgment.

6. And, in general, to observe with intelligence and faithfulness, all the social relations under which he shall be placed.

In other words, a well-educated citizenry can "choose with discretion" the elected representatives who are the holders of our government that protects our rights, and hold those politicians accountable "with diligence, with candor and judgment."

Ronald Reagan, on the other hand, promised during his election campaign of 1980 to "eliminate the Department of Education" from the federal government; and he appointed his friend William Bennett, who had campaigned and written extensively about destroying the federal Department of Education, as secretary of education—akin to asking the fox to guard the chicken coop. Between Reagan's ax hacking at the roots of our educational systems and his tax cuts to "starve the beast" of government, we are now left with the highest illiteracy rate in the developed world and an electorate that is spectacularly vulnerable to demagoguery and cynical political manipulation.

The experiment of Reaganomics and Reagan's anti-intellectual worldview are demonstrably disordered and dead; we must put them behind us and build anew our country on the solid Jeffersonian foundation of good and free education for all.

Combine that with breaking up the media monopolies in this country and fostering competition and its attendant innovation through intelligent regulation of the "natural monopolies" in our nation, and we would have a more informed citizenry with better and faster access to *real* news and information—including information about our body politic.

These "radical" concepts of free public education all the way up to graduate degrees, breaking up companies that vertically integrate entire markets (particularly in the media), and requiring infrastructure-owning companies to offer their infrastructure to a wide variety of competitors work quite well in dozens of countries around the world. They can here too.

From *Rebooting the American Dream: 11 Ways to Rebuild Our Country* by Thom Hartmann, © 2010, published by Berrett-Koehler.

Whatever Happened to Cannery Row?

From Buzzflash.com

ARGUABLY, THERE'S NOTHING POLITICAL ABOUT JOHN STEIN-beck's novel *Cannery Row*. It chronicles the lives of some of the residents of Monterey, California, in the early twentieth century, before the great ecological disaster (mostly overfishing—it's still debated) of the mid-1940s that wiped out the sardine harvest and threw the boom-town into bust. There's Doc, the central focus of the novel, based on a close friend of Steinbeck's, Edward F. Ricketts, one of America's most famous marine biologists; and Mack, who's always trying to do good and never quite making it; and an entire cast of characters who reflect the aura of America in the 1930s.

On the other hand, one could argue that the book is entirely political, today, because it shows us a slice of America before the Great Corporate Homogenizers got hold of us; before we walled ourselves into our highly mortgaged houses to stare for hours, alone, at our TVs, eating the mental gruel of multinational corporations; when the real American Dream was grounded in community, safety, friendship, and a healthy acceptance of eccentricity.

In 1968 I hitchhiked from Michigan to San Francisco, lived there for half a year, and then hitchhiked back. Every city and every Main Street was different. Restaurants were locally owned. Hotels and motels had eccentric names. It was fascinating, an exploration in a very literal sense, discovering hundreds of communities that were uniquely different from one another.

Then came Reagan's "revolution." When he stopped enforcing the Sherman Antitrust Act for all practical purposes, mega-corporations moved in. For much of the 1990s, I made a living in part as a consultant to a variety of organizations, leading me all around the United States (and the world). I logged more than 7 million miles just on Delta Air Lines. And I saw the quirky, unique, personality-rich cities of America being replaced by chain stores, chain restaurants, chain hotels, and franchises. Today, if you were to parachute randomly into any town or city in America, it might take you days to find a commercial landmark that would uniquely identify the place. In this regard, in that it shows us how different the pre-Reagan America was from the post-Reagan America, *Cannery Row* is a political book.

I didn't go looking for *Cannery Row*. As I sat with my father in the summer of 2007, helplessly watching him choke and gag on his own blood as he died from asbestos-caused mesothelioma (thanks in part to one of Dick Cheney's companies) while my brothers and I tried to comfort him, I saw the book beside his bed. He was an inveterate reader—there are about 20,000 books in his basement—and he'd often read and reread his favorites over and over again. After his funeral I picked up *Cannery Row* and took it with me to read on the plane ride home from Michigan to Oregon.

What I found in *Cannery Row* was a time and an America that my parents had often spoken of to me. It reminded me of my mother's stories about squeezing the last of the toothpaste from the tube in a doorjamb because there was barely enough money for toothpaste or toilet paper much less cosmetics. I was reminded of my dad's stories of going down to one of Al Capone's speakeasies as a kid on the South Side of Chicago to get a pail of bootleg beer to bring to his father and uncles as they sat on the stoop in the row houses.

It was a time of challenge and a time of opportunity. It was America before Reagan.

In one of my dad's last e-mails to me, he talked about that era:

> Thank you for the wonderful dedication in *Screwed*. It made me think of what I did in life other than try to lead a good life and do no harm to others. I'm happy with my life, although it was selfish

because I did the things I did with no sacrifice on my part. Then I thought of your mother. She was the one who gave up all her early ambitions and dreams for me and her family.

She wanted to be a writer—worked her way through college to complete her dreams. I still have many of her early writings (if she hasn't tossed them), which were very good. She worked at an airport for money and flying lessons, she took care of a family for room and board, plus all summer with a bunch of girls to earn tuition money. After she graduated she turned down a great job working for the oil companies in Saudi Arabia just so she would not leave her mother alone. . . . After we were married she started to write again. But then you came on the scene. . . . I have hoped that you could and would write about her as you have about me. I think she deserves it much more. She is the true hero of our family.

They were the last words of his I ever heard, and those in an e-mail, as he couldn't speak by the time I got to Michigan.

I realize that telling you a story about my hitchhiking across America, or about my father, isn't telling you the story of *Cannery Row*, but in a way it's very much the story of *Cannery Row*. The stories are meta to the novel. My dad was a huge fan of Steinbeck, presumably because he knew so well the America about which Steinbeck wrote.

Beyond that, telling you the storyline of *Cannery Row* would be a disservice. It's a novel, and one shouldn't have even an inkling of where a novel is going when one starts to read it. It was only after I finished the book that I began to research its history and found a rich treasure trove of information on the web about the real Cannery Row, the real Monterey of the 1930s, and the real Ed Ricketts. I hope you will, too.

But first indulge yourself in a bit of old-fashioned escapism—step back to the time of the Republican Great Depression and meet a wonderful cast of characters in a story that will leave you smiling, wistful, and newly informed.

Maybe, hopefully, we'll all live to see that true spirit of America—its people so brilliantly drawn by Steinbeck in *Cannery Row*—again emerge as we Americans awaken from our dream-fog of consumerism and hellish wars and rediscover the sense of self and community and purpose and the egalitarian values of community on which this nation was founded.

PART II
Brainstorms

A COLLEAGUE OF THOM HARTMANN'S ONCE REMARKED THAT there's never a dull moment in the Hartmann brain. A glance at even a partial list of his achievements bears this observation out. In addition to his years in radio and television broadcasting and print journalism, he's run at least seven successful businesses, among them an advertising agency and a travel agency, and he's been a private detective, a practitioner of homeopathic medicine, and on the Vermont roster of psychotherapists. He's a former ham radio operator and a private pilot, and he used to be a skydiver. There's seemingly nothing that doesn't interest Hartmann and seemingly no topic he hasn't thought about, researched, or even written a book about. With one year of formal college under his belt, he is a true citizen-scholar in the mold of his hero, Thomas Jefferson. If you were to observe, in jest, that the guy seems hyperactive, or maybe easily bored, you would be correct. Or you could call him, to use his own term, a *hunter.*

When Thom and Louise's son Justin was a boy, he was diagnosed with attention deficit disorder. The news sent Hartmann not into a well of gloom, as it might some parents, but into an intensely focused search for information and answers. His research led him to the realization that he too had attention deficit disorder, followed by the writing of seven books on ADD and the invention of a fascinating original theory on the meaning and the origins of ADD: *hunter in a farmer's world,* described here in "The Edison Gene."

Hunter in a farmer's world is a powerful metaphor, and it reframed the conversation about ADD forever. Hartmann's first book on the subject, *Attention Deficit Disorder: A Different Perception,* published in the early nineties, was the first to come out and say that attention deficit is not a disorder or a defect but an evolutionary adaptation. The creativity, distractibility, and risk-taking that are characteristic of people with attention deficit are part of a unique skill set that was critical to the survival of our hunter-gatherer ancestors. However, traits that were advantageous in a hunting culture—constantly scanning the environment, impulsivity, distractibility—became a liability when human society switched to farming, which required patience and self-discipline. In 2002 gene researchers identified the genes associated with "hunter" behavior, confirming that Hartmann's model was a scientific reality.

Taking the hunter/farmer model further, Hartmann developed the paradigm described in "Older and Younger Cultures." One of his keystone theories, this pivotal idea is a lens through which we can view human behavior and find solutions to some of society's most pressing ecological and sociopolitical problems. This piece also introduces two men whose friendship and ideas would have a profound influence on Hartmann's intellectual and spiritual development: Gottfried Müller, the founder of the humanitarian organization Salem International; and the Coptic master Kurt Stanley.

Hartmann's background in advertising, psychology, and progressive talk radio informed his book *Cracking the Code: How to Win Hearts, Change Minds, and Restore America's Original Vision.* After spending years observing Republicans making huge strides in messaging, he realized that progressives needed help learning how to tell their stories to convey their vision to America. In the lively essay "Framing," he describes the art and the science of political persuasion using tools and techniques from the advertising industry. Mastering these communication strategies will do much more than just allow you to frame your message—it will show you how to distinguish and rebut right-wing propaganda wherever you find it.

The last piece in this section, "Walking the Blues Away," describes yet another breakthrough Hartmann theory: walking as bilateral therapy. Hartmann contends that walking, throughout human history, has been the brain's method of healing itself from psychological trauma.

It's a natural form of bilateral therapy that humans have used for centuries to alleviate emotionally charged memories. Just as our bodies can heal with time, our brains are designed to be psychologically self-healing. Walking "gives you access to healing powers, creative states, and emotional and psychological resilience beyond what you may have ever thought possible."

The Edison Gene

From *The Edison Gene: ADHD and the Gift of the Hunter Child*

> In the space of less than 40,000 years, ever more
> closely packed cultural "revolutions" have taken
> humanity from the status of a relatively rare large
> mammal to something more like a geologic force.
>
> —RICHARD G. KLEIN AND BLAKE EDGAR

I WAS IN INDIA IN 1993 TO HELP MANAGE A COMMUNITY FOR orphans and blind children on behalf of a German charity. During the monsoon season, the week of the big Hyderabad earthquake, I took an all-day train ride almost all the way across the subcontinent (from Bombay through Hyderabad to Rajahmundry) to visit an obscure town near the Bay of Bengal. In the train compartment with me were several Indian businessmen and a physician, and we had plenty of time to talk as the countryside flew by from sunrise to sunset.

Curious about how they viewed our children diagnosed as having attention deficit hyperactivity disorder (ADHD), I asked, "Are you familiar with those types of people who seem to crave stimulation yet have a hard time staying with any one focus for a period of time? They may hop from career to career and sometimes even from relationship to relationship, never seeming to settle into one job or into a life with one person—but the whole time they remain incredibly creative and inventive."

"Ah, we know this type well," one of the men said, the other three nodding in agreement.

"What do you call this personality type?" I asked.

"Very holy," he said. "These are old souls, near the end of their karmic cycle." Again the other three nodded in agreement, perhaps a bit more vigorously in response to my startled look.

"Old souls?" I questioned, thinking that a very odd description for those whom American psychiatrists have diagnosed as having a particular disorder.

"Yes," the physician said. "In our religion we believe that the purpose of reincarnation is to eventually free oneself from worldly entanglement and desire. In each lifetime we experience certain lessons, until finally we are free of this earth and can merge into the oneness of God. When a soul is very close to the end of those thousands of incarnations, he must take a few lifetimes to do many, many things— to clean up the little threads left over from his previous lives."

"This is a man very close to becoming enlightened," a businessman added. "We have great respect for such individuals, although their lives may be difficult."

Another businessman raised a finger and interjected. "But it is through the difficulties of such lives that the soul is purified." The others nodded in agreement.

"In America they consider this behavior indicative of a psychiatric disorder," I said. All three looked startled, then laughed.

"In America you consider our most holy men, our yogis and swamis, to be crazy people as well," said the physician with a touch of sadness in his voice. "So it is with different cultures. We live in different worlds."

We in our Western world have such "holy" and nearly enlightened people among us and we say they must be mad. But they may instead be our most creative individuals, our most extraordinary thinkers, our most brilliant inventors and pioneers. The children among us whom our teachers and psychiatrists say are "disordered" may, in fact, carry a set of abilities—a skill set—that was necessary for the survival of humanity in the past, that has created much of what we treasure in our present "quality of life," and that will be critical to the survival of the human race in the future.

Genetics and Differences

The long history of the human race has conferred on us—some of us more than others—a set of predilections, temperaments, and abilities carried through the medium of our genetic makeup. These skills were ideally suited to life in the ever-changing world of our ancient ancestors and, we have now discovered, are also ideally suited to the quickly changing modern world of cyberspace and widespread ecological and political crises that require rapid response. I will call this genetic gift the Edison gene,* after Thomas Edison, who brought us electric lights and phonographs and movies and—literally—10,000 other inventions. He is the model for the sort of impact a well-nurtured child carrying this gene can have on the world.

While I'm principally referring to the DRD4 gene, the science of genetics is embryonic, with new discoveries being made every day. No doubt sometime soon we'll have a better, more complete list of specific genes that make up what Dave deBronkart first called the "Edison trait" back in 1992 and Lucy Jo Palladino expanded on considerably in 1997 in her wonderful book *The Edison Trait: Saving the Spirit of Your Free-Thinking Child in a Conforming World.* For the moment, however, I'll use the useful shorthand the *Edison gene.*

When Edison's schoolteacher threw him out of school in the third grade for being inattentive, fidgety, and "slow," his mother, Nancy Edison, the well-educated daughter of a Presbyterian minister, was deeply offended by the schoolmaster's characterization of her son. As a result, she pulled him out of the school. She became his teacher from then until the day he went off on his own to work for the railroads (inventing, in his first months of employment, a railroad timing

---

*The Edison gene, of course, is not just a single gene. As is true for all characteristics, particularly those having to do with personality, those related to the Edison gene are actually the result of a complex interaction of many genes. While there is one gene that's been most often associated with what psychiatrists call ADHD—and this one is my best candidate for the Edison gene—there are many others that work with it in different configurations, shading its nuance and power to create the personality of an inventor, explorer, or entrepreneur.

and signaling device that was used for nearly a century). She believed in him and wasn't going to let the school thrash out of him his own belief in himself. As a result of that one mother's efforts, the world is a very different place.

"Ah, but we mustn't coddle these children!" some say. Consider this: Edison invented, at age 16, that device that revolutionized telegraph communication. It started him on a lifelong career of invention that led to the light bulb, the microphone, the motion picture, and the electrification of our cities. Would the world have been better off if he'd been disciplined into "behaving himself"?

The children and adults who carry this gene have and offer multiple gifts, both individually and as members of society. Sometimes these gifts are unrecognized, misinterpreted, or even punished, and as a result these exceptional children end up vilified, drugged, or shunted into Special Education. The result is that they often become reactive: sullen, angry, defiant, oppositional, and, in extreme cases, suicidal. Some Edison-gene adults face the same issues, carrying the wounds of school with them into adulthood, often finding themselves in jobs better adapted to stability than creativity.

What exactly defines those bearing this genetic makeup? Edison-gene children and adults are by nature enthusiastic, creative, disorganized, nonlinear in their thinking (they leap to new conclusions or observations), innovative, easily distracted (or, to put it differently, easily attracted to new stimuli), capable of extraordinary hyperfocus, understanding of what it means to be an "outsider," determined, eccentric, easily bored, impulsive, entrepreneurial, and energetic.

All of these qualities lead them to be natural explorers, inventors, discoverers, and leaders.

Those carrying this gene, however, often find themselves in environments where they're coerced, threatened, or shoehorned into a classroom or job that doesn't fit. When Edison-gene children aren't recognized for their gifts but instead are told that they're disordered, broken, or failures, a great emotional and spiritual wounding occurs.

This wounding can bring about all sorts of problems for children, for the adults they grow into, and for our society.

I and many scientists, educators, physicians, and therapists believe that when these unique children don't succeed in public schools it's often because of a disconnect between them—their brains are wired to make them brilliant inventors and entrepreneurs—and our schools, which are set up for children whose brains are wired to make them good workers in the structured environments of a factory or office cubicle.

Those children whom we call "normal" are more methodical, careful, and detail-oriented and are less likely to take risks. They often find it hard to keep it together and perform in the rapid-fire world of the Edison-gene child: they don't do as well with video games, couldn't handle working in an emergency room or on an ambulance crew, and seldom find themselves among the ranks of entrepreneurs, explorers, and salespeople.

Similarly, Edison-gene children have their own strengths and limitations: They don't do well in the school environment of repetition, auditory learning, and rote memorization that has been set up for "normal" kids, and they don't make very good bookkeepers or managers. Genetically, these kids are pioneers, explorers, and adventurers. They make great innovators, and they find high levels of success in any field where there's a lot of change, constant challenge, and lots of activity. Such personalities are common among emergency room physicians, surgeons, fighter pilots, and salespeople.

There are many areas in which such people can excel—especially when they make it through childhood with their belief in themselves intact.

1993: The Hunter Gene

Dozens of studies over the years have demonstrated that ADHD is genetically transmitted to children from their parents or grandparents. From the 1970s, when this link was first discovered, until 1993, when my first book on the topic was published, conventional wisdom held that ADHD, hyperactivity, and the restive need for high stimulation—all were indications of a psychiatric illness that should be treated with powerful, mind-altering, stimulant drugs.

But could it be that ADHD, this psychiatric "illness," has a positive side? I proposed in 1993 that these behaviors and temperaments—often misunderstood in schools—were once, in fact, useful skills for hunter-gatherer people (which I'll refer to simply as *hunters*) and also have a place in the modern world of emergency rooms, police departments, entrepreneurial businesses, and sales, to which the skills of the hunter can been transferred.

A year later the metaphor entered the popular culture with a *Time* magazine cover story on ADD and a sidebar article about my hypothesis, titled "Hail to the Hyperactive Hunter."[1] I contrasted the hunter skill set with the skills of the very first farmers, or agriculturalists, which have become those most favored in our schools and most workplaces.

Of course, when I referred to farmers in my comparison, I wasn't talking about modern agriculturists who contend with all the equipment and challenges of agriculture today. Instead I was considering the skill set of the first settled people who engaged in agriculture, those who had to spend hour after hour planting, cultivating, and harvesting crops by hand.

To engage in such early farming activity, three basic behaviors—which we now know are genetically determined and are related to brain dopamine levels—would have to be minimized: *distractibility, impulsivity,* and *risk-taking.* These three behaviors, however, would have been assets to hunters.

Because they are at the core of the ADHD diagnosis—and relate to those with the Edison gene—these behaviors are worth briefly exploring, along with their history in human societies.

Distractibility

Distractibility is often incorrectly characterized as the inability of a child or an adult to pay attention to a specific task or topic. Yet people with ADHD can pay attention, even for long periods of time (it's called *hyperfocusing*) but only to something that excites or interests them.

ADHD experts often noted that it's not that those with ADHD *can't* pay attention to anything; it's that they pay attention to everything. A better way to characterize the distractibility of ADHD is to describe it as *scanning.* In a classroom the child with ADHD is the one who notices the janitor mowing the lawn outside the window instead of focusing on the teacher's lecture on long division.

But while this constant scanning of the environment is a liability in a classroom setting, it may have been a survival skill for our prehistoric ancestors. A primitive hunter who couldn't easily fall into a mental state of constant scanning would be at a huge disadvantage. That flash of motion on the periphery of his vision might be either the rabbit that he needed for lunch or the tiger or bear hoping to make lunch of him.

When the agricultural revolution began 12,000 years ago, however, this scanning turned into a liability for those people whose societies changed from hunting to farming. If the moon was right, the soil held the perfect moisture, and the crops were due to be planted, a farmer couldn't waste his time wandering off into the forest to check out an unusual movement he noticed. He had to keep his attention focused on the task at hand and not be distracted from it.

Impulsivity

Impulsivity has two core manifestations among modern people with ADHD. The first is impulsive behavior—acting without thinking things through or the proverbial "leap before you look." Often this takes the form of interrupting others or blurting things out in conversation. Other times it's reflected in snap judgments or quick decisions.

To the prehistoric hunter, impulsivity was an asset because it provided the ability to act on instant decisions as well as the willingness to explore new, untested areas. If the hunter were chasing a rabbit through the forest with his spear and a deer ran by, he wouldn't have time to stop and calculate a risk/benefit analysis. He would have to make an instant decision about which animal to pursue, then act on that decision without a second thought.

Thomas Edison purportedly said that his combined distractibility and impulsiveness helped him in his "hunt" for world-transforming inventions. He said, "Look, I start here with the intention of going there [drawing an imaginary line] in an experiment, say, to increase the speed of the Atlantic cable; but when I have arrived partway in my straight line, I meet with a phenomenon and it leads me off in another direction, to something totally unexpected."

The second aspect of impulsivity is impatience. For a primitive farmer, however, impatience and impulsivity would spell disaster. A very patient approach, all the way down to the process of picking bugs off plants for hours each day, day after day, would have to be hardwired into the brain of a farmer. The word *boring* couldn't be in his vocabulary. His brain would have to be built in such a way that it tolerated, or even enjoyed, sticking with something until it was finished.

Risk-Taking

Risk-taking or, as Dr. Edward Hallowell and Dr. John Ratey describe it in their book *Driven to Distraction: Recognizing and Coping with Attention Deficit Disorder from Childhood through Adulthood,* "a restive search for high stimulation," is perhaps the most destructive of the behaviors associated with ADHD in contemporary society. It probably accounts for the high percentage of people with ADHD among prison populations and plays a role in a wide variety of social problems, from the risky driving of a teenager to the infidelity or job-hopping of an adult.

Yet for a primitive hunter, risk and high stimulation were a necessary part of daily life. In fact, the urge to experience risk, the desire for that adrenaline high, would have been necessary among the members of a hunting society because it would have propelled their members out into the forest or jungle in search of stimulation and dinner.

If a farmer were a risk-taker, however, the results could lead to starvation. Because decisions made by farmers had such long-ranging consequences, their brains would have to have been wired to avoid risks and to carefully determine the most risk-free way of going about their work.

So the agricultural revolution highlighted two very different types of human societies: farmers and hunters. Each group lived different lives, in different places. Those with the ADHD gene in farming societies were probably culled from the gene pool by natural selection, or they became warriors for their societies, "hunting" other humans as various tribes came into conflict. In some societies—evolving into the countries of India and Japan, for instance—this role was even institutionalized into a caste system. History is replete with anecdotes about the unique personalities of the warrior castes such as the Kshatriya in India and the Samurai in Japan.

Where Have All the Hunters Gone?

If we accept for a moment the possibility that the gene that causes ADHD was useful in another time and place but has become a liability in our modern society based on the systems of agriculture and industry, these question arise: How did we reach a point in human evolution where the farmers so massively outnumber the hunters? If the hunter gene was useful for the survival of people, why have hunting societies largely died out around the world, and why is ADHD seen in only 3 to 20 percent of the population (depending on how you measure it and whose numbers you use) instead of 50 percent or more?

Recent research from several sources shows that hunting societies are always wiped out by farming societies over time. Fewer than 10 percent of the members of a hunting society normally survive when their culture collides with an agricultural society—and it has nothing to do with the hunter's "attention deficits" or with any inherent superiority of the farmers.

In one study reported in *Discover* magazine,[2] the authors traced the root languages of the peoples living throughout central Africa and found that at one time the area was dominated by hunters: the Khoisans and the Pygmies. But over a period of several thousand years, virtually all of the Khoisans and Pygmies (the Hottentots and the Bushmen, as they've been referred to in Western literature) were wiped out and replaced by Bantu-speaking farmers. Two entire groups of people were rendered nearly extinct, while the Bantu-speaking farmers flooded across the continent, dominating central Africa.

There are several reasons for this startling transformation. First, agriculture is more efficient at generating calories than hunting. Because the same amount of land can support up to 10 times more people when used for farming rather than hunting, farming societies generally have roughly 10 times the population density of hunting societies. In war, numbers are always an advantage, particularly in these ratios. Few armies in history have survived an onslaught by another army 10 times larger.

Second, diseases such as chicken pox, influenza, and measles, which virtually wiped out vulnerable populations such as native North and South Americans, who died by the thousands when exposed to the illnesses of the invading Europeans, began as diseases of domesticated animals. The farmers who were regularly exposed to such diseases developed relative immunities; though they would become ill, these germs usually wouldn't kill them. Those with no prior exposure and thus no immunity, however, would often die. So when farmers encountered hunters, the latter were often killed off simply through exposure to the farmers' diseases.

Finally, agriculture provides physical stability to a culture. The tribe stays in one spot while their population grows, which allows its members to specialize in individual jobs. Some people become tool and weapon makers, some build devices that can be used in war, and some create governments, armies, and kingdoms—all of which give farming societies a huge technological advantage over hunting societies, which are generally more focused on day-to-day survival issues.

So now we have an answer to the question: Where have all the hunters gone?

Most were killed off, from Europe to Asia, from Africa to the Americas. Those who survived were brought into farming cultures either through assimilation, kidnapping, or cultural change—and provided the genetic material that appears in the small percentage of people with ADHD today.

Further evidence of the anthropological basis of ADHD is seen among the modern survivors of ancient hunting societies.

Indigenous Hunters Today

Cultural anthropologist Jay Fikes points out that members of traditional Native American hunting tribes normally behave differently from those who have traditionally been farmers. The farmers such as the Hopi and other Pueblo Indian tribes are relatively sedate and risk-averse, he says, whereas the hunters, such as the Navajo, are "constantly scanning their environment and are more immediately sensitive to nuances. They're also the ultimate risk-takers. They and the Apaches were great raiders and warriors."

A physician who recently read my first book on the subject, *Attention Deficit Disorder: A Different Perception,* and concluded that he saw proof of the hunter-versus-farmer concept in his work with some of the Native Americans in southwest Arizona, dropped me the following unsolicited note over the Internet:

> Many of these descendants of the Athabaskan Indians of western Canada have never chosen to adapt to farming. They had no written language until an Anglo minister, fairly recently, wrote down their language for the first time. They talk "heart to heart," and there is little "clutter" between you and them when you are communicating. They hear and consider everything you say. They are scanning all the time, both visually and auditorily. Time has no special meaning unless it is absolutely necessary (that's something we Anglos have imposed on them). They don't use small talk, but get right to the point, and have a deep understanding of people and the spiritual. And their history shows that they have a love of risk-taking.

But what sent humankind onto the radical social departure from hunting to farming? Few other animals, with the exception of highly organized insects such as ants, have developed a society that is based on anything that approaches agriculture.

In *The Ascent of Man,* Jacob Bronowski points out that 20,000 years ago every human on earth was a hunter and forager. The most advanced hunting societies had started following wild herd animals, as is still done by modern Laplanders. This had been the basis of human and pre-human society and lifestyle for several million years.

Until 1995 the earliest hard evidence of human activity (and hunting activity, at that) came from the Olduvai Gorge in Tanzania, Africa, with fragments of stone tools and weapons that dated back 2.5 million years. More recently, University of Southern California anthropologist Craig Stanford was quoted in the *Chicago Tribune* as saying that recent research he conducted in Africa indicates that early hominids may have been tribally hunting as early as 6 million years ago.

So for 6 million years, our ancestors were hunters, and then, suddenly, in a tiny moment of time (10,000 years is to 6 million years what less than three minutes is to a 24-hour day), the entire human race veered in a totally new direction.

The Agricultural Revolution

The reason for the change, according to Bronowski and many anthropologists, probably has to do with the end of the last ice age, which roughly corresponds to the beginning of the agricultural revolution. (Bronowski and most authorities place the agricultural revolution as occurring roughly 12,000 years ago.) At that time mutated grasses appeared simultaneously on several continents, probably in response to the sudden and radical change in climate. These grasses were the first high-yield, edible ancestors of modern rice and wheat and provided the humans who lived near them an opportunity to nurture and grow these staple foods.

Those people with the farmerlike patience to grow crops evolved into farming societies that emptied their ranks of the impulsive, sensation-seeking hunters among them. Those persons who were not patient enough to wait for rice to grow maintained their hunting tribes, the last remnants of which we see today in a few remaining indigenous peoples on the earth. The Old Testament, for example, is in large part the story of a nomadic hunting tribe moving through the wrenching process, over several generations, of becoming a settled farming tribe.

Our Society's Hunters

In 1996 the *Journal of Genetic Psychology* published an article titled "Attention Deficit Disorder: An Evolutionary Perspective," which suggested that, "Although no theory entirely explains the occurrence of ADHD, it is worthwhile to note that, at least historically, ADHD may have served an adaptive function and may have been selected by the environment for survival."[3]

In 1997 Peter S. Jensen, the head of the Child and Adolescent Psychiatry division of the National Institutes of Mental Health (NIMH), was the lead author of a paper published in the peer-reviewed *Journal of the American Academy of Child and Adolescent Psychiatry.* In that paper, titled "Evolution and Revolution in Child Psychiatry: ADHD as a Disorder of Adaptation,"[4] Jensen and his co-authors strongly argued that ADHD children shouldn't be told they have an illness but that instead parents and teachers should emphasize their positive characteristics. "In reframing the child who has ADHD as 'response ready,' experience-seeking, or alert," they wrote, "the clinician can counsel the child and family to recognize situations in modern society that might favor such an individual, both in terms of school environments, as well as future career opportunities, e.g., athlete, air-traffic controller, salesperson, soldier, or entrepreneur."[5]

But it was all just speculation until 2000, when the article "Dopamine Genes and ADHD" appeared in *Neuroscience and Biobehavioral Reviews.* This paper, by lead author James M. Swanson and 10 other scientists, noted that, "The literature on these candidate genes and ADHD is increasing. Eight molecular genetic studies have been published, so far, about investigations of a hypothesized association of ADHD with the DAT1 and the DRD4 gene."[6]

Soon other scientists were saying that the "hunter gene" may be a good thing. Dr. Robert Moyzis said of an NIMH-funded study of the gene, which he helped conduct, "We found a significant positive selection for the genetic variation associated with ADHD and novelty-seeking behavior in the human genome. This study strengthens significantly the connection between genetic variations and ADHD. It also provides a clue as to why ADHD is so pervasive."[7]

Numerous other scientific journals over the years have published similar reports or studies. There's a growing consensus that such children are carrying a gene for a behavior set that's really a skill set, a collection of *useful adaptations*. And a growing number of voices, such as Howard Gardner (*Frames of Mind: The Theory of Multiple Intelligences*) and Daniel Goleman (*Emotional Intelligence: Why It Can Matter More Than IQ*), are calling for a wider definition of the kinds of "intelligence" and talent our schools accept and teach to.

The Edison Gene

All these discoveries have led me to a new hypothesis built upon my earlier work with the hunter/farmer model.

The early development of this came, in part, from Michael Garnatz, who, with his wife, Heidi, has founded and runs the website www.hypies.com, one of the largest and most well-known ADHD sites in Germany. Michael confronted me one day with the essential inconsistency of a theory that suggests the Edison gene, which emerged in full form only about 40,000 years ago, was useful for hunters when humans had been hunters for 100,000 years before that. Although I'd never called it the farmer gene, Michael pointed out that its emergence in the human genome seemed to coincide with some of the earliest documented examples of ancient peoples' experimenting with agriculture. So how could I continue to call it the hunter gene?

I thought about this for some time, trying to figure out how to put together all the pieces in a way that was scientifically consistent and not merely some glib renaming of an older theory. Nothing seemed to work.

And then I read William H. Calvin's book, *A Brain for All Seasons*. Calvin had synthesized some of the most remarkable science of the last decade of the twentieth century and had done so in a way that gave sudden and clear meaning to the appearance and the persistence of the Edison gene.

The Crisis-Survival Gene

It's amazing what science can learn in a decade. In the early 1990s, most paleoclimatologists believed that climate change was a gradual phenomenon and that ice ages lasting 10,000 or more years were gradually alternated with periods of warmth. Nobody understood what caused the ice ages or even our current warmth, although variations in solar radiation were suspected.

Similarly, paleoanthropologists had known for decades that fully modern humans emerged from Africa about 200,000 years ago and, about 40,000 years ago, began behaving in highly organized and cooperative ways. Scientists had figured out that if they could take a child from the world of 38,000 years ago and raise him in today's world, he would be indistinguishable from the rest of us.

The problem was that nobody could understand why it took these "modern" people so long—up until about 10,000 years ago—to begin building city-states and engaging in intensive agriculture. Of course, people pointed to the ice age that had North America, northern Asia, and Europe in its grip up until 10,000 years ago, but this didn't explain why civilizations weren't being built in still-warm Africa or other equatorial areas of the world.

In part this confusion was due to the common assumption that ice ages were relatively constant phenomena that had come on slowly throughout ancient history, with the glaciers of the most recent one gradually melting about 10,000 years ago, leading to today's weather.

A decade later, however, scientists discovered that what they thought to be true was actually wrong. As William Calvin documents so brilliantly in *A Brain for All Seasons,* it turns out that each and every one of the transitions between the cold, dry, windy ice ages and today's wet, warm weather happened not gradually, over hundreds or thousands of years, but suddenly—in fewer than a dozen years.

The weather might have become strange one year, with a cold summer and a hard winter, and then the next year, or the one after that, the summer simply never returned. The winters then became so harsh that very few humans could survive them (with the exception, it seems, of the Neanderthals, who could—and did—more easily because their bodies were better adapted to cold).

Although ice gripped the north during these times, the weather changes also hit Africa and southern Asia: when it became cold in the north, drought struck the equatorial regions. Waterholes dried up, rivers stopped flowing, and jungles and rain forests turned to tinder and then blazed in massive, continent-consuming wildfires.

When, a thousand or so years later, the worldwide weather switched to being wet and warm, ice in the north thawed and monsoonlike floods swept Africa, tearing away what life had managed to hang on to survival during the cool, dry, windy period.

This is the cauldron in which humans evolved. When we look at a graph of worldwide temperatures, we discover that in the past 150,000 years—virtually the whole of human history—there has rarely been a period of 10,000 years (or even as much as 2,000 years) of steady, warm, comfortable weather. The single exception is the past 10,000 years, which is referred to as the Holocene period.

Hunters before the Holocene

When the climate is stable, farmers are at an advantage. During the summer they can plant and harvest crops, which they can eat during the winter. Life is good, and they're able to extract at least 10 times the calories from a given area of land that hunter people can. When the climate is constantly changing, however, farming becomes impossible. Hunters rarely suffer from the affliction of farmers—famine—because when a hunting area is hit by drought or flood, heat or cold, such people simply move to another place. When one primary food plant or animal dies off, they switch to others. When the pickings get slim, hunters expand their range.

The diet of hunters is incredibly diverse because of their ranging and nomadic existence. This is why, until the development of antibiotics around the time of World War II, no agricultural peoples in the 8,000-year history of agriculture had achieved the health of hunters. Both modern *and* ancient hunters consistently have had stronger bones and taller bodies, have lost fewer teeth, and have lived longer than typical Europeans from the earliest cities until as recently as 50 years ago.

While popular culture portrays the lives of hunter people as harsh and miserable, the ones I've met and known on four continents enjoy high-quality lives. Indeed, according to anthropologists, hunters represent the original leisure society, typically working only two to four hours a day to secure all their food and shelter needs and spending the rest of the time playing with their families, talking, singing, and building community.

Thus we find that hunters were ideally suited to the climate of the world for most of its history, just as agricultural peoples are well suited to it as it is today. In both of these cultures, there is and has always been a place and a need for those creative, nonconformist individuals who are best adapted to change, especially when the climate undergoes one of its regular flip-flops (to use Calvin's term).

During ancient hunter times, it was the creative nonconformists who broke with 100,000 years of tradition and invented ostrich shell beads to exchange with other tribes as a way of sealing mutual deals for hunting rights. During more recent agricultural and industrial times, it was the creative nonconformist Thomas Edison who brought us electric lights, movies, and 10,000 other inventions.

The gene for wanderlust, adventure, and innovation is relatively rare, carried by fewer than 10 percent of our population. But it's incredibly valuable, and it's even possible that one day the survival of the human race will depend on it.

From *The Edison Gene* by Thom Hartmann, © 2003,
published by Inner Traditions International.

Older and Younger Cultures

From *The Prophet's Way: A Guide to Living in the Now*

> The man who sat on the ground in his tipi meditating
> on life and its meaning, accepting the kinship of all
> creatures and acknowledging unity with the universe
> of things was infusing into his being the true essence of
> civilization. And when native man left off this form of
> development, his humanization was retarded in growth.
>
> —Chief Luther Standing Bear

I N MY EARLIER BOOKS ON ADD, I POINTED OUT HOW FROM THE earliest times humans were hunter-gatherers and that some of those behaviors that were survival skills for our ancestors are now problems in many modern schools and workplaces.

The picture that this model paints for some people is one of noble hunters who have been systematically tracked down and destroyed by the ignoble farmers.

While it's true that there are now only a very few hunting societies left on the earth, as I delved deeper I came to realize that the real paradigm is deeper than just hunters and farmers.

While that does a fine job of explaining why some kids excel or fail in school, or why high-stimulation-seeking people are drawn to jobs like being an emergency medical technician while low-stimulation-seeking people are drawn to jobs like accounting, it misses a larger and more important point.

That point is the one that prophets from Jeremiah to Jesus to Nostradamus to Edgar Cayce have gone to great lengths to indicate to us: "modern" (post–agricultural revolution, since 10,000 BCE) humankind is destroying the world in which we live.

One explanation often put forth for this is that there is a basic flaw in human nature. This concept of original sin is often pointed to as being demonstrated in the biblical story of Eve and the apple.

The problem with this concept, however, is that there have been human societies around for hundreds of thousands of years—people just like you and me—who did not destroy the world. Instead they lived in harmony with it.

I first encountered this possibility as a teenager, reading Margaret Mead's *Coming of Age in Samoa: A Psychological Study of Primitive Youth for Western Civilisation*. There were detractors and counter-arguments to her view of the noble primitive, however, and even when I first read her book it occurred to me that her Samoan "primitive" people were lacking basic and important things like advanced medical care and communications, which, I assumed, would make their lives better if they'd had them.

My assumption was then, as it had been all my life, that our culture, what we call Western civilization, was inherently better and more valuable than what we called the primitive cultures that preceded it.

Then while in Bogotá for Gottfried Müller, at the Salem program in the La Paz slum, I first heard the story of the Kogi tribe, who live at the top of one of the Andes mountain ranges.

When I heard of the message of the elder brothers, I thought it an interesting spiritual story but figured that the average person would have little interest in it. After all, how could a primitive people who live on simple crops have something important to teach us? We have, after all, conquered the earth. We've conquered disease, hunger, space, and even the atom.

I also noticed that the elder brother people, to use my hunter/ farmer metaphor, very much exhibit the characteristics of farmers. And it was on the farmers that I'd been mentally blaming much of the mess of modern civilization.

Yet these elder brothers lived in harmony with the world and had for thousands of years. They trod lightly upon this earth, and even in their architecture they didn't damage the ecosystems but instead guaranteed their survival over millennia.

And now I was being told that they are warning us, their younger brothers, that we are on the verge of bringing about a global catastrophe.

So, if the elder brothers, and other ancient civilizations that have lived in peace with the world, were farmers and yet didn't create a civilization that (like other farmer societies of Europe, Africa, and Asia) would ultimately lead to the death of the world, what was different? How could it be that some farmer peoples would leave behind a planet relatively unscathed, whereas others would wreak such incredible damage that it would put all life on earth at risk?

I had similarly paradoxical questions about hunters. Many primitive hunting people (using my metaphor) left only gentle footprints on the planet. Elaborate cave paintings from 30,000 years ago in France and 20,000 years ago in Australia are the remnants they have left us—not piles of nuclear waste that will be lethal for more than a million years into the future.

But other hunting people were exploitative. They burned forests to drive out animals or, more commonly, turned their hunting efforts against their neighbors and became hunters of humans. The Mongols and the Tatars, originally nomadic hunting tribes, rose to conquer most of Europe and ruled it with a brutal iron fist for centuries, every bit as cruelly as had the Roman Empire, which had evolved from an agricultural society.

So, with ADD it may well be something as simple as hunter and farmer material remaining in our genetic code. But from a larger view, the view of the past and the future of the planet, there was a third picture that I began to see only after first visiting the Apaches in 1995.

This is the idea of cultures that are "old" and "young."

The old cultures, be they agricultural or hunting/gathering, live with an intrinsic connection to the earth. For them the planet on which we live is itself a living organism. It has its own life, its own destiny, and, in a way that the younger cultures could never understand, its own consciousness. Things that run counter to the earth's nature will (naturally) not work in the long run—although the damage may be too slow to be noticeable on the younger-culture time scale. All we have to do, to tell which is which, is look at what's happening on the planet.

And that's why what I've seen in my travels is so disturbing.

The younger cultures live quite different lives: they view themselves as separate from the earth, with "dominion" over it, and see the earth's resources only as things to be used and then discarded. Nature is the enemy, not the mother, father, or brother/sister of these younger peoples, and their disregard for it is so visceral, so intrinsic to their worldview, that many live their entire lives without ever once questioning their own cultural assumptions about humankind's place in the universe.

The older peoples are so clear in their understanding of humankind's place on earth that they often pray for the soul of an animal as they kill it for food. Daily they thank God for the life given them and the life around them—all of which is viewed with reverence.

The younger peoples, on the other hand, are so egocentric that in the recent past they tenaciously fought—killed and tortured—to preserve their belief that our planet was at the center of all creation. Many of these younger-culture descendants still argue that the creation of humans marked the creation of all things, and even today they fight to insert such teachings into public schools. They are so ethnocentric that they make it an article of faith to seek out and convert older cultures to their view of the world—or to obliterate them entirely, as was done across much of North and South America, Africa, Australia, and Europe. Their view was so short and their arrogance so great that they believed their "conquest" of disease and hunger with modern medicine and agriculture were signs of a blessing by God.

Older cultures the world over are warning younger cultures of the danger and the stupidity of their ways. I was told by the Apaches and received the message in Colombia. Tribal village elders in Africa asked me to "warn the world" that the famine I was seeing there in

Uganda in 1980 would one day be worldwide, the fate of the white man as well.

I cannot imagine it is mere coincidence that *the same message* would come from all of these disparate peoples, who have no conventional way of communicating with one another.

And all I'd seen of death, famine, children suffering, warfare, and extermination was because of the arrogance, the greed, the limited vision, and, ultimately, the immaturity of the younger cultures. We discovered and developed technology but do not have the wisdom to consistently use it responsibly; we've infected the earth's landmasses like an encrusted sore, and now we're filling the seas with the pus of our waste.

Gottfried Müller pointed out to me how Jesus warned against this. The earliest Jews had been an older culture, and we can see this in the story of Cain and Abel. The farmer (Cain) killed the earth-respecting herder brother, so God cursed his future agricultural efforts. Surely this was the story of an older-culture peoples and a warning to those who would follow.

But along the course of time, the ancient Hebrews encountered more and more younger peoples and began to adopt their ways. The prophets railed against this and warned over and over about the inevitable results; but as the record of the Bible tells us, the prophets were almost always ignored.

Then came Jesus who, it now appears from the Dead Sea Scrolls and other sources, was a member of the Essenes. The Essenes were an older-culture Jewish fragment that still remained in his day, which was dominated by younger-culture Judaism. And his message, not at all well received in his time, was an older-culture message: stop worrying (God will provide), trust others to the point of not fighting them in court, respect and see God in everybody, forgive people no matter how many times they harm you.

Absolutely, the older-culture message is one of harmony and living together. It is not a message of separation, of "us or them," and it has not a word about dominating others.

He directly challenged the younger-culture notions of destroying one's enemy, of exploiting the earth with intensive agriculture, and—the ultimate younger-culture idea—that man is independent of God and that human "thinking" is the same as "consciousness."

These teachings showed older-culture insights that man is *not* separate from God and nature and that even our thoughts have meaning and impact—and are known to God. We are all a part of a larger, more encompassing consciousness.

In a younger culture, it's assumed that God is distant, that heaven is far away in time and space, that humans are separate and unique and have to grab what they can, and that the ancient laws that protected the earth, such as a Sabbath for the land, are merely quaint. Jesus challenged all of these and did so with such conviction that it led to his being sentenced to death.

But after his crucifixion, a man who was an enthusiastic member of the younger culture of the then-modern Jews and who circulated freely and comfortably in the younger culture of the Roman conquerors was visited by the Holy Spirit or Christ himself or both and began an aggressive ministry. This man, Saul, later renamed Paul, took much of Jesus's messages to the far parts of what was then his known world, and the messages he carried became the basis of what was to be today's Christian Church.

But there were also parts of Jesus's message—those older-culture warnings and admonitions—that Paul could not understand because of his own cultural upbringing, so he overlooked or ignored them.

Some years ago Herr Müller commented to me that he preferred to read the four Gospels, the Psalms, and the Prophets over the writings of Paul.

It wasn't until I understood this fundamental difference in worldviews that Paul's writings represent that I understood his comment. A man who worries about the lives of even the tiniest of living creatures certainly has an older-culture view of the world—a view that's now nearly extinct planetwide.

How many pastors of today, for example, would survive in their position if they preached that people should not have savings or charge interest, should not gather into barns, should trust God totally for tomorrow even if it meant their death, and should not only not fight against their enemies but help them and pray for them?

In the small view, those are all recognized as good words and often cited from the pulpit. But they're cited only as quaint stories, or perhaps metaphors, or lessons in humility—not as instructions to an entire culture about how it must reform itself if it is to avoid destroying itself and the world.

Herr Müller's commitment to peace (that's what *Salem* means, after all) is so complete he will not eat the products of violence. His older-culture understanding teaches that food must be grown organically—not just to be healthier but out of respect for the earth itself. As we pollute and destroy the earth and ourselves (from our drunkenlike consumption of oil and energy to the very personal pollution of our bodies through nicotine and other drugs), we show how totally disconnected we are from the life we were bred for and the spirit that's part of it.

Once when Herr Müller embraced a huge pine tree, hugging it, talking with it, giving it his blessing and asking it for its blessing, I asked: "Do trees have souls?"

He shrugged. "I do not know. But the light of God's life is in all living things."

"So you see God all around you?" I asked.

"Yes, of course."

"But some would call that animism or say that you're worshipping nature spirits or something like that."

"We are humans, in the image of God, but we are also part of nature," he said simply. "I save the life of a worm, I have saved life. I touch the life of the tree, I have touched life. Of course, we have a highest obligation to human life, but it is the stupidity of people who do not see the light of God in all living things that has led to this."

He waved his hand above his head at the browning pine trees, victims of acid rain and pollution. "Who could kill off a forest for a few dollars if he knew that the forest was alive with the light and the presence of God? Only a stupid man, and that is what we have become. Because people do not see the light of God in all life, they are so ready to destroy the world for profit and power. And this is what will end with the end times: in the new times to come, people will know that all life is sacred."

And so I saw it clearly, at last.

As an enthusiastic member of our science-worshipping modern culture, I'd felt a shock when I first realized as a youth that there might be buried within my religion and education the remnants of an older and wiser culture. This older culture seemed inexplicable and odd: its most famous ancient spokesperson (Jesus) said that we should forgive people regardless of what they did, that we should not worry about the future, and that we should bless and love those who have hurt and used and exploited us. Nobody I'd ever known lived that way.

At the time I didn't know what to make of this, and I carried the dissonance with me as the years went by.

You can imagine the effect on me when I later did meet a human who actually lived the principles of that older and more mature culture: Kurt Stanley. The things Master Stanley did and taught were inexplicable in the context of my scientific worldview: they were miracles or madness. Yet I knew what I'd seen, whether or not I could explain it. And I later met Herr Müller, who had similar insights and powers.

As I delved into Master Stanley's and Herr Müller's lives and teachings, I saw that their older-culture beliefs were firmly anchored in things I had always told myself were the basis for our younger (Jewish and Christian) culture: the words and the acts of Jesus and the prophets who preceded him.

But I also discovered that even *these* teachings had been turned by the younger culture into machines, mechanistic steps and rituals to be manipulated to suit the purposes of those in power, into do-this-and-you'll-get-that-result formulas.

We had kept the information, but we'd lost the wisdom.

This loss of wisdom has led to terrible human suffering in our past and has set up potentially severe difficulties in our future.

The early colonists of the United States were fond of the Calvinistic notion that those who won in battle or commerce did so because it was manifest destiny or the will of their god. This rationalization satisfied their consciences as they slaughtered the natives who already occupied the land that the colonists had "discovered" and as they bought, sold, and used human slaves—as had their younger-culture dominator predecessors all the way back into the earliest records of human history.

It's clearly a story of younger, immature cultures interested in themselves (like any immature entity) to the exclusion of the larger community in which they live. The view was well articulated by Aristotle and Descartes. It holds that those who survive are, ipso facto, better suited for survival. By this logic it follows that those who conquer, who destroy, are superior; otherwise they wouldn't be around to write the history books.

Further, because better machines make better conquerors, a culture that views the entire universe and all of life as a machine will make the best machines and thus be the best conquerors.

Unfortunately for our culture, this works only in a world of abundant resources. When human populations and their needs outstrip the resources available to them, this cultural viewpoint most often leads to war and famine. If our standard way of interacting with the world is to dominate and subdue it, our first response to other peoples' competing for resources is to dominate and subdue *them* too.

Older cultures, on the other hand, view living things as interrelated and interconnected. The world, in the words of an Apache medicine woman I met, "flows from the web of life." The earth is alive, and all humans are a part of its life, not separate from it. And the valued skills are not machine-building or conquest but love, mercy, forgiveness, and a connection to the power of life.

In a younger culture, consciousness means *thinking,* considering with a purpose in mind.

In an older culture, consciousness touches an *experience beyond thought* that has to do with *being,* with the way we are—the power of life.

From *The Prophet's Way* by Thom Hartmann,
© 1997, published by Inner Traditions International.

Framing

From *Cracking the Code: How to Win Hearts,
Change Minds, and Restore America's Original Vision*

Every word evokes a frame.

—GEORGE LAKOFF

WITH STARTLING REGULARITY, EVERY MONTH OR TWO SOMEONE will call in to my radio program with a very specific story about why they oppose gun control. The story nearly always goes like this:

> A friend of mine was shopping at the supermarket, and when she came back from shopping she found a black guy (it's always a black guy) trying to break into her car. As she walked up to her car, he pulled a knife on her. Fortunately, she always carries her gun with her. She pulled her gun out of her purse and he ran away. That's why we need guns.

That's a very powerful story. So every time I hear it, I say, "Wow, that's a powerful story. Tell me more. Who is your friend?" And the caller will say, "Well, actually, it didn't happen to my friend; my friend told me the story about someone else that he knows." Turns out, the caller doesn't actually know anyone who pulled a gun on a carjacker in a supermarket parking lot. The story is not a personal story at all. But it has such power, even as a friend-of-a-friend story, because it's a story that gives us a way of understanding an issue.

There are other stories about gun control. In my case, it really is a personal story.

My best friend in high school, Clark Stinson, went off to the army during the Vietnam War. He came home for the Christmas holiday after basic training and told me how much he hated the army and the prospect of going off to a war he didn't believe in. He was feeling really depressed, went to a gun shop, bought a gun, put it in his mouth, and blew the back of his head all over his bedroom wall. If he hadn't been able to get a gun so quickly and easily, he might have been able to get help and still be with us.

Here's another gun control story, synthesized from several articles in the paper over the past few years:

A family in our community just suffered a terrible tragedy. The father was a gun owner who forgot to lock his gun safe. His five-year-old son had a friend over, and they found the open safe. The man's son took out the gun, and the boys decided to play cops and robbers. The gun was loaded, and the boy ended up shooting his little friend.

All of these stories are persuasive. They all have strong visual and kinesthetic elements and appeal directly to our feelings, and feelings always come first in our decision-making.

When we probe the stories deeper, the handgun-control story has the advantage of being true.[1] I'm not saying that someone, somewhere didn't pull a gun on a carjacker. I'm sure that has happened, and the National Rifle Association probably issued a hundred press releases about it. But easily available handguns do lead to an increase in suicides and an increase in deaths of innocent bystanders. For example, one in six parents say they know a child who accidentally shot him- or herself with a handgun. Guns kept in the home for self-protection are 43 times more likely to kill a family member or friend than to kill in self-defense. And suicide is nearly five times more likely to occur in a household with a gun than a household without a gun.[2]

Handgun ownership makes a society more dangerous. A Montreal-based gun control group, for example, uses a statistical comparison between the United States and Canada to bolster the case for increasing gun control in both countries:[3]

> The US has a higher rate of gun ownership, particularly of handguns, than any other industrialized country in the world. Approximately 40 percent of US households have firearms and it is estimated that there are more than 200 million firearms owned, one-third of them handguns. In Canada, it is estimated that there are approximately 7 million firearms, only about 450,000 of them handguns.

Approximately 18 percent of Canadian households have firearms. Rates of homicide without guns in the US are only slightly higher than in Canada whereas rates of homicide with guns are much higher. This suggests that the availability of firearms is a critical fact in the high US homicide rate.

Truth is always the most powerful form of persuasion, and it offers the most useful and durable (ecological) frame.

Framing John McCain

The conservatives had a hard time going into the 2008 election. None of the Republican frontrunners was a dyed-in-the-wool abortion-hating, war-loving, welfare-bashing, corporatocracy supporter—at least not reliably and all at the same time. Unlike the Democrats, who tend to encourage debate among their candidates, the conservatives began in May 2006—two years before the election—to push potential frontrunners toward particular, uniform, conservative views. They wanted to code their communications from the very first moment of the presidential campaign.

One target of this early effort at political persuasion was John McCain. McCain was reliably pro-war and anti-abortion, but he seemed to have some trouble supporting the wealthiest 1 percent of all Americans. Outrageously, McCain had voted to retain the estate tax for estates over $5 million. If someone dies and leaves more than $5 million to heirs, McCain actually thought it was a good idea for their rich children to pay taxes on the money they're getting by accident of birth that exceeded the first 5 million bucks. The conservatives—who care a lot about people who have $5 million at their disposal—were not happy with McCain. So, when McCain was running to retain his Senate seat back in 2006, they created an ad just for the conservative blogosphere designed to get McCain to change his mind.

The ad is a masterpiece of future pacing, incorporating trance techniques to push McCain into a future in which he will vote against the estate tax. It ties those techniques together with a strong *frame* to code its message.

Here's how the ad goes:

> [picture of John McCain smiling]

"American family business owners and farmers are counting on John McCain . . ."

> [a white flash, like a camera flashbulb, then a picture
> of a man holding a boy against a blue sky]

"counting on McCain to protect the jobs they create and the legacy they leave their children . . ."

This is a very friendly opening, designed to establish a rapport with McCain and with McCain supporters. Americans, families, farmers—all "are counting" on McCain. That suggests they will support him, but the emphasis is on what he does in the future.

The flash that comes between pictures is almost unnoticeable. That fast flash is designed to help put McCain supporters into a learning trance. It registers on the unconscious while the conscious is trying to process the words and the images that are more readily visible. The brain has to focus harder to get the visual process going.

> [Flash, then a picture of the *Chicago Sun-Times* against a black
> background with a quote from McCain circled. The visual sub-
> modalities change quickly as the image is shown far away, then
> brought close. The auditory submodalities shift as the music
> changes and becomes darker, even dirgelike. For some the visual/
> auditory connection may suggest a funeral announcement and
> evoke a powerful kinesthetic feeling/response of dread.]

"counting on John McCain to keep his promise and show the leadership he's known for . . ."

Now the insistence on the future grows stronger. He's made a promise, and the question is whether he will keep it. The modality changes to kinesthetic.

> [No flash here—the image changes at a slower pace to a dark
> blurred-out picture on a black background. The picture—
> which may not be consciously recognized the first time one

> sees the ad—depicts mourners carrying a casket in the rain,
> with the logo www.nodeathtax.org in white in front of it.]

"counting on him to cast the deciding vote to end the IRS death tax
forever."

Here, finally, is the promise. It's a promise to "end the IRS death tax forever." Go back to Newt Gingrich's anchor words. What words could trigger negative emotions more strongly than "IRS" and "death"? Nothing, perhaps, except "IRS death *tax.*" Here those very powerful words are themselves anchored in death both visually—through the black background established in the previous shot and the barely visible funeral picture—and auditorily, through the music. McCain is thrown into the future of his promise. What we've been counting on him to do is end this terrible thing, the IRS death tax.

Notice the many different ways the ad simultaneously is working to create a trance. Aside from the intermittent flashes, the ad shifts submodalities from auditory to visual to kinesthetic. The effect is that by the time this final, dramatic picture shows up, the viewer must focus very hard to figure out what is happening onscreen. By now most viewers will be deeply in a learning trance.

Notice also that this image gets the viewer to key in particularly on the words *death tax* in the URL www.nodeathtax.org. At the unconscious/emotional level, the viewer won't pick up the negative *no* and will unconsciously read only *death tax* and shudder.

> [The ad flashes again, a flash that is longer and brighter.
> The picture then goes back to the exact same image the
> ad began with—an image of John McCain smiling.]

"Ask John McCain to keep his promise and vote to end the death tax."

Now that the viewers are in a learning trance, they are taken back to the start of the ad, as though the rest of the ad never happened. In this trance they are given a task in the immediate present and the near future: "Ask John McCain to keep his promise."

At the same time, the ad uses future pacing to throw McCain and his followers into the future. He must keep his promise because all of his supporters will be counting on him. The emotional/irrational mind will "understand" that he was smiling at the beginning of the ad because he kept his promise. That's the future we can imagine. Now, the ad says, we have to go back and make sure that future happens.

> [Picture of McCain smiling zooms in, so his face is closer to us.
> On top of the image are the words *Tell him it's important. . . .*]

"Tell John McCain it's important."

> [Picture of McCain smiling zooms in more, so he is even closer.
> On top of the image are the words *Tell him we're watching. . . .*]

"Tell him we're watching."

> [Picture of McCain zooms in again, even closer. On top of
> the image are the words *Tell him we'll **remember**. . . .*]

"Tell him we'll remember."

This is pacing used both to create a trance and to modify the future. The visual effect of the same picture zooming in, closer and closer, enhances the trance that the viewer is already in. In this trance the viewer is given more commands. The commands appear to be directed to McCain ("Tell him") but are also directed to the viewer: "remember." The ad wants viewers to remember how McCain votes on the estate tax and to base their support on how he votes. And, as a powerful and useful side benefit, it directs viewers to emotionally anchor the "IRS death tax" with powerful negative states for their own future.

The ad is a direct attempt to change the future by modifying the behavior of a candidate—and the electorate. The target of the ad was John McCain himself. If McCain votes against the tax, he will get support. If he votes for the tax, viewers will "remember" and vote against him. The outcome is assured by the ad itself, which has put its viewers into a trance and directed them to take those steps—including the viewer named John McCain, who is imagining all those other people out there looking at him and wondering about the . . . *er* . . . size of his vote.

Just in case you are interested, the ad worked. The ad appeared in May 2006. On June 8, 2006, John McCain voted to bring bill H.R. 8, advocating abolishing the estate tax, to a vote.

Framing Your Worldview

If all that the "death tax" ad had done was use future pacing to throw McCain and his supporters into a future in which he supported abolishing the estate tax, it would have been effective. If the ad had done that and also put viewers into a learning trance so they would "remember" how McCain voted, it would have been effective. Both those effects, however, would have had a direct political impact only on John McCain. The ad would have been a powerful tool to change McCain's vote and no more.

But this ad did something more. It told viewers how to think about the estate tax. It told them to "remember" that the estate tax is an "IRS death tax." That's a powerful frame.

We experience the world through our senses. We remember through pictures, sounds, tastes, and touch. We then sort those sensations through our feelings. That's the brain's folder system. It's not easy to distill the very complex world around us down to these very simple elements, but that's what we have to do because that's how the brain works.

We move from complexity to simplicity by using frames.

A *frame* is a simple way of understanding a complex set of feelings and sensations. "My family" is a frame I use to think about the people with whom I have a very particular kind of deep and complex relationship, largely based on love but also on interdependence and mutual support. The frame doesn't actually tell other people anything about who is in my family. I may think my family includes only my wife and children, or I may think of my family as an "extended family" that includes my mother, my in-laws, my siblings, and so forth. It may even include deceased relatives, like my father and my grandparents. For some people "my family" includes people who are not related to them by blood or marriage—they have become family by virtue of close and lasting ties.

A frame won't tell you about any particular content. If we speak of the frame "my family," it won't tell you who I think is in my family, and it won't tell me who you think is in your family. What a frame will disclose, however, and very powerfully, is how to think about a certain set of people. When people say, "My dog is a member of my family," we understand immediately the strong feelings those people must have for their dog. They don't have to explain those feelings at all. They just have to use the word *family* and we get it. That's because "my family" is a frame we all understand at a visceral level, even though its content is highly variable.

Politics is all about frames. When I was in high school, the debating instructor would talk about the importance of framing an argument. He'd say, "How do you frame an argument? What position are you taking? How is that position—that frame—constructed?" He knew that once you've defined a frame, you've colored or changed the meaning of everything that is contained within that frame.

Democrats have finally gotten wise to the power of framing, largely through the work of George Lakoff, a linguistics professor and the author of *Don't Think of an Elephant: Know Your Values and Frame the Debate.* Before Lakoff, Democrats thought that the best way to frame an argument was to describe the argument as accurately as possible. They thought that you convinced people by talking about content. What Lakoff taught them—and what the conservatives already knew from having listened to people like Newt Gingrich and Frank Luntz and Karl Rove—was that what matters is our *feelings* about the content. Remember: feeling comes first.

Frames are powerful because they can quickly bring up a whole set of feelings. When we communicate, frames give us a simple way to elicit a particular response to what can be a very complex issue or idea.

The conservatives' "death tax" frame is a perfect example.

The Frame on Taxes

John McCain upset conservatives because of the position he took on the inheritance, or estate, tax.

The United States was founded in opposition to a monarchy supported by a landed aristocracy. Our country's Founders wanted to make sure that their radical idea—a country governed by We the People—would never be replaced by a king and a bunch of nobles.

Writing more than 200 years ago, Thomas Jefferson argued for a tax on accumulated wealth because he knew that if wealth was passed down from one generation to the next, those lucky inheritors would turn into new aristocrats. You don't hear about the Founders passing on fortunes because most of them didn't believe in doing so. Thomas Jefferson himself died in debt.

Despite Jefferson's warnings about the danger to "the state" of the accumulation of "excessive wealth," such a tax was not actually put into place until 1916. The estate tax was one of the many reforms put into place during the Progressive Era, a period from 1896 to 1918 when ordinary people rose up against the robber barons and the monopolists who had created an aristocracy of wealth, power, and privilege in this country. President Theodore Roosevelt, a Republican, advocated for the estate tax in 1906, arguing, "The man of great wealth owes a particular obligation to the State because he derives special advantages from the mere existence of government."

Teddy Roosevelt, in that simple sentence, gave us the liberal frame on the estate tax and in fact on all taxes. Taxes are the means we use to fund our society, which includes the government institutions that make it possible for people to accumulate wealth.

I often talk to people on my radio show who say they shouldn't have to pay taxes.

"Why not?" I ask them.

"Well, I'm a self-made man," they reply. "I've earned all of my money by starting my own business, and I don't see why I should pay any of it to the government." That's the conservative core story, that self-interest trumps the public interest.

"Okay," I say. "Well, do you have plumbing and electricity in your business?"

"Of course."

"Do your employees and customers use the highway and street system to drive to your business or take public transportation to get there?"

"Of course."

"Okay. And do you use money for your transactions and keep that money in a bank that you trust?"

"Yes."

"Well," I say, "it seems to me you've relied pretty heavily on the government institutions and government-built infrastructure of our society to build your business. You've used public utilities and the public transportation infrastructure; you rely on the public regulation of banking and finance; you probably also are relying on public education to train the people who work for you and on public programs like Social Security and Medicare to cut the cost to you of employee benefits. Seems to me like you owe society a pretty large bill for all the services you use to make your business possible and profitable, and the way we pay that debt is through taxes."

That's the traditional liberal American story on taxes, and it's a powerful one. It works even better for the estate tax.

Estate Tax or Death Tax

Most of us would like to be able to pass along enough money to our children to ensure that they will be able to put food on the table and perhaps even to avoid working for a living for a few generations. We don't, however, want to create a permanent overclass in America simply because someone got lucky and had a very good businessman for a grandfather or a very good investor for a grandmother. Family dynasties—in our day, the Rockefellers, Kennedys, and Bushes spring to mind—are ultimately not healthy for democracy and largely didn't even exist in this nation until after the Civil War, when incorporation and taxation laws were changed to allow the massive accumulation of wealth using the corporate form.

Nor are they healthy for capitalism. Many wealthy businesspeople believe that a powerful class composed mostly of people of inherited wealth cripples innovation and ingenuity, creating a disincentive to work among the best educated. Warren Buffet is a good example of a self-made man who has decided to give his massive estate away rather than give it to his children (the kids don't become paupers— they each will inherit millions).

He's in good company, which includes the father of Bill Gates as well as businessman Bill Foster, who will owe the tax.

"The proponents of estate tax repeal are fond of calling it the 'death tax.' It's not a death tax; it's a rich kids' tax," Foster has said. "The estate tax is one of our time-tested and best tools in preventing the aristocracy of an 'Old Europe' from establishing itself on our shores."[4]

Understood as an inheritance tax or, as Foster calls it, a "rich kids' tax," this tax makes sense. An inheritance tax is a kind of tax even a Republican might be willing to support. And that posed a problem for conservatives, who actually want to create a new aristocracy. So they changed the frame.

The frame "inheritance tax or estate tax" gave people the positive message that We the People helped create the wealth of the rich, and We the People have a right to use some of that wealth to pay for the institutions that keep our nation strong. It reminded people of the aristocrats of old Britain and of how in America we have a democracy rather than an aristocracy.

The conservatives replaced that nice-but-not-very-powerful frame "estate tax" with a new frame: "death tax." *Death* is one of Gingrich's anchor words. No one wants to die. It also reminds us that this tax is levied when a loved one dies. Finally, it suggests that everyone will have to pay the tax—because everyone dies—rather than just the 0.27 percent (less than three-tenths of 1 percent) of Americans who actually paid it in 2006.[5]

Here's how powerful the frame "death tax" is. When pollsters asked Americans whether they thought the estate tax should be reformed or repealed, 57 percent favored keeping the tax as it was or reforming it, while only 23 percent favored repealing it.[6] When those same pollsters, joined by Frank Luntz's company, later asked voters if the "death tax" was "fair," they got a very different answer: 80 percent of voters polled thought the tax was unfair and should be repealed.[7]

"Death tax" is effective not because it is the best description of the tax. In fact, it is quite misleading. "Death tax" is effective because it triggers a picture of death and raises a whole constellation of negative emotions that arise for us around death. Those negative emotions become anchored to this tax. Once our feelings have changed, the way we think about an idea changes as well. It's an incredibly powerful—albeit deceptive—frame and was promoted in large part by several heirs of the Walton family, who spent millions on front groups that promoted the "IRS death tax" frame to save those few people tens of billions of dollars when their estates move to their heirs.

War versus Occupation

Some frames can be hard to see or hear. When George W. Bush sent troops into Iraq, he told the American people we were at war. That seemed to be a fact, not a frame.

"War," however, is a frame, and it's one of the most powerful in our culture. In the case of Iraq, using the "war" frame was the way that Bush, Rove, and their cronies helped persuade Americans that they were pursuing a noble strategy. Few Americans like to oppose a president when the country is at war.

The fact, however, is that the war in Iraq ended on May 1, 2003, when George W. Bush stood below a "Mission Accomplished" sign aboard the USS *Abraham Lincoln* and correctly declared that we had "victoriously" defeated the Iraqi army and overthrown its government.

Our military machine is tremendously good at fighting wars—blowing up infrastructure, killing opposing armies, and toppling governments. We did that successfully in Iraq in a matter of a few weeks. We destroyed its army, wiped out its air defenses, devastated its Republican Guard, seized its capital, arrested its leaders, and took control of its government. We won the war.

After we won the war, however, we stayed in Iraq. That is called an *occupation*.

The distinction between the "war" frame and the "occupation" frame is politically critical because wars can be won or lost but occupations most honorably end by redeployments.

We won World War II, and it carried the legacy of Franklin D. Roosevelt to great political heights. We lost the Vietnam War, and it politically destroyed Lyndon B. Johnson, Richard Nixon, and Gerald Ford.

Americans don't like to lose or draw at war. Even people who oppose wars find it uncomfortable, at some level, to lose; and Republican strategists have used this psychological reality for political gain. When wars are won—even when they're totally illegal and undeclared wars, like Reagan's adventure in Grenada—it tends to create a national good feeling.

On the other hand, when arguably just wars, or at least legally defensible "police action" wars, like Korea, are not won, they wound the national psyche. And losing a war—like the German loss of WWI—can be so psychologically devastating to a citizenry that it sets up a nation for a strongman dictatorship to "restore the national honor."

When using the "war" frame, it's not politically possible to push to end the war: losing a war is too psychologically damaging. When using the frame of "occupation," however, it is very possible to push to end the occupation, and in fact that end is welcomed. In this case, how you frame the US troop presence in Iraq has everything to do with how soon that troop presence ends.

Here's a scenario—fictitious—of how Democrats could have played out the change of frames:

> **Tim Russert:** So, Senator Reid, what do you think of this most recent news from the war in Iraq?

Senator Harry Reid: The war ended in May 2003, Tim. Our military did its usual brilliant job, and we defeated Saddam's army. The occupation of Iraq, however, isn't going so well, in large part because the Bush administration has totally botched the job, leading to the death of thousands of our soldiers and dragging our nation into disrepute around the world. I'd like to see us greatly scale down the current occupation of Iraq, redeploy our occupation forces to nearby nations in case we're needed by the new Iraqi government, and get our brave young men and women out of harm's way. Occupations have a nasty way of fomenting civil wars, you know, and we don't want this one to go any further than it has.

TR: But isn't the war in Iraq part of the global "War on Terror"?

SR: Our occupation of Iraq is encouraging more Muslims around the world to eye us suspiciously. Some may even be inspired by our occupation of this Islamic nation to take up arms or unconventional weapons against us, perhaps even here at home, just as Osama bin Laden said he hit us on 9/11 because we were occupying part of his homeland, Saudi Arabia, at the Prince Sultan Air Base, where Bush Sr. first put troops in 1991 to project force into Kuwait and enforce the Iraqi no-fly zone. The Bush policy of an unending occupation of Iraq is increasing the danger that people will use the tactic of terror against us and our allies; and, just as George W. Bush wisely redeployed our troops from Saudi Arabia, we should begin right now to redeploy our troops who are occupying Iraq.

TR: But the war . . .

SR: Tim, Tim, Tim! The war is over! George W. Bush declared victory himself, in May 2003, when our brave soldiers seized control of Iraq. That's the definition of the end of a war, as anybody who's ever served in the military can tell you. Unfortunately, our *occupation* of Iraq since the end of the war, using a small military force and a lot of Halliburton, hasn't worked. We should take Halliburton's billions and give them to the Iraqis so they can rebuild their own nation— the way we helped Europeans rebuild after World War II—and go from being an occupying power to being an ally of Iraq and the Iraqi people, like we did with Japan and Germany.

TR [bewildered]: I can't call it a war anymore? We have to change our NBC "War in Iraq" banners and graphics?

SR [patting Russert's hand]: Yes, Tim. The war is over. It's now an occupation and has been for three years. And like all occupations, it's best to wrap it up so Iraq can get on with its business. I'm sure your graphics people can come up with some new logos that say "Occupation of Iraq." It'll be a nice project for them, maybe even earn them some much-needed overtime pay. The "War in Iraq" graphics are getting a bit stale, don't you think? After all, soon we'll be able to say that we fought World War II in less time than we've been in Iraq. Wars are usually short, but occupations—particularly when they're done stupidly—can be hellish.

TR [brightening]: Ah, so! Now I get it! I even wrote about wars and occupations in my book about my dad. Thanks for coming on the program today and clarifying this for us.

Frames matter and have consequences, sometimes life-and-death consequences. If the Democrats had been able to shift the media's discussion from "war" to "occupation" back in 2003, we could have prevented the deaths of many, many Iraqis and thousands of US soldiers.

From *Cracking the Code: How to Win Hearts, Change Minds, and Restore America's Original Vision* by Thom Hartmann, © 2007, 2008, published by Berrett-Koehler.

Walking the Blues Away

From *Walking Your Blues Away: How to Heal*
the Mind and Create Emotional Well-Being

Never trust a thought that didn't come by walking.

—FRIEDRICH NIETZSCHE

THE HUMAN BODY IS A SELF-HEALING ORGANISM. WHEN YOU CUT your finger, it heals. If you break your leg, it heals. Even if part of you is cut out in surgery, the surgeon's wound heals. We heal from bacterial and viral invasions, from injuries, and from all variety of traumas. The mechanisms for healing are built into us. Five million years of evolution, or the grace of God, or both, have made our bodies automatic healing machines. So why wouldn't the same be true of our minds and emotions?

All of the traumas that we experience in life leave their wounds; if humankind hadn't had ways of healing from those emotional and psychological blows, over time society would have become progressively less functional. Instead history shows us that people usually recover from even the most severe psychological wounds, often learning great lessons or gaining important insights in the recovery process.

The famous Kauai longitudinal study of children raised in stressful, disadvantaged conditions found that a higher percentage of the children grew up "highly resilient" than did a middle-class comparison group.[1] The generation that survived the Republican Great Depression and the Nazi Holocaust in Europe went on to create important social institutions, build nations, and offer comfort and hope to humankind. Elie Wiesel's experience specifically comes to mind: although he would never have wished on another the horrific experience of being in one of Hitler's death camps, through his writing of that experience he has given a particularly inspiring model of resilience and healing to the world.

The reality is that although adversity breaks some people, it strengthens others. And when people heal from adversity, the old cliché *What doesn't kill you makes you stronger* usually rings true.

But, just as with the production of scar tissue in the healing of a wound to the skin—a process involving millions of cells producing very specific compounds in response to the trauma in the tissue—there must be an inborn mechanism for healing the mind and the emotions. And just as healing from a cut can be speeded up by keeping the wound clean and dry or can be slowed down by letting the wound get wet or dirty, this emotional healing is also a process that can be either stimulated or thwarted by our interventions.

I've identified a specific healing mechanism and process that nature has built into the human mind and body that enables us to process trauma in a way that is quick, functional, and permanent. Just like the skin's mechanism for forming scabs and scars and eventually even making the scars vanish, this mechanism is simple, fundamental, and elegant.

In its simplest form, this mechanism involves rhythmic side-to-side stimulation of the body. This side-to-side motion, or *bilateral movement*, causes nerve impulses to cross the brain from the left hemisphere to the right hemisphere and back at a specific rate or frequency. This cross-patterning produces an organic integration of left-hemisphere "thinking" functions with right-hemisphere and brain-stem "feeling" functions. This integration is a necessary precursor to emotional and intellectual healing from trauma.

This steady movement of nerve impulses across the hemispheres of the brain is stimulated in the bilateral-movement processes of a variety of modern forms of psychotherapy, such as Eye Movement Desensitization and Reprocessing, Emotional Freedom Technique, and Thought Field Therapy. In its purest form, however, I've discovered that the natural and rhythmic left-right-left-right process of walking, while performing a simple mental exercise, can also stimulate this same internal integration process.

This, I posit, is the way humans have healed themselves from trauma for the hundreds of thousands of years of human history, and it is only because so few of us walk anymore that we have to resort to office-based psychotherapeutic processes to produce the same result.

And that result is impressive. When we stimulate the nervous system in this bilateral manner while calling to mind a persistent emotional distress, the emotional "charge" associated with that memory quickly and permanently dissipates. This isn't a process of producing amnesia or forgetting; instead it's a way of reframing the past, a way of re-understanding, of putting into context that which has been so "unnerving" for us. When we perform this bilateral process correctly, the pictures of painful past events in our memory transform from stark, scary, sound-filled color movies into black-and-white still pictures that are flattened out and lose their sound. The internal dialogue we have about the events—the "tagline" that we tell ourselves and actually hear in our own heads in our own voices—changes, usually from something like *That was a painful experience that still scares me* or *I was victimized in that relationship* to a more productive synopsis, such as *Yes, that happened to me, but it's well in the past now and I've learned some good lessons from the experience. I can let go of it.*

Inciting the movement of nerve impulses across the brain hemispheres helps people to come to terms with their past. They stop being frightened by their imagined futures and feel comfortable and empowered in the present. Walking while holding a traumatic memory in mind in a particular way can produce this result in a very short time.

This is not new. Rhythmic bilateral activity as a healing agent has been known to aboriginal peoples for millennia, and in the past few hundred years the secret of using bilaterality to heal emotional and psychological wounds—particularly those that produced psychosomatic physical results—was most famously discovered by Franz Anton Mesmer in the 1700s (called *mesmerism*), refined by Dr. James Braid in the early 1800s (and renamed *hypnosis* by Braid), and brought into widespread and mainstream use in the late 1800s by Sigmund Freud.

In an odd historical event in the late 1890s, however, the growing power of yellow journalism (sensationalized "news" by publishers such as William Randolph Hearst) merged with European anti-Semitism, and the synergy of those forces compelled Freud to abandon these techniques. Freud spent the rest of his life searching in vain for a replacement for hypnosis that actually worked, experimenting with cocaine, developing his early concepts of penis envy and the Oedipal complex, and finally promulgating his largely unsuccessful "talk-therapy" systems. When Freud committed suicide in 1939, he still hadn't found anything that worked as well as the beloved bilateral therapies he'd been forced to abandon by the amazingly synchronous and unusual events of the 1890s.

From the 1890s until the past few decades, hypnosis and the bilateral therapies on which it is based were for the most part ignored or shunned by medical and mental health professionals, in large part because of the uproar of the 1890s. Only with the development of neuro-linguistic programming (NLP) in the 1970s, the NLP development of eye-motion therapies, and the 1987 development of Eye Movement Desensitization and Reprocessing by Francine Shapiro did bilateral therapies begin to make a comeback.

There is now a whole spectrum of variations on these systems for integrating brain function and thus encouraging healing from emotional and psychological trauma. They all involve stimulating one hemisphere of the brain, then the other, then back to the first, then back again, and repeating this bilateral stimulation over and over. You can accomplish this same kind of stimulation using the simple process of walking. This bilateral stimulation gives you access to healing powers, creative states, and emotional and psychological resilience beyond what you may have ever thought possible.

Why Bilaterality Is So Important

Bilaterality is the ability to have the left and the right hemispheres of the brain fully functional and communicating with each other. It represents an optimal way of functioning for the brain, a way that reflects how most animals' brains operate.

Many people in our society are stuck in a groove of habitual emotional response, with only one hemisphere of the brain taking responsibility for much of the brain's functioning. Even though they're "normal" and "sane," they're carrying around a mind full of unresolved emotion and pain. Bilateral exercises have been demonstrated to encourage healthier brain functionality. Now we're finding that walking can also perform this healing.

As recently as 30 years ago, before the availability of sophisticated brain-imaging equipment such as PET, SPECT, and MRI scanners, it was widely believed that the left hemisphere of the brain—which controls the right side of the body—was responsible for logic and thinking, and the right hemisphere—which controls the left side of the body—took charge of emotions. Though we now know that it's not quite that simple, we also know that there is a significant grain of truth in this longstanding belief.

A healthy person operates with both hemispheres of the brain fully engaged and able to hand off information to each other in such a way that we can think about our emotions and evoke feelings with our thoughts. Evidence of this dual-hemispheric functioning can be recognized by simply watching an able-bodied person walk or talk—both sides of the mouth open the same amount when the person speaks, and both legs and arms swing comfortably and reach the same distances when they walk. A person who is said to "speak out of one side of his mouth" is showing signs either of single-hemispheric brain damage (such as from a stroke) or of serious emotional or psychological illness. One hemisphere has taken over the brain's functioning. Depending on which hemisphere has taken charge, such people often either are overly emotional (usually left-side-of-the-mouth speakers) or are lacking the ability to easily experience emotions (right-side speakers). Our culture has intuited this for hundreds of years—thus the old expression about a person "talking out of the side of his mouth."

Hemispheric dominance—one side of the brain controlling the functions of both—is no small matter, and it not only has an effect on individuals but, some scientists suggest, actually shapes society and culture itself. In a very real way, even though most of us talk out of both sides of the mouth, a *cultural* hemispheric dominance is reflected in societies that we call "civilized," whereas indigenous/aboriginal societies (Jean-Jacques Rousseau's "noble savages") are more bilateral in their overall cultural brain functioning.

Just as a person with a severe hemispheric imbalance can be badly disconnected from emotions such as empathy, and thus sanction or even encourage actions such as the mass murder that is war, so too can an entire society. In the opinion of some researchers, societies that are hemispherically unbalanced are more likely to be patriarchal, hierarchical, and violent, whereas societies that are hemispherically balanced are more likely to be egalitarian and democratic and employ violence only in self-defense.

What we now call *civilization*—the earliest example of an entire culture becoming left-hemisphere dominant—can be traced back to the oldest written tale, *The Epic of Gilgamesh,* a story set 6,000 to 7,000 years ago in ancient Mesopotamia (now Iraq) about the first ruler to defy the gods and seize control of others in the process. Gilgamesh was history's first warlord. His epic tale, which predates the Bible, describes not only a hierarchical social order but a hierarchical religion as well: it tells the story of a good man named Utnapishtim who was told by his god, Ea, to build an ark and put into it two of every animal. By doing this, Utnapishtim survives a great flood that Ea brings upon the city of Shurippak because its people aren't sufficiently worshipful of Ea.

Gilgamesh's culture established, in many ways, the prototype for later agriculture-based (and violence-based) social and political systems. A ruling king or queen with the power to remove the head of any person who dared defy him or her ruled every civilization from Gilgamesh's Mesopotamia to today's Saudi Arabia. Whether east or west, north or south, from China to Europe to the Inca, violent dominator societies have emerged over the past few thousand years. With millennia of this history as background, by the turn of the nineteenth century Charles Darwin and others of his era reasoned that Gilgamesh's dominance-based model must be the way humans were *meant* to live.

In his 1871 book, *The Descent of Man,* Darwin summarized the notion, common at the time, that society is best held together by dominance rather than true democracy, by the elite few rather than the unwashed masses, by those most willing to wield force rather than those willing to compromise or sacrifice. Darwin was making the case that most humans are biologically predisposed to living under the dominance of others.

The assumption of conquerors has always been that they are superior in every way to the conquered. How else does one justify the conquest?

Darwin, however, had a problem making his view fit into what he was learning about the social models of the tribal peoples he and his contemporaries called "savages." Reports were beginning to trickle in to the scientific and political communities from explorers and colonists in the New World and the African and Indian colonies that these so-called savages—tribal peoples from the Americas to Africa—weren't the stupid, selfish, and violent characters they'd been portrayed as in European literature and philosophy. Instead they often displayed altruistic behavior and had social and political systems that were highly sophisticated and in many cases far more democratic than was England in Darwin's day.

At the time there were about as many indigenous peoples living tribally around the world as there were "civilized" people. They were living the way all humans had lived for most of human history (and thus were often referred to as "Stone Age people"), and yet their societies were troublingly democratic. Pesky Americans such as Thomas Jefferson and Benjamin Franklin had written and spoken extensively about the lessons to be learned from the democratic forms of governance of the savages of North America. And the savages of Asia and Africa often lived peacefully, cooperatively, and with elaborate and sophisticated—but egalitarian—social organizations, as well.

Presumably, Darwin's ancestors had once been savages, too. Why, Darwin wondered, hadn't the modern-day savages being found in the Americas and elsewhere developed into "civilized" societies, as Darwin's fellow Englishmen had?

"It is, however, very difficult to form any judgment," Darwin wrote, "[as to] why one particular tribe and not another has been successful and has risen in the scale of civilisation. Many savages are in the same condition as when first discovered several centuries ago. As Mr. Bagehot [the economist and political writer Walter Bagehot] has remarked, we are apt to look at progress as the normal rule in human society; but history refutes this."[2]

Why did modern tribal peoples of the time live the way they did, even when offered an opportunity to become "civilized"? The stories of Native Americans brought up in white communities who later escaped back into the "savage wilds" were legendary; similarly, Africans fiercely resisted being taken into white communities as slaves, even though it represented a "civilized" improvement over their tribal conditions. As well, it was not uncommon during colonial days for Europeans to escape to Indian communities to live among them, becoming "white Indians" and never returning to "civilized" society. This intrigued Thomas Jefferson, who began a detailed analysis of Native American peoples and societies. As Jefferson wrote in his autobiographical *Notes on Virginia:*[3]

> Founded on what I have seen of man, white, red, and black, and what has been written of him by authors, enlightened themselves, and writing among an enlightened people, the Indian of North America being more within our reach, I can speak of him somewhat from my own knowledge, but more from the information of others better acquainted with him, and on whose truth and judgment I can rely. ... [H]e is brave, when an enterprise depends on bravery; education with him making the point of honor consist in the destruction of an enemy by stratagem, and in the preservation of his own person free from injury; ... also, he meets death with more deliberation, and endures tortures with a firmness unknown almost to religious enthusiasm with us; that he is affectionate to his children, careful of them, and indulgent in the extreme; that his affections comprehend his other connections; weakening, as with us, from circle to circle, as

they recede from the centre; that his friendships are strong and faithful to the uttermost extremity, that his sensibility is keen, even the warriors weeping most bitterly on the loss of their children, though in general they endeavor to appear superior to human events; that his vivacity and activity of mind is equal to ours in the same situation; hence his eagerness for hunting, and for games of chance. . . .

They raise fewer children than we do. . . . It is said, therefore, that they have learned the practice of procuring abortion by the use of some vegetable; and that it even extends to prevent conception for a considerable time after. . . . An inhuman practice once prevailed in this country, of making slaves of the Indians. . . . To judge of the truth of this, to form a just estimate of their genius and mental powers, more facts are wanting, and great allowance to be made for those circumstances of their situation which call for a display of particular talents only. This done, we shall probably find that they are formed in mind as well as in body, on the same module with the "Homo sapiens Europaeus."

As suggested by Jefferson's description of Native peoples and their character and customs, there had to be something Darwin was missing in the theory of why "savages" didn't want to become "civilized," but Darwin couldn't figure out what it was. A theory suggesting that "savages" had actually begun as "civilized people" but had deteriorated or degenerated over the eons was put forth by the duke of Argyll, although Darwin found that wanting. "The arguments recently advanced by the Duke of Argyll and formerly by Archbishop Whately, in favour of the belief that man came into the world as a civilised being and that all savages have since undergone degradation, seem to me weak in comparison with those advanced on the other side," Darwin wrote in *The Descent of Man.*[4] And yet he had no way to account for the apparent nobility and quality of life among the savages.

Darwin was a scientist, and he knew that meant sometimes bringing forward unpopular views. Flipping Argyll's theory upside down, Darwin began to consider that perhaps civilized people had once been savages, too. But if civilized people *had* once lived as savages, why didn't we remember those times?

The Cultural Dissociative Barrier

In his brilliant *Ishmael* books, Daniel Quinn popularizes the idea of a memory barrier between modern civilization and what Darwin called the "savage" state.[5] Quinn calls this "The Great Forgetting," a cultural amnesia so strong that we're unable even to *imagine* how our ancestors lived.

For example, when we think of another "civilized" country, we imagine our stereotypes of people in full color: Greeks dancing like Zorba, or French women and men sipping wine, or Italians eating pasta in a café in Venice. Even if we don't speak their language, we can hear fragments of it and can easily imagine them speaking the language. We can bring to mind the smells, tastes, and even the feel of their world because on the whole it is so culturally similar to our own.

But when we think of our own ancestors' preliterate history, our mindscape often turns to black-and-white. Our ability to imagine language or other sounds from that time is minimal. (Indeed up to the past decade, some anthropologists speculated that our "savage" ancestors were mute, suggesting that the development of civilization coincided with a recent evolutionary mutation that increased the size of the nerve bundles that control the human tongue.) Most people have never tried to conjure up a sense of what the food of our prehistoric ancestors must have tasted like; what sorts of herbs, seeds, and pollens they used as spices; how their living areas smelled; or what brought them joy.

We all have a collection of different "selves," or roles, that we necessarily play in life: parent, teacher, employee, spouse, friend. Each role requires us to move slightly different skill sets and personality attributes front and center when engaging one of these selves. When a person loses the ability to remember that he or she carries the same identity when acting out various roles, that person is said to have developed a dissociative disorder. Multiple-personality disorder is the most well known of these.

Collectively, it appears that we've erected a cultural dissociative barrier that is so complete that we believe Darwin was right in his assumption that a dominance- and violence-based culture is biologically based and has grown and thrived because of natural selection.

Whether bilateral walking therapy in and of itself is enough to cure many of the violent ills of society is doubtful but conceivable. The Indians of North America were pedestrians before the introduction of the horse from Europe in the 1500s, and available anthropologic evidence indicates that their societies were rarely violent.[6] With the widespread use of nonwalking forms of transportation in Europe and the Middle East 7,000 years ago (primarily the horse and the horse-drawn carriage and chariot), it's possible that the loss of walking made society more violent.

Even glimpses we get today of societies that still depend entirely on walking for transportation—such as the San of southern Africa, who were featured in the movie *The Gods Must Be Crazy*—find that "walking" people are rarely as violent or as hierarchical as "riding" people.

Although all of it is speculative at this moment, the evidence is accumulating that both social and personal mental health depend on people's having regular bilateral stimulation and that we are evolutionarily designed to derive that from daily walking.

From *Walking Your Blues Away* by Thom Hartmann,
© 2006, published by Inner Traditions International.

PART III

Visions and Visionaries

W HEN THOM HARTMANN WAS 17 OR 18 YEARS OLD, HE AND TWO
friends set out to spend the summer living in a tipi on the
shores of a lake in Michigan's Chippewa National Forest. During the
period he relates in "Life in a Tipi," he learned to identify edible plants,
swam in the lake daily, and walked for miles through the forest, com-
muning with the lush voices of nature. Welcoming the silence and the
solitude, the three friends went days without speaking, communicating by chalkboard when necessary. He'd brought a stack of books with
him: Ram Dass, his grandmother's Bible, several books on Hindu and
Christian mysticism, and the works of Thomas Merton. Heady stuff
for a teenager, and Hartmann later admitted that he couldn't make
heads or tails of the Hindu *Vedas,* but he spent hours studying or sitting under a tree and meditating. For the first time in his life, he cul-
tivated stillness instead of activity, and, slowly but surely, he began to
find the inner anchor that would sustain him for decades to come.

Here were planted the intellectual seeds that would later take
shape as his hypothesis of older and younger cultures. Hartmann also
began to appreciate the power and the capacity of his own mind and
to believe that a single person's thoughts could be the pivot that leads
to the transformation of the world. This idea recurs throughout his
work, and long after that summer in the tipi he made it the mission
statement of his nationally syndicated talk radio program: *Saving the
world, by awakening one person at a time.* It's not an original idea, as
Hartmann readily concedes, but it's a critical one. True and lasting

social change has to begin with an idea. Movements gain momentum as ideas spread through enough people to reach a critical mass.

This is the underpinning of *The Prophet's Way: A Guide to Living in the Now,* the most personal of Hartmann's books. Part spiritual autobiography, part travelogue, part self-help manual, *The Prophet's Way* is also a colorful portrait of the remarkable Gottfried Müller, Hartmann's mentor and longtime friend. Müller, the founder of Salem International, started a network of communities for orphans and abused children in Stuttgart, Germany. (*Salem* is pronounced "sah-*lem,*" from the Hebrew and Arabic words for peace, *shalom* and *salaam.*) A Christian mystic, Müller devoted his life to healing people and the environment and working for peace. He believed there was great power in practicing small, anonymous acts of kindness and that these acts become "culturally contagious," spreading the way a YouTube video spreads virally on the Internet. Since meeting Müller in 1978, Hartmann has helped Salem set up hospitals and schools in Australia, Colombia, India, Israel, Russia, Uganda, and several other countries as well as the residential treatment program he describes in "Starting Salem in New Hampshire."

With Hartmann's passion for knowledge, it's no surprise that his ideas on public education are both visionary and provocative. Why, he asks, have so many modern people lost access to their intuition? Why are so many people disconnected from their emotional lives? And why is our society, while on the cutting edge of intellectual development, so often lacking in empathy and tolerance? Grounded in his research on neurobiology, "How to Raise a Fully Human Child" tackles these questions, describing how children are psychologically harmed by schools that treat them like items on an assembly line. The obsession with good grades, academic success, and high-stakes tests extinguishes kids' natural curiosity. Kids aren't the ones who are failing school; school is failing kids.

Two essays from *The Last Hours of Ancient Sunlight*—"Younger-Culture Drugs of Control" and "The Secret of 'Enough'"—make it clear why that book has had such a galvanizing effect on readers. The premise of *The Last Hours of Ancient Sunlight* is that the global crises we face stem primarily from our younger-culture way of thinking, and the only lasting solution is to relearn the lessons of older cultures, our ancient ancestors who lived sustainably for thousands of generations. Hartmann names and analyzes our problems, and then he offers a new way of thinking about the world that is original, powerful, and nothing short of visionary.

Life in a Tipi

From *The Prophet's Way: A Guide to Living in the Now*

Every day people are straying away from
church and going back to God.

—Lenny Bruce

M Y BEST FRIEND THROUGH SCHOOL WAS CLARK STINSON. WE
met when we were 13, and instead of pursuing the normal pas-
times of teenagers we spent our time studying Sanskrit (we had an old
study-guide book I found in my father's library), reading *The Tibetan
Book of the Dead,* and arguing minutiae of the Bible. Clark's mother
was interested in metaphysics and shared with us a book called *Autobiography of a Yogi.* Years later, when I went to Detroit with her and
Clark to attend an initiation in Kriya yoga by Yogacharia Oliver Black,
the oldest living disciple of Yogananda, I recognized Yogananda's Kriya
technique as identical to an ancient Coptic exercise that Kurt Stanley
had taught us years earlier, called the Cobra Breath.

I introduced Clark to Master Stanley, and Clark and I began a
serious study of spirituality. We were both in our late teens by then,
and Clark had recently married. I was recovering from a painful
breakup with a girlfriend, and we agreed that to do our spiritual work
best we should seek isolation.

So, Clark and his wife bought a tipi, and I bought one, and we
three gave away everything else we owned in the world except some
clothes and our spiritual books. We bought 100 pounds of wheat, 100
pounds of dried fruit, and some basic camping equipment and got a
ride up into Michigan's Upper Peninsula, where an old trapper led us
on a three-day trek back into the Chippewa National Forest to a small
lake that isn't on most maps.

We spent the summer there, Clark and his wife on one side of the lake, me on the other. We practiced silence three days a week, and we did meditation and prayer every day for hours.

I had a pet tachinid fly, a small insect that looks like a honeybee but is actually a fly. When I'd meditate in the morning on my blanket outside my tipi, he'd come and hover just above my right hand, as if he were drawing nourishment from me. Sometimes he'd hover there for as long as 20 minutes; occasionally, he'd land and walk around with careful steps like an astronaut exploring a distant but friendly planet. I also shared my tipi with a large and furry brown-and-black wolf spider, who came out at night as the sun set and picked the sleeping mosquitoes off the canvas on the west side of my tipi; I watched the play of life and death, predator and prey.

One cold and rainy afternoon, Clark and I were walking through the woods, looking for berries and edible plants. We'd gotten pretty skilled at identifying what was safe and what wasn't and were filling a bag with leaves and fruits.[1]

"This must be what our ancestors lived like," Clark observed. "Hunting and gathering."

"Except that we're vegetarians, so we're just gathering," I said, joking.

But to Clark it wasn't a joke. "Seriously. What we call civilization started when humans started farming. But humans like us were around for tens and maybe hundreds of thousands of years before that. Fully conscious, awake and aware, thinking and feeling just like us. But they were hunters and gatherers instead of farmers."

"Without agriculture there would be no civilization?" I asked. It was an interesting thought.

"Remember Miss Hemmer?" Clark said. Miss Hemmer had been our eighth-grade biology teacher and one of the best teachers I've ever known. Clark and I conspired to make her life difficult, but we also loved her and learned more from her each month than from any of our other teachers in a year. And she was a huge fan of Margaret Mead.

"She said that in primitive societies there isn't suicide, depression, drug addiction, all that stuff."

"The noble savage," I said, shivering. "I'm skeptical. And cold. And the Indians who once lived here were probably cold, too."

He shrugged and said, "This life seems much more natural to me."

At least I had to agree with that.

A few days later, Clark came running over to my tipi with his Bible, all excited. "Look at this," he said, pointing out Genesis 4:2. "It says, 'Cain was a tiller of the ground.' The Bible is talking about how the first murderer was also the first farmer. And in the twenty-fifth verse, it makes it clear that Abel, the brother who was not the farmer, was the one whom God loved the most."

"So what? It's a classic archetype of the oldest child being the most beloved but also the one who screws up; it's all over, from Greek mythology to Shakespeare."

"Don't you see? Adam and Eve were gatherers, like we are now. They walked around the Garden of Eden and picked up food. But then they tasted of the knowledge of good and evil, of life and death. That's your food supply—you live or die by it. When you live as a gatherer, you live by the whim of nature: if there's no food, you die. When you begin to store up food, you can defy nature and survive a drought. You then have the power to control life: the knowledge of life and death, or good and evil. So the tasting of the apple must mean that Adam and Eve experimented with agriculture, that they defied the god of nature. It's a warning. It's saying that the primitive life of hunting, gathering, and herding was more in accord with nature's way than is agriculture.*

Clark dove deeply into the issue, but I didn't consider it all that important at the time. I couldn't see how when people started farming after the end of the last ice age it could have been a bad thing—after all, it brought us modern society and science. Clark, however, was totally certain that agriculture and what he called "the organized ones" (whom I'd later call, in writing about attention deficit disorder, the

---

*Reading Daniel Quinn's novel *Ishmael* in 1995 brought Clark's personal obsession into a clearer light for me.

"farmers") were responsible for the coming death of the earth. I wasn't to seriously consider the issue again, though, for more than 20 years.

I was also told during that time, quite clearly and directly in several dreams and strong intuitions, that my ultimate spiritual teacher would not be a yogi from India or any of the other Eastern religions (even though I was studying these too) but a Christian from Europe. I was amazed by this, as the Maharishi and all the other teachers seemed to be coming out of India, but the message was unmistakable. And ever since I'd first read Carl Jung's writings (particularly his autobiography), I'd paid careful attention to my dreams and took seriously their content.

At the time I assumed it must have meant Master Stanley, as he was Swiss. But I later learned that, as Master Stanley had said, he was not my ultimate teacher.

That summer in the tipi was profoundly transformational for me, a time of preparation for what would come next. It taught me that I should never be afraid to lose or give away everything (as I've done more than once since then), that possessions can be meaningless, and that there is great peace in solitude. As a "gifted but hyperactive" young adult, I learned for the first time how to truly and profoundly relax and gain control over the wild racing of my mind. I learned to look within for strength and discovered that the forest is afire with life. I felt truly alive, truly connected to my creator, in a more real and visceral way than I'd ever before experienced.

From *The Prophet's Way* by Thom Hartmann,
© 1997, published by Inner Traditions International.

How to Raise a Fully
Human Child

From *The Edison Gene: ADHD and the Gift of the Hunter Child*

WHY HAVE SO MANY MODERN PEOPLE LOST ACCESS TO WHAT Albert Einstein called the "gift" of our intuitive minds and are thus less capable of critical and deep thought? Why is our society rich in intellectual rationality but seems too often to be lacking in compassion, insight, and understanding?

When we go back to developmental neurobiology, we discover that building a brain is somewhat parallel to building a computer. A computer system is made of obvious parts—the monitor, the power supply, the tower, and the keyboard—and the more sophisticated parts of the computer's motherboard and its chips for audio, video, and processing function. There are its memory chips, which determine in speed and capacity via their interaction with the processor chip or "brain" of the computer the ability the computer will have. If the memory chips are too slow in their ability to handle data, no matter how fast or fancy the processor chip we build into it, the computer will never go faster or farther than the limits of the slower memory chips.

Similarly, every stage of brain development builds on those that came before it, all the way back to the first pruning of the brain in utero. The baby in utero has determined to some extent whether the world outside is safe or hostile. This process continues from birth into the early twenties, during which time half the total mass of synapses— more than 500 trillion—are pruned away and discarded.

At every stage the brain must decide which of the two poles—safe or hostile—to emphasize. On this foundation is built the earliest of the brain's structures, and these depend to a significant degree on the level of care and nurturing the child experiences with his mother. On this experience are built the toddler and later brain structures that depend on a child's having nonhostile, supportive interactions with his father and mother, siblings, extended family, and the larger world. Throughout childhood, daily experiences such as stress in a school environment or living in a war zone continue to determine the nature and the shape of the brain the child will have when he achieves adulthood.

If we want to produce children who are deep and thoughtful in their emotions and intellect, every step along the way requires that they receive full reward and nurturing and avoid more than the occasional burst of cortisol from an occasional brush with a tiger.

Invasion of the Lizard People

I have a friend who, in all seriousness, once took me aside to assure me that "the lizard people have taken over the United States."

"And who are the lizard people?" I asked. This friend has multiple graduate school degrees (including a master's in psychology) and a very high IQ, but recently I'd begun to wonder about his reading habits.

"Lizard people!" he said. "Some people think they live under the earth and then zip into human outfits when they come up to the surface; others think they're some sort of incubus that inhabits the bodies of regular people, like in *The Invasion of the Body Snatchers*. But it's obvious they've taken over. How else would you explain the current state of world affairs? I'll bet that the president gets up every morning, zips on his human suit, and then starts his day. Have you noticed how sometimes his features seem like they're not quite right, like his smile is phony and might even slide off his face? It's the rubber suit he wears over his lizard body."

"And where are these lizard people from?"

"Again, there's some controversy," he said. "Some people think they're from a distant star, maybe explorers marooned here tens of thousands of years ago. Others think they're simply the first highly intelligent beings to have evolved on this planet, probably during the time of the dinosaurs, and it was when we started evolving that they figured out how to infiltrate us and take control of our societies.

They became our first kings and leaders and are to this day. What we call *history* is really the history of the lizard people's control of the human race."

In a way my friend may be partially right. From just before birth all the way into the early twenties, the brain is constantly facing the decision of whether to produce a mind that is more lizard (reptile brain–dominant) or more human (forebrain- or prefrontal lobe–dominant). More than 500 trillion synapses are pruned away to leave dominant either one structure or the other, and all of adult life is then based on that dominant structure.

It's not surprising that hierarchical, power-based cultures, from warrior tribes to feudal societies to modern empires, are stressful places for most of their inhabitants. Even those individuals who rise to the top of the power and wealth structure experience regular stress because of their constant need to defend what they have.

Thus we see that reptile brain–dominant people are the ones best adapted to fight and claw and climb their way to the top of the social, political, and economic ladders—after all, that's what reptiles do best. *Survival of the fittest!* is their slogan. *Might makes right!* is their marching theme. Compassion and insight are for wimps: *Get while the getting is good!*

Those mothers and children hit by the greatest stresses are often at the most survival-oriented end of our social structure—the economic bottom. But the stresses echo all the way up the ladder, particularly in high-pressure households or among children exposed to high levels of advertising. Even though the changes induced at the level of the individual brain are subtle and small, when expressed over a nation of millions of people, their effects are amplified and become broadly visible.

Are We Stuck in a Loop?

It would seem that this is a never-ending loop; once a culture enters into it, there's no clear way out. The culture restrains its members from developing into the most evolved state humans are capable of because each generation is birthed in stress, forming reptile brain–powered brains instead of those powered by transcendence and intuition. Children who have been born in stress, whose neural pruning favors the reptile brain, become the adults that control and maintain ever more rigid hierarchical and wealth- and power-centered governments, companies, and social institutions as well as more and more violent and rapid-fire media. In this way more stress is produced for new mothers and the next generation of developing children and young adults. And on the cycle goes.

When a society or nation goes into decline because of a loss or lack of resources and fighting over the crumbs begins, the stresses in the culture produce more and more children whose brains defer to the survival mechanisms of the reptile brain. These children, in turn, grow up to produce cultures that are less feeling, less intuitive, more power oriented, and—as is seen in both ancient and modern feudal societies—very stable and persistent. The culture feeds the neurology, and the neurology sustains the culture.

Triggering Events

In *The Biology of Transcendence: A Blueprint of the Human Spirit*,[1] Joseph Chilton Pearce suggests that some sort of triggering event drove societies worldwide into this cycle of domination, stress, and proliferation of children whose reptile brains are dominant. This echoes the work of Allan N. Schore in his book *Affect Regulation and the Origin of the Self*[2] and the similar works of others. The science behind it is solid. Stressors alter brain development, and the modified brain, in turn, has the potential to change culture in ways that make life more stressful.

There is no shortage of possible stressors: They range from war, cycles of global weather change, and Riane Eisler's theory that the violence associated with eating domesticated animals has required a change in the brain, to the theory first presented by Walter Ong[3] in 1982 and Robert Logan[4] in 1986, and later brilliantly developed by the physician Leonard Shlain in his 1998 book *The Alphabet versus the Goddess: The Conflict between Word and Image*,[5] that the development of the alphabet created a rewiring of the brain, which led to hierarchical behavior when the alphabet was taught to children younger than seven years old.

Books have been written about how World Wars I and II were caused, in part, by late-nineteenth- and early-twentieth-century German childrearing practices that advocated violence toward children to break their wills and teach compliance. In the 1950s psychologist Erik Erickson wrote a brilliant analysis of how the early American Puritan practice of "breaking the will of the child" prior to the age of two led to a generation of violent, angry, and even paranoid Puritans who were so incapable of living and working together without strife that they sowed the seeds of the end of Puritanism.[6]

But the pattern can be—and is being—changed. In 1946 Dr. Benjamin Spock first published his groundbreaking *Baby and Child Care,* a book that contradicted the remnants of American Puritan conventional wisdom that believed that children should have their will broken at an early age. Instead, Spock persuasively argued, children should be treated with respect and shouldn't be subjected to physical violence as a way of guiding or controlling their behavior.

Spock didn't have the benefit of the knowledge we now have about the impact of stress on the developing brain. He didn't realize that the growth of the uniquely human prefrontal lobes can be slowed or even stunted simply by angry words or regular spankings from Mom or Dad. But he knew intuitively that for children to grow to their full potential, they must, from the earliest age, receive recognition of their humanity and personhood.

Schools May Be the Key

In the huge body of literature on stress, cortisol, and childhood brain development, there is virtually no mention of the single largest presence in a child's life: school. Thousands of studies have been done over the past 50 years on the consequences of child abuse and neglect and on how substance abuse changes brain structures, but the only publication I have been able to find on the topic of the impact of school stress was published in India.

When I asked a physician and researcher about this (who asked that his name not be used), he said:

> I wouldn't touch that topic with a 10-foot pole. You can't get funding if there's any indication that your study is going to end up suggesting that our schools need to be changed in a way that may be more expensive. Government won't support it, industry won't support it, and true foundation support that's not promoting a specific agenda is nearly invisible. . . . If you want to do a study that will probably conclude that giving schoolchildren drugs is a good idea, I can get you cash tomorrow from a dozen sources, mostly in the pharmaceutical industry or the government agencies that respond to their lobbying. But even the people who criticize our schools as a device to support their advocacy of school vouchers don't want anybody looking into how much it might cost if we were to *really* provide both teachers and children with a high-quality, stress-free educational environment. Forget it.

We know about the impact of the hour or two the average family with a school-age child spends together. We've even begun to discover—although it's not widely publicized on television—the neurological impact of the four hours per day that the average school-age child spends watching TV or playing video games. But when was the last time you heard about a study on the neurological impact of the six hours a day the average child spends in school?

Children attend state-run schools six hours per day, nine months per year, from, on average, ages five to 18—the largest chunk of time in the most neurologically critical developmental period of their lives. (Throw in daycare, and the amount of time becomes even more significant.) By simply looking at the time spent in school—and considering that it's the time of day of peak awareness and brain activity—it would be impossible not to conclude that school must have a huge impact on how a child's brain forms, on the neural pruning process, and on whether he ends up as an adult with a dominant reptile brain or dominant prefrontal lobes.

That said, I want to be on record as a strong supporter of public education and our public school system. There are many excellent teachers in our schools and much innovative work being done, but this institution that is so critical to a free society is under daily attack by radical so-called conservatives who want to privatize education, destroy teachers' unions, and starve government assistance to public education. While I philosophically object to "compulsory" education, I strongly agree with Thomas Jefferson that one of the most important functions of government in a democracy must be to provide a high-quality, comprehensive, and free public education—from the earliest years up through college—to any student who wants it. My goal is to improve public education, not destroy it.

School as Torture

I've noticed an interesting pattern in all three of my own children, in my three younger brothers, in many of the children we've had in our care, and even among the many teachers we've had as friends, acquaintances, or employees over the years.

The pattern goes something like this: When kids (and new teachers) start school for the first time, they're incredibly excited. They can hardly wait for the year to get under way; they believe it's going to be new, stimulating, and exciting—a wonderful opportunity and a great new experience. By the second or third year of school, however, both kids and teachers are beginning to balk. The teachers are tired and frustrated; the kids are stressed and wounded.

Somewhere in the middle of the 13 years of their public school incarceration, some children begin to complain and rebel. And after their first decade of teaching, many teachers I have met have become complete cynics.

Condemnation

Some of the nation's most well-promoted ADHD researchers have stated that people with attention deficit disorders have "stunted" frontal or prefrontal lobes, implying that these stunted prefrontals are the cause of ADHD and similar problems involving self-regulation and self-control. They further suggest that the reason why stimulant drugs help such people increase their self-control is because they increase blood flow to this particular part of the brain.

But the most recent science shows that these stunted prefrontals (and the lack of inhibition that comes with them) may well be the result of children's being psychologically harmed by the mismatch between the way they learn and the way some of our schools teach. Scientists now know that when a child receives predominantly punishment, criticism, and other fear- and anxiety-inducing feedback from the world around him, the development of his brain's prefrontal lobes is stunted. Research demonstrates that such cortisol-producing negative input causes a child's brain to emphasize the development of the survival-oriented reptile brain and sacrifice the development of the emotional and intuitive prefrontals involved in inhibition and higher function.[7]

So, a child who's developing normally but who may have some differences from others—perhaps she takes a bit longer to understand questions or to process language, or she needs to mentally rehearse her answers before giving them—may find herself in a school environment that doesn't tolerate those differences. Unlike the adult world, in school generally what is most valued is the ability to quickly memorize and instantly repeat things that may not even seem to have any value or context.

While a number of our schools emphasize rote memorization and test taking, the real world rarely demands these as primary skills. Anyone who's been to a twentieth high school reunion knows that there are many surprises—late bloomers as well as people who did well in school but went nowhere in life. The fact is, very few careers require sitting in one place for hours a day, switching topics every hour or two, although our schools seem locked into this as their singular model of education.

One result can be that the child who functions differently is criticized or condemned for her learning style. The condemnation produces stress in the form of the disapproval of teachers, the jeers of classmates, and the disapproval or concern of her parents, and this stress increases cortisol levels. This in turn slows the development of her prefrontal lobes with their regulatory system and increases development of her instinctual, rapid-response reptile brain. After a few years of this daily stress in school, the child's brain has been sculpted into something different from what it could have been: It's more functional for survival—fight or flight—and less functional for deep or long-lasting thinking processes. She now has attention deficit disorder.

School as Work

Some of you may know how hard it is to sit, day after day, through a job you hate. A number of things could be making it difficult for you: Maybe your boss constantly puts you down—and your co-workers know it. Or perhaps you do your work poorly every single day because it isn't something you know how to do well, even though there are other jobs you can do quite well. Maybe you're a petite woman with exquisite handiwork skills who's trying to move hundred-pound sacks of cement all day. Or perhaps you have to solder miniature components on a circuit board, but your fingers are thick and you don't see very well.

Imagine that everybody knows you're no good at your job and many of your co-workers make fun of you for it. Maybe your boss reminds you of it all the time and even regularly reports to your family on how poorly you're doing. But if, after all this, you try to quit this job, the police will come and get you and take you back to it; and when you protest, they say that you are being oppositional and give you drugs to eliminate your reaction or put you in jail. How would you (or do you) exist in such an environment? What kind of attitude do you have toward the world after a few months in this situation? How about after a few years?

This, in reality, is the world many of our children face each day: It's daily life for Edison-gene children in many public schools. On the first day of kindergarten, they're so excited to go to school that they can hardly wait. In the first days, weeks, or months, they love school.

And then the mismatch starts to show up, the difference between their learning style and their teachers' techniques. And they begin not to like school. They beg not to be sent, but they're sent anyway (with the best intentions). Being in school begins to hurt, to be unpleasant; they're being wounded by it. Whether it takes months or years, they begin to hate school. And out of those wounds come all sorts of problematic behaviors.

Of course, there are some teachers and some students who love our schools just as they are. Their genetic profile and neurology matches up perfectly with the instructional style required in most modern educational environments, and they have fun. But school becomes little more than imprisonment for those teachers who thought they could innovate to make their work positively transformational and for those children who began by seeing school as a wonderful new opportunity for learning but then realized they would be criticized, punished, and given what they experience as painfully boring work to do for no apparent reason.

The predictable result for an Edison-gene child whose learning style is mismatched with our public schools' teaching style is stress and its accompanying flood of cortisol, hour after hour, day in and day out, year after year, through the largest part of a child's developmental years.

Comorbidities

When Edison-gene children have trouble in school, they're often described as oppositional (argumentative), or having a bad attitude, or behaving as if they think the world owes them something. Having been treated as misfits and outcasts by the school, such children may have problems making and sustaining friendships among peers. These become additional diagnostic criteria for psychiatric conditions, and in the delightful language of the medical world the new behaviors are called *comorbid conditions* or *comorbidities.**

School can be hell for a child who doesn't fit in and can't perform as well as his peers. The experience can leave scars that last a lifetime. In my experience, however, these comorbidities are a natural and predictable result of the daily wounding these children receive in the classroom environment.

Cultures determine which behaviors will be considered good or bad, which will be rewarded and which will be discouraged, and then they impose those determinations on their children.

When I went into the advertising business in the 1970s, I learned that the first job of effective advertising is to tell a viewer (child or adult) that he's incomplete or imperfect and thus unhappy. Television images flash so quickly between product shots and smiling faces that even preliterate babies can get the idea: You're unhappy now, but this product will bring you happiness.

An Edison-gene child faces a double whammy in that he's also confronted with a school system that says he must fit in with the teaching and testing style in common use in order to be accepted. Failure and the blame associated with it, Schore's research shows, can produce a stress-driven cortisol response that inhibits the normal maturation process of the prefrontals and other structures in the most recent (human) parts of the brain and strengthens the fight-or-flight reptile brain.

The result is that the child's intellectual development is slowed—which produces more stress that further slows the process of brain growth, which leads to more developmental delays. Ultimately, the child becomes clearly and definably both different from and developmentally inferior to his peers. The "different" part is something he was born with and, in another time and place, could be a great asset to

---

*In everyday language the word *morbid* connotes "dying," but in medical terms *morbidity* refers to how often something occurs, and *comorbid* refers to diagnoses that occur together.

him. But the "developmentally inferior" part is a tragedy: it's the result of the mismatch between his learning style and the school's teaching style, and it doesn't have to happen.

Breaking the Loop

When Edison-gene children are misunderstood and endure years of stressful negative experiences, they are at particular risk of stress-induced developmental brain damage. When allowed to continue through school under such circumstances, it's just common sense to infer that they're at greater risk of drug abuse, promiscuity, anti-social behavior, relationship troubles, and a whole range of failures and problems in the teenage years and adult life—the range of problems that are usually attributed to their genetic difference but in fact are more directly the result of that difference colliding with a hostile school environment.

It's particularly critical, then, to break the cycle of damage to these children as early and as quickly as possible so that their normal brain development can continue through their early twenties. There are two actions we can take: we can create for a child a new way of interpreting events, and we can put a stop to any wounding he may be experiencing.

Offering a New Story

To begin creating a new way of interpreting events, the first step is to offer a new story, a new way for the child—and the adults around her—to view what her behavior signifies: Instead of thinking of an Edison-gene child as having a genetic mental problem or "disorder," tell her—and yourself—that she is the descendant of the explorers who moved across the world discovering and populating new lands and of people like Thomas Edison, who invented all sorts of ways to make life better, healthier, or easier. Then tell her about the latest research that shows that this is more than just a story you've made up. Children love hearing this and begin to view their inner tendencies in a completely new light. Instead of being seen as an evil from within, the itch to be active begins to feel glorious. Think of the difference!

Point out the positives of his genetic trait: energy, enthusiasm, creativity, fearlessness, and the ability to think on his feet. Suggest that such things are a skill set that will suit him well in adult life *if* he can learn to channel them well and to perform basic "farmer" tasks; remind him that "You don't have to *change* how you are."

One of the most primal of human instincts is to form a tribe, an instinct that's subordinated only by the need for family. Tribes are rightly self-centered: I've sat with Apaches who made jokes about the Hopi, and with Hopi who told unflattering stories about the Navajo. Tribalism emerges in our culture in sports and sports talk—"my" team is better than "yours" is—and in politics. And it's powerfully visible among genetic and religious minorities in our culture. It holds them together, makes them strong, and keeps them going in the face of adversity.

Tribalism is healthy when one tribe says, "Our tribe is better for people like us than your tribe would be," but it becomes unhealthy when one tribe says to another, "and therefore we have the right to invade or harm your tribe." Thus, frankly and openly, I'm recommending that you tell your child about the noble tribe of hunters, of Edison-gene people, she has descended from and how, from her viewpoint, they're better than those farmers. Tribal pride is not a bad thing: it's a social and psychological survival mechanism.

As for putting a stop to any wounding an Edison-gene child may experience, when you catch yourself wanting to criticize or punish him for Edison-like behaviors, reframe his actions in terms of the positive message you're trying to instill. Thus, "Johnny, quit running around knocking over the lamps!" becomes, "Johnny, you have a lot of energy! Someday you'll use it to change the world. But your energy shouldn't be indoors where there are so many things to break! How about going outside to play or finding some other way to let it out if you want to be inside?"

Much of the time you won't need to be so explicit—but what's most important for a parent or other adult to realize is that you can't change a child's story for the child until you change it for yourself. This is not in any way a recommendation that inappropriate behaviors be overlooked or ignored. Instead I'm suggesting that the consequences for such behaviors or the reasons for telling a child to change them be delivered not in a "bad child" way but in the context of an Edison-gene story.

From *The Edison Gene* by Thom Hartmann, © 2003, published by Inner Traditions International.

Starting Salem in New Hampshire

From *The Prophet's Way: A Guide to Living in the Now*

He who helps in the saving of others, saves himself as well.

—HARTMANN VON AUE

IN JULY AND AUGUST 1978, GOTTFRIED MÜLLER'S CHILDREN'S orchestra came for four weeks to the United States and toured the halls he had requested and which Louise Sutermeister and I had set up and publicized; they also took a trip to Florida. I traveled with him and the kids, and in each city Herr Müller gave speeches to groups of invited guests.

In one city only two people showed up to hear him. He knocked himself out, giving a powerful and enthusiastic speech about Salem, the coming times, and the work he was doing. He was dramatic, dynamic, and moving.

Afterward I asked him why he'd gone to so much trouble for just two people; he could have just sat with them and talked.

"When only a few people show up, then you know it is the most important speech you must give," he said. "Just as when a person donates only $1 to Salem, that is the most important donation." It reminded me of the story Jesus told in the Bible about the widow who could afford to give only a few mites (pennies) and how her contribution was more important and spiritually powerful than those of the wealthy elite. Similarly, one person has often been at the pivot point of world changes. If that one person happened to be in an audience that had only a few people—or even only that one person—giving that speech may be the event that could eventually lead to the transformation of the world.

The last week of July, I flew home to help my wife, Louise, give birth to our second child. After the horrific experience we had had with our first in a suburban Detroit hospital, where the doctor showed up late and drunk (it was Christmas Eve) and the nurses tied Louise down to the bed and forced her knees together until he arrived, we decided to deliver our second at home. A friend who was a midwife joined us, and another friend who was an MD and lived nearby was "on call" for us. In preparation Louise had attended several births with our midwife friend, and I'd joined in helping our neighbors deliver their baby at home. After two hours of labor, about three in the morning, Justin slid out into my hands. It was a miracle! We gave him the middle name of Noah because Herr Müller so often referred to Salem villages as "arks in a sea of chaos and turbulence," and his birth seemed to signal a turning point in our lives in that direction.

A week later Louise, Justin, and I flew to Washington to see the Salem orchestra perform at Kennedy Center and attend a dinner for Herr Müller that Louise Sutermeister had arranged at the Watergate Hotel. It was a gala event, with some of the biggest names in Washington society as sponsors, including Maestro Mstislav Rostropovich and Celeste Holm.

It was the end of the tour, and the logical end of my association with Herr Müller. I'd done the job he'd hired me to do (although I never ended up sending him a bill because of the events that followed shortly), and the reasonable thing to do now would be to return to Michigan and continue with my radio program, the advertising agency, and the herbal company; back to my old, crumbling mansion built by R. E. Olds (founder of Oldsmobile) and our new Volvos; back to making money and being spiritually unfulfilled. But I wasn't prepared to do that and had been wondering if and how I could reorganize things to work more closely with Herr Müller.

As we ate delicious vegetarian meals prepared by the hotel's staff, Herr Müller turned to me and said bluntly, "Why don't you sell your business and join us in this work?"

I felt like he had put a knife into my heart. It was everything I wanted and yet also so many things that I feared—so much change, so much to leave behind.

I looked at my wife. Louise, breast-feeding Justin, smiled and nodded in affirmation.

"Okay," I said. "What should we do?"

He shrugged. "Start out by helping Louise Sutermeister raise money for Salem here in America."

And so we went back to Michigan. We arranged to sell and transfer our businesses, I quit my part-time job at WITL radio station, and in October 1978 we moved to New Hampshire. For the first half-year, I tried to raise money for the Maryland program, but it was not to be. I gave speeches and visited donors, but nobody wanted to give money to somebody who wasn't "doing the work" themselves. So, my wife and I decided we should start our own Salem program in New Hampshire.

We began by taking three foster children into our home. Louise did most of the child care, while I did fundraising, gave speeches, and wrote grant applications. I created a nonprofit corporation and jumped through the hoops the state provided in order to get a license as a group home and, eventually, a residential treatment facility.

Over the next few years, as word spread, we drew some wonderful people to help us, and donations came as a result of our PR and fundraising efforts. We moved up north to a rental property on Stinson Lake in Rumney, and in 1979 opened several houses for kids.

The first of the two houses was an old, white building that once was a summer camp and at another time a school. It had started out as a farmhouse overlooking the lake, but several additions followed in the hundred years or so since it was first built. Children and houseparents lived in the old house part, and staff and a school we started filled the other quarters. It was located several miles up a long, winding mountain road to nearly the top of Stinson Mountain, where Stinson Lake settled like a filled-in volcanic caldera.

Next door to "the white house" was "the brown house," an old four-bedroom vacation house that we reinsulated and that became home to a second "family" of six children.

The edges of the road were the beginnings of the White Mountain National Forest, about 20 miles west of Plymouth, and, local lore said, the woods extended without a stop all the way up through the state, into Canadian forestland, and all the way up to the Arctic Circle. Bears, moose, foxes, deer, and wild turkeys would occasionally show up in our yards or forage through our trash.

The children we took in were, in Herr Müller's paraphrasing of the Bible, the least of the least. They were the children who had been rejected by one foster family after another, often rejected by other institutions, and some even came to us from the state mental hospital or the state-run prisons for children. As one of our house-parents told J. Tevere MacFadyen, who wrote a marvelous article about us for *Country Journal* magazine,[1] "These kids here are those who by definition couldn't make it in a family. That's why they're in a group home. We've had one girl, 13 years old, who'd been through 29 foster homes before she got here. At the last one she broke her foster mother's leg with an iron. These kids eat foster parents for breakfast. They just run right through them, burn them out, and when it becomes evident to the social worker that they're not going to make it in a foster home, they go into an institution."

On the other hand, the reason these kids are so tough is because they've been given nothing but hell all their lives. They arrive with dossiers an inch thick, often with broken bones, cigarette burns, or the psychic scars of emotional or sexual abuse. One boy came into the program after having been drugged in another institution to the point of drooling with Thorazine, a powerful antipsychotic, and was often tied to his bed for days at a time. After a few years with us, without drugs or restraint, he graduated from high school with honors.

The "magic" part of our formula, in my opinion, was Herr Müller's revelation about the need for family. Those of us who grew up in a "normal" home tend to take family for granted. As Robert Frost said in "The Death of the Hired Man":[2]

> Home is the place where, when you have to go there,
> They have to take you in.

I've always known that if worse came to worst, I could turn to my parents, siblings, and extended family for help and support. That knowledge has enabled me to take chances and step out into areas that others may consider adventurous, and it has provided me with a lifelong sense of security.

But these children usually have no place to call home, no safe place where they can return and be accepted. Such a reality is unthinkably frightening to most of us, even as adults: imagine how terrifying it must be for a child.

So instead of being thrown out of the program when they reach 17 or 18 and the funding stops, kids are told that they're always welcome. They can stay if they need (although, as in a normal family, we work to help them become self-reliant out in the real world and make the transition to adult independence). If they hit a rough time in their lives in the future, they're always welcome to come back.

In 1981 I went into Uganda for Salem with comedian and social activist Dick Gregory. On our way to Africa, we stopped at the Salem Children's Village in Stadtsteinach, Germany. It was a week or two before Christmas, as I recall, and we had dinner with one of the families. In addition to the six or seven children in the home with their house-parents and helpers, there were two young men in their early twenties at the table.

"Who are they?" Dick asked the house-parents.

"They grew up here," the housemother answered, "and one is now in the army and the other has a job in Frankfurt. But they came home for Christmas."

Home was the core, the central and most-effective therapy.

Our treatment plans drew heavily on the work of Alfred Adler, Rudolf Dreikurs, and others who advocate "logical consequences"

instead of punishment. Children must learn that there are consequences to their actions and that they have choices in life. When they
grow up, there won't be people to follow them around and dose them
with drugs or restrain them if they get out of control. Life's lessons
began at Salem with learning to put away the bicycle, clean up one's
own messes, and interact rationally with other children and adults.

Within a year of the time we moved up to Rumney, we had three
sets of house-parents, 12 children, a teacher, a cook, a carpenter, a
child-care assistant, a secretary, and a therapeutic program director,
and I was the executive director. We hired part-time therapists, psychologists, and psychiatrists to work with the children individually
and to train and consult with our staff regularly.

We were blessed with some truly brilliant individuals: Ken, our
cook, ended up writing numerous hot-selling cookbooks in later
years; Barbara stayed in child care and teaching; one of our house-
parents earned his PhD in divinity school; and others moved into
related social-work fields. A man in his late sixties, Grandpa Irving,
stayed with us for nearly a year; he lent a multigenerational flavor to
the program and taught us all about how to most efficiently gather
firewood from the forest and plant vegetables. At that time everybody
was earning between $25 and $112 per week, plus room and board.
We became a community as much as an institution, and there was an
intense sense of camaraderie.

As word about us spread and we were written up in *Country
Journal, East-West Journal, New Age Journal, Mother Earth News, Pre-
vention,* and other similar publications, we drew an advisory board of
famous vegetarians. I spent several evenings in New York at the apartment of Gloria Swanson, who lent her name to our work and loved
to cook vegetarian meals with me. Dennis Weaver and his family did
two fundraising concerts for us, as did Dick Gregory. National Public
Radio sent Sanford Ungar and Nina Ellis up to do a report on us, and
that 18-minute segment—the longest they'd ever run up to that time
on the *All Things Considered* show—drew what Ungar later described

to me as "one of the biggest responses we've ever had to that type of piece on the show."

As time went on, we learned that 137 acres on the other side of the lake were for sale, and, through a series of events I can only call miraculous, we were able to buy the land and begin building houses.

A half dozen or so young men and women, most in their early twenties, volunteered for the brutal job of building a passive solar house from scratch throughout the course of the harsh New Hampshire winter. These courageous volunteers, particularly Daniel, Sam, Anita, and Michael, referred to themselves as "the Siberians" and lent an even stronger sense of mission to our work as they labored in the freezing temperatures, often for 10 or more hours a day, until the first house was completed and we were ready to move the program from one side of the lake to the other.

Once Herr Müller commented to me: "I live like a king. I have the best food, the best friends, horses to ride, a forest to walk in, and a work that I would pay to do if I had to. What could be better?" This is a man who owns only his clothes and books and a bit of furniture.

But the fact is that Salem work (or any type of service work) should be done only for the fire in the work, the joy of doing it that's derived *right then and there*.

People who do things because they expect to be rewarded in heaven are often not alive: they're living in a future that has not yet come. (Those who avoid things because of a fear of hell are not living in the moment, either.)

While heaven may be a useful side effect of the work, it's only a small part of why one should do the work.

The clearest, most real motivation comes from the knowledge that the quality of the work we do, the spiritual vibration it spreads around, is based on the reasons for our doing it. If we do things as martyrs, we are merely spreading around martyrdom. The value of that is pretty minimal and, as in the case of the suicide bombers we've seen so much of lately, can even be profoundly destructive.

But if we do our work out of joy, love, and an enthusiasm born of the work itself—be it meditation and prayer, feeding the hungry, caring for the sick, building community, or whatever—we're pumping into the world joy, love, and a general lightening of the vibratory universe in which we all live.

For example, when Herr Müller decided he wanted to reduce the number of animals who were unnecessarily suffering because of medical and cosmetic experimentation (vivisection), he didn't go out and bomb research laboratories or try to portray scientists as evil people. He didn't go out into the world with hatred or anger.

Instead he created the Salem Research Institute, hired a biochemist and a few other scientists, and compiled a 2-inch-thick hardcover book published in English that chronicled tens of thousands of experiments where working with human tissue in culture (in a petri dish) was a more effective—*and cheaper*—way of doing research than using live animals. (One of the best examples: human tissue sample tests showed that Thalidomide had the potential to cause mutations, but the studies on rabbits required by the British equivalent of the US Food and Drug Administration didn't show such activity. So, the product went to market as a "proven safe cure" for morning sickness even as some scientists working with human tissues were worrying out loud that it might cause birth defects.)

After compiling all this research, and other books with information about how and where to obtain human tissue cultures and how to do research on them, Herr Müller sent his scientists out to all the big drug and cosmetics companies to talk with their directors of research about ways they could both save money and produce more-valid research results. As a result, many companies changed their policies, and millions of animals were spared from vivisection.

They were campaigning against vivisection, but not in a way that spread the vibration or energy of war and opposition. Herr Müller reframed the idea of research and thus changed the world for the better. And he did it from a place of cooperation and help, not of saintliness or martyrdom or a crusader's zeal.

Salem's efforts to reform the child-care systems in Europe and the United States were similar: When we'd speak at conferences about the advantage of family-based residential treatment models, we didn't talk much about how it was "right" or "good" or anything like that. Instead we talked about how it would reduce the number of children in care who would grow up to become "institution-created criminals" and thus add to the financial and social burdens of the government organizations funding child care.

Similarly, when I talk about teaching meditation or doing the Salem work, even the painful things such as working in the slums of Bogotá or ducking bullets in war-torn Uganda, please don't think of me (or think that I think of me) as a saint or martyr. I do these things because they're more self-actualizing than anything else I've ever known and because I love to be fully alive in the moment. I hope that that was the vibration I was spreading through both the work and the world as I was doing those things—and that I am now helping to create in showing and talking about them to people.

The years at Salem in New Hampshire taught Louise and me more about ourselves and our capabilities than any other time of our lives. They gave us a vivid insight—a powerful feeling—of our purpose for incarnating into this earth.

The people we worked with have shared with me, both at that time and in conversations in later years, similar comments about their own experience of working at Salem.

From this I've come to firmly believe that when we help others, even in small ways such as by sharing smiles or unnoticed acts of kindness, we come closer to our own enlightenment, our own salvation. As so many before us have found, serving others is one of the most useful routes to spiritual transformation.

From *The Prophet's Way* by Thom Hartmann,
© 1997, published by Inner Traditions International.

Younger-Culture
Drugs of Control

From *The Last Hours of Ancient Sunlight:*
Waking Up to Personal and Global Transformation

> It is not heroin or cocaine that makes one an addict, it is
> the need to escape from a harsh reality. There are more
> television addicts, more baseball and football addicts,
> more movie addicts, and certainly more alcohol addicts
> in this country than there are narcotics addicts.
>
> —SHIRLEY CHISHOLM (B. 1924)

POLITICIANS AND WRITERS OFTEN REFER TO OUR CURRENT ERA AS the Information Age. The average person alive today, they say, knows more than anybody at any time in the past. Through the Internet, encyclopedias on CDs and DVDs, and 700-channel television, the collective knowledge of the planet is available instantly to even the most ordinary of citizens, they say. It's a wonderful thing, and we're spectacularly well informed.

But is this really so?

If we are so well informed, why is it that when you ask most Americans simple questions about the history of the world, you get a blank look? How many of our children have read even one of Shakespeare's plays all the way through? How many people know with any depth beyond the 15-second sound bites served up on the evening TV news the genesis and the significance of the wars in, for example, Afghanistan or the Congo? Or that the United States government is still stealing Indian lands in Alaska, Arizona, Minnesota, Nevada, New Mexico, Wyoming, and a dozen other states?

Information Deficits

We may be living in an "information age" with "information overload," in some sense. But when it comes to what actually gets into people's heads, we're living in an age of "knowledge scarcity." People no longer know information that's vital to sustain life, such as how to grow their own food; how to find drinkable water; what's in their food; how to build a fire and keep warm; how to survive in the natural environment; how to read the sky; when the growing seasons begin and end; what plants in the forest and the fields are edible; how to track, kill, dress, eat, and store game; how to farm without (or even with) chemicals and tractors; how to treat broken bones and other common medical emergencies; and how to deliver a baby.

Because of this information deficit, we are out of touch with reality and are also standing on a dangerous shelf of oil-dependent, corporate-induced information starvation. In the 1930s during the Republican Great Depression, far more people lived in rural areas than in cities. The information about how to grow and preserve food, how to survive during difficult times, and how to make do with less was general knowledge. Today we know the names of the latest movie stars and how much their movies grossed, or what level the Dow Jones Industrial Average is at, but few of us could survive two months if the supermarkets suddenly closed. In addition, according to the Barbara Bush Foundation for Family Literacy, fully 27 percent of all American adults are "functionally illiterate" . . . although fewer than 1 percent of American homeowners lack a television set.

This works to the tremendous advantage of anyone who'd benefit from our being dependent on their systems, information, fuel, and food. We've become easy to manage and easy to control. We'll vote for whomever has the best 10-second sound bite on the evening news or the most powerful and expensive advertising.

We're Not Just Asleep; We're Intoxicated

As a teenager growing up in the sixties in college towns and San Francisco, I made the acquaintance of several heroin addicts. By and large they were nice people—not the stereotypes we see on TV and in literature but relatively normal middle-class kids who got in over their heads with a drug that was stronger than they'd ever expected or believed. Later, as I grew through my twenties and thirties, I met my share of alcohol addicts. Similarly, most were good people at heart but had found themselves in the grip of a drug that consumed their lives. And I've known many tobacco addicts over the years, most similarly well intentioned, who always thought they could one day just say no and then discovered it was unbelievably difficult.

One thing that I noticed about these addicts was that keeping the supply of the drug flowing into them had become the most important thing in their lives. It was at the core of their existence. They'd wake up in the morning, and their first thought would be how to get that day's supply of their particular drug. The day was drenched with the drug, and eventually they'd go to sleep with the drug.

Another thing you notice about addicts is that they will sacrifice things for their drug that they might otherwise consider important. They may have great plans for career, education, or relationships, but somehow those things end up subordinated to the enjoyment of their drug. Long after the drug has stopped producing a "high" but is just keeping them from flipping over into painful withdrawal, they're still spending hours every day immersed in it.

From the point of view of those running our culture, this is considered a good thing: younger-culture governments have traditionally regarded getting people addicted as desirable.

For instance, consider that the US government continues to give millions of dollars in subsidies (a nice euphemism for *gifts* or *corporate welfare*) to tobacco producers. In the more distant past, 30 years after losing the American Revolutionary War, the British fought a war with China to protect their "right" to sell opium to the more than 12 million addicts they'd created in China. They won the war, and took Hong Kong as part of their booty, and the British Empire made billions on opium trade and opium taxes. Many historians believe that the British were successful in winning the Opium Wars in large part because so many members of the Chinese royalty and bureaucracy were themselves addicted to opium. This reduced both their effectiveness as military opponents and their enthusiasm for making the British—and their opium—go away.

In dominator younger cultures, the first goal of the culture itself, as acted out most often by the cultural institutions of government and religion, is to render the citizenry nonresistant. What typically happens to peoples who won't "adjust" is that they're exterminated. Many native peoples have shared this fate; the result is that the only conquered peoples who survive tend to be docile. (If it sounds like conquerors treat the conquered like animals to be domesticated, you're getting my point precisely.) As every heroin dealer, tobacco salesman, and liquor store owner knows, if you have people who depend on a daily dose of your product for a sense of well-being, you have people who are not going to give you much trouble. (They may cause problems for others, but generally the dealers are left alone.)

Similarly, our technological culture has found a technological drug to maintain docility.

One measure of a drug's addictive potential is what percentage of people can take it up or put it down at will and with ease. This behavior is called *chipping* a drug—occasionally using it but also walking away from it without pain or withdrawal for months or years at a time. Research reported in *Science News* found that while large percentages of people could chip marijuana—and medium percentages of people could chip alcohol, cocaine, and even heroin—very, very few people (less than 5 percent) could chip tobacco. But imagine a "drug" that fewer than even 5 percent of Americans could walk away from for a month at a time without discomfort. Such a drug, by the definitions of addiction, would be the most powerfully addictive drug ever developed.

In addition to discouraging chipping behavior, this drug would also have to stabilize people's moods. It would put them into such a mental state that they could leave behind the boredom or pain or ennui of daily life. It would alter their brainwaves, change their neuro-chemistry, and constantly reassure them that their addiction to it was not, in fact, an addiction but merely a preference. Like the alcoholic who claims to be only a social drinker, the user of this drug would publicly proclaim the ability to do without it—but in reality would not even *consider* having it be completely absent from his home or life for days, weeks, or years.

Such a drug exists.

Far more seductive than opium, infinitely more effective at shaping behavior and expectations than alcohol, and used for more minutes every day than tobacco, our culture's most pervasive and most insidious drugging agent is *television*. Many drugs, after all, are essentially a distilled concentrate of a natural substance. Penicillin is extracted from mold; opium, from poppies. Similarly, television is a distilled extract—super-concentrated, like the most powerful drugs we have—of "real" life.

People set aside large portions of their lives to watch a flicker-ing box for hours every day. They rely on that box for the majority of their information about how the world is, how their politicians are behaving, and what reality is, even though the contents of the box are controlled by a handful of corporations, many of which are also in the weapons and tobacco and alcohol business. Our citizens wake up to this drug, consume it whenever possible during the day, and go to sleep with it. Many even take it with their meals.

Most people's major life regrets are not about the things they've done but about the things they've *not* done—the goals they never reached, the type of lover or friend or parent they wished they'd been but know they failed to be. Yet our culture encourages us to sit in front of a flickering box for dozens (at least) of hours a week, hundreds to thousands of hours a year, and thereby watch, as if from a distance, the time of our lives flow through our hands like dry sand.

The Sickness of "Living in Boxes"

Psychologists agree that being separate from others is generally harmful to our mental health and well-being. To be well, we must connect with others.

Louise and I live with a cat named Flicker, a beautiful black female with a thick gray mane that makes her look like a miniature lion. Flicker is nuts. The person we got her from told us that Flicker is quite certain that every human in the world is out to kill her and, we found, that appears to be true. A "scaredy-cat," she is paranoid, in the clinical sense.

Yesterday, on my way to the living room via the kitchen, I came across Flicker in the hall. She looked at me in bug-eyed fright, spun around, and ran toward the kitchen. I was heading in the same direction, so I kept walking: now she was *certain* that I was coming to get her. In the kitchen she paused for a moment, but I kept coming, as the way to the living room is through the kitchen. She glanced around with a panicked look, then ran toward the living room. I was still behind her. I tried purring at her, making soft sounds, and calling her, but nothing works with this cat: she knew that I was coming to hurt her. In the living room, I encountered her again, which sent her flying up into the air and then out to the safety of another hall that leads to the front door. Flicker's world is a hostile place filled with malevolent giants. In the few months we've had her, we've managed to get close to her from time to time, but there is always that wildness in her, that latent certainty that she can trust only herself for her own safety.

I was a guest on a nationally syndicated radio show a few weeks ago, and a man called in from someplace in Kansas.

"Do you mean to say," he said, "that plants and animals have a *right* to life on this planet?"

"Yes," I said. "That's exactly what I mean to say."

"You know that that's the position of the 'deep environmentalists,' don't you?" he said. "The radical tree-huggers?"

"Yeah, I've heard that," I said. "What's your position?"

"That we have to assign a value to things, using science and economics. Some forests are worth keeping and others are not. Some species can survive along with us, like cows and dogs and deer, and others can't, and so we shouldn't worry about them."

"So where do you draw the line?" I asked. "How do you know which species we should keep and which we should wipe out to make more room for the ones we like or to make more room for more people?"

"Keep the ones that are useful!" he said, as if the answer were obvious. "Who needs a spotted owl or a snail darter, for God's sake? We need jobs, economic security, clean streets, and safe cities. Those are the important things."

I pointed out to him that even if his assumption (that the world is only here for humans) were true, such massive tinkering as wiping out hundreds of thousands of species and altering the chemistry of the atmosphere might still create unintended results that would end up making the planet inhospitable to our "master species." And, in fact, there's plenty of evidence that that's exactly what's happening.

If we were to set aside our assumption of supremacy and instead adopt the older-culture view of all things having value and a sacred right to live on this planet, the odds of our unwittingly taking planet-scorching actions plummet.

Like Flicker, the caller to this radio show sees only one world. That world is populated by bright and colorful and "real" human beings, and every other living thing has a dimmer presence. Every "thing" is here to serve us, and we are given the knowledge and the power over what shall live and what shall die. If it is to our advantage to strip the world naked, down to a single species of tree and grain and vegetable and fish, so be it. We have decided that it is right because we see and understand the world as it really is. And for those who don't believe it's possible, we have the words of several of our gods, reported by humans who are incapable of error, to prove it.

This is the logic of the mentally unhealthy or ill.

Just as Flicker is certain she has the world figured out and that my walking from the bedroom to the living room—regardless of what I may think my motives are—is proof positive of the malevolent intent of all humans, the caller is certain that everything he sees in the world was put here for him; and if I assert it has its own right to existence, I am conspiring to take it away from him.

Paranoids construct a detailed and well-organized world where everything makes sense and is self-reinforcing. That man on the corner who is looking at you is the CIA spy who put the transmitter in your brain. He looks away because he doesn't want you to know that he is the spy. He glanced at you not because you were staring at him but because he is wondering if you have figured out that he is responsible for the transmitter. He gets on the bus not to go to work but to follow you. And on and on.

Similarly, whatever our worldview, we collect evidence to support it. Flicker believes that people are chasing her, and she sees signs of it everywhere. So if you believe that everything is a resource that we can use to our advantage, you'll see signs of that everywhere, too.

Sigmund Freud, the father of psychoanalysis and the man to whom many today look for definitions of what is "sick" and what is "healthy" mentally, made some interesting observations along these same lines in the years before he died. He pointed to his belief that what our civilization refers to as a "healthy ego" is, in fact, "a shrunken residue" of what we had experienced early in life when the ego experienced a "much more inclusive" and "intimate bond" with the world around it.[1] Many psychologists say that one result of this "shrinking process" is that the third most common cause of death for Americans between 15 and 27 years of age, according to the National Institutes of Mental Health, is suicide.

This shrinking into separateness, this breaking of the intimate bond with the world around us, this separating ourselves into isolated boxes, was largely unknown for the first 100,000 years or more of human history. It is still largely unknown by tribal people around the world, who, among those who have little contact with younger-culture people, have a suicide rate so low as to be almost immeasurable.

Historian Theodore Roszak uses the word *ecopsychology* to define the study of the relationship between humans and the natural environment. In his books *The Voice of the Earth: An Exploration of Ecopsychology* and *Ecopsychology: Restoring the Earth, Healing the Mind,* Roszak eloquently shows how the physical, mental, and spiritual disconnect of modern people may be responsible for entire realms of personal and cultural mental illnesses and how reconnecting with nature can be a powerful therapeutic process for both the individual and society.[2]

But this disconnect from nature has been at the core of "civilized" human experience since the formation of the first such "civilization" seven millennia ago. It was celebrated by Aristotle in his writings on how the universe and the natural world were merely collections of simple particles (atoms) that humans could manipulate once they understood them; and it was refined by Descartes, who argued that the entire universe was a giant machine, and this machinelike nature echoed all the way down to the smallest level. If we could just figure out where the levers and switches were, we could always figure out a way to control the machine. We withdrew from the natural world and created an artificial world around us, in our cities and towns, which is quite alien from that in which we first evolved. We even asserted that animals were just biological machines, incapable of feelings or emotions. As time went by, we decided for ourselves that various things were right and wrong with the rest of the planet, and we set about organizing things "out there" to comply with our needs "in here."

We placed our planet at the center of the universe and ourselves at the top of the hierarchy of our world. Our younger-culture religions and philosophers proclaimed, both explicitly and implicitly, that all of creation is made only for man. Galileo even went so far as to propose that if humans were not present to observe the world, it would cease to exist. When it was finally accepted that our planet wasn't the pivot point of all creation, we simply shifted our language to accommodate a fundamentally unchanged worldview: it is now the assumption of almost every "religious" citizen of any "civilized society" that we are at the *spiritual* center of the universe.

From this story, this view of the world—that our manmade cities are civilized and the natural world is wild and people who live in it are primitive or uncivilized or savages—we have developed a psychology that acknowledges and praises only itself and its own culture and has lost contact with the real physical world and its extraordinary powers and mysteries.

When the early European/American settlers fanned out across the prairies and killed every buffalo they could find, the Native Americans watched in shock and horror at what they considered an act of insanity. How could the settlers take the life of the plains? How could they parcel up the flesh of Mother Earth? How could they be so crazy as to cut down every tree in sight? The settlers looked at the Indians and thought they were crazy to not take and eat all the buffalo they could. How could they have sat on this valuable resource for 10,000 years and not have used it? They had to be savages, uncivilized half-humans who didn't have the good sense to know how to use nature's bounty for the good of the human race.

For a while this worked for the conquering "Americans." Just as Gilgamesh could cut down the cedars of Lebanon, just as the Greeks could destroy their own forests, just as Americans could strip half their topsoil from the land, the rapid consumption of "out there" to satisfy the needs of us "in here" worked for more than a few generations.

But it's working no more, as we're seeing in the "early warning system" of the developing world. In our inner cities, where people are afraid to drive with their doors unlocked or their windows down; on our farms, where dioxin or PCB-laced waste is spread across food plants as fertilizer; in our hospitals, where the primary waste from the manufacture of nuclear weapons (yttrium) is being promoted as an experimental "cure" for cancers (which are caused in large part by the air and food and drugs of our civilization)—in all these places we see that this world we have created can work for only a very few. It is the nature of hierarchical, dominator systems to end up this way.

Older cultures are older because they have survived for tens of thousands of years. In comparison, younger cultures are still an experiment, and every time one has been attempted (Sumeria, Rome, Greece), however great its grandeur, it has self-destructed, while tribes survive thousands of years.

Younger cultures are built on a foundation that is psychologically and spiritually ill: Freud's "shrunken residue" of the true and historic beauty of human life lived in intimate connection with the natural world. Increasingly, we live in isolation, in "boxes"—and we suffer for it.

What It's Like to Be in Touch with the World Again

It's possible to climb out of the box and get back in touch with the world.

Over the past 25 years, I have taken several classes in wild edible or medicinal plants. Usually, the courses involved one or more trips into the forest and the fields in search of the plants being studied. One of our teachers carried with her a small bottle of yellow cornmeal. She said, "When I uproot a plant or cut off a leaf, I put some cornmeal on the earth as my way of acknowledging the spirit of the plants and giving an offering back to them for their giving some of themselves to us."

In *The Origin of Consciousness in the Breakdown of the Bicameral Mind,* Columbia University psychology professor Julian Jaynes puts forth the concept that in prehistoric times (more than 7,000 to 10,000 years ago) people actually heard the voices of the gods.[3] When they looked out into the natural world, they saw fairies, sprites, spirits, and other entities. This was because, Jaynes posits, the two hemispheres of the brain were more fully connected, so the auditory regions of the left hemisphere were directly connected to the hallucinatory regions of the right hemisphere (Wernicke's and Broca's areas) that, in modern people, are normally active only during dreaming or in schizophrenics.

Because of this direct connection, Jaynes suggests what we now call hallucinations probably were a common part of the everyday experience of ancient peoples.

It was the rise of the Mesopotamian city-state empire, Jaynes suggests, and its use of written language that was largely responsible for the breakdown of this connection between the two hemispheres of the brain, causing all of us except the occasional mystic or schizophrenic to lose contact with much of the right hemisphere during our normal waking consciousness. Jaynes's arguments are persuasive, particularly where they draw on historical record and contemporary neurology. If his perspective is accurate, we would expect that people living today in the same way all humans did 10,000 years ago would live in a world alive with spirits, energies, and voices. When people are removed from that world and "civilized" by learning to read and write, they quickly (in as little as one generation, perhaps within an individual's life span) lose contact with that other world.

Another view is advanced by Terence McKenna in *Food of the Gods: The Search for the Original Tree of Knowledge.*[4] McKenna believes that the reconnection of the bicameral mind in cultures ancient and modern was and is brought about by the ingestion of certain plant substances. Hallucinatory plants are used by numerous cultures to open the doors to the world of the gods, McKenna points out. He even goes so far as to suggest that the rigidity, pain, and sterility of modern life are largely the result of our having lost access to those worlds because of the regulation and the control of these substances that once grew throughout humanity's habitat. McKenna proposes that the use of these plants helped catalyze the birth of human consciousness in early primates. This in turn spurred the development of the thinking and mystical brain/mind and gave the human species the mental power to set about replacing the plants with its own ways of controlling the mystical or divine experience, principally through the force of law promoted by organized religions.

Both Jaynes and McKenna contribute significantly to our understanding of the history of consciousness. McKenna has lived among and studied tribal peoples who today use these plants to meet and talk with the spirits of their world, and Jaynes has extensively studied the writings of past civilizations and people who said they heard the voices of their gods within their own heads. Regardless of the technique or method, there is a consensus among them and others that ancient and "modern primitive" people share the ability to see, feel, and hear something that we in modern Western society generally do not.

When a Shoshone looked about for food, he listened to what the land told him, the voices of the plants and the animals and the earth itself. They showed and told him where his day's meal would be found and also what types of ceremony would be appropriate to thank the world for this gift.

Contrast this with how European kings lived in the Middle Ages and how the dominator mind-set of that era has led us into an ironically unaware pseudo-information age and, perhaps unwittingly, into what author Daniel Quinn and the Australian Aborigines call "the great forgetting."

Our minds and our cultures created our situation. There's great insight in understanding this and much power in realizing how much of a role we can play in redefining the future of the planet for ourselves and our children.

The Secret of "Enough"

From *The Last Hours of Ancient Sunlight:*
Waking Up to Personal and Global Transformation

For I have learned, in whatsoever state
I am, therewith to be content.

—Saint Paul, Letter to the Philippians, 4:11

FIRST, THE TRUTH.

If you are naked, cold, and hungry and somehow you get shelter, clothing, and food, you will feel better. Providing for these necessities creates a qualitative change in life and could even be said to, in some ways, produce "happiness." You feel comfortable and safe. Your state of mind and emotional sense of well-being have improved as a result of these external changes, the result of your having acquired some stuff. Let's refer to this as the "enough point." It represents the point where a person has security, where their life and existence are not in danger.

Now, the lie or myth.

"If some stuff will make you happy, then twice as much stuff will make you twice as happy, 10 times as much will make you 10 times as happy, and so on into infinity."

By this logic, the fabulously rich such as Prince Charles, Bill Gates, or King Fahd must live in a state of perpetual bliss. "Greed is good," the oft-repeated mantra of the Reagan era, embodied the religious or moral way of expressing this myth. More is better. He who dies with the most toys wins.

Many Americans who lived through the Republican Great Depression discovered in that time that "More is better" is a myth. My wife's grandmother, who died in her nineties and was still living frugally but comfortably, owned a farm during that time and was able to provide for nearly all of her family's needs by growing her own food, burning wood, and making their clothing. Recycling wasn't a fad to save the environment but a necessary part of staying alive and comfortable. Great-grandma had enough money in investments and from the sale of the farm to live a rather extravagant lifestyle, but she still bought her two dresses each year from the Sears catalog, collected rainwater to wash her beautiful long hair, wrote poetry, and found joy in preparing her own meals from scratch. She saw the myth for what it was and was unaffected by it.

Some, of course, came through the Great Depression so scarred by the experience that they went in the opposite direction and totally embraced the myth. The excesses of Howard Hughes, for example, are legendary—as is the painful reality that almost limitless resources never bought him happiness.

Similarly, the myth has become a core belief in the cultures of America, much of Europe, and most of the developing world. Advertisers encourage children and adults to acquire products they don't need, with the implicit message that getting, having, and using things will produce happiness. Often the advertising message of "Buy this and you will be happier" is so blatant as to be startling to a person sensitized to the myth. "Forget about the 'enough point,'" these sellers say, "this product or service will be the one that finally brings you fulfillment."

The Meaning of Wealth

But we are the people—both those who feel that "enough" is a humble level of comfort and those who crave great wealth—of our culture. Like the air we breathe, it's often easy to forget that we are members of a culture that is unique and that has its own assumptions. This younger culture is based on a simple economy: you produce goods or services that have value to others and then exchange them with others for goods or services they produce that you want or need. Money arose as a way of simplifying the exchange, but this is the basic equation. This concept of wealth as a measure of goods or money owned is intrinsic to these cultures; so, in this regard you could say that all of

these different cultures around the world are really the same, variations on a single theme, different patterns woven of the same cloth.

The Wealth of Security

Although they number fewer than 1 percent of all humans on the planet,
the result of a relentless five-millennium genocide by our worldwide
younger culture, members of older cultures are still alive on earth.
There are also people whose older-culture ways have been so recently
taken from them—such as many Native American tribes—that while
they may no longer live in the older-culture way, they remember it.

In these older cultures, the concept of "More is better" is
unknown. They would consider "Greed is good" to be the statement
of an insane person. One person's eating near another who is hungry
is an obscene act.

These values and norms of behavior are quite different from
those we see in our own world today. But why? The reason is simple:
security is their wealth, not goods or services.

In older cultures the goal of the entire community is to bring
every person in the community to the "enough point." Once that is
reached and ensured, people are free to pursue their own personal
interests and bliss. The shaman explores trance states, the potter makes
more-elegant pots, the storyteller spins new yarns, and parents play
with and teach their children how to live successfully.

But Aren't They Dirt-Poor?

Because older-culture people usually work together to create enough
food, shelter, clothing, and comfort to reach the "enough point" and
then shift their attention and values to other, more internal pursuits
(such as fun or spirituality), they appear to us in younger cultures to
be poor.

I remember spending a few days with a Native American healer
who taught me about a particular ritual I've promised not to reveal in
my writing. He lived in a mobile home in the desert, on reservation

land that was pitifully lacking in everything except scrub brush, cactus, and dust. His car, a 1970s Chevy, was missing major body parts, and he traded healing ceremonies with the locals for food, gasoline, clothes, and nearly everything else he needed. His income in actual cash was probably less than $500 per year; and if you added up the total market value of everything else he took in during the course of a year, it was probably less than $5,000. By any standard of contemporary Western culture, he was about as poor as you can be in America and still stay alive. And his lifestyle was nearly identical to the other 200 or 300 families who lived within 20 miles of him and were members of his tribe: they were all "poor."

But he had things that most of the people I knew back in Atlanta living in upscale suburban homes lacked.

If he became ill, people would care for him. If he needed food or clothes, they'd give them to him. If he was in trouble, they were there with him. When his only child needed something, somehow it always materialized from the local community. When he got old, he knew somebody would take him in; if he lost his home, others would help him build or find another. No matter what happened to him, it was as if it happened to the entire community.

As we got to know each other and I met people in his small "town," I discovered that his riches of security and support from his neighbors weren't unique to him just because he was the community's healer. The same was true of every person in the "town," from the guys who did part-time carpentry work in the city 122 miles away to the town drunks. *Everybody* had cradle-to-grave security, to the maximum extent that it could be provided by the members of the tribe.

Our Poverty

After returning from my first trip to New Mexico, I had dinner with a friend who is a successful attorney with a big law firm in Atlanta.

"What would happen if you lost your job?" I asked him.

He shrugged. "I'd probably get another one."

"What if the job market was bad? If there was a recession or depression? Or what if you lost your job because of some monumental screw-up you did on a case?"

He looked at his plate of spaghetti with a troubled expression, staring at the twisted strands as if his future were there. "I don't know," he said softly. "I suppose I'd lose my house first—the mortgage payments, insurance, and taxes are well over $2,000 a month. And the car is another $500."

"And if your health went bad?" I asked. "If you had some serious disease?"

He looked up. "You mean without the insurance from my employer?"

"Yeah."

"I'd die," he said. "I have a colleague who spends most of his time defending insurance companies who've done that to people who got sick. They then start looking through the insurance applications to see if there was anything on there the people forgot to mention when they filled it out, like a pre-existing condition, or that they'd once been turned down for insurance. If they find it, they dump them. I know of several people who've died, who could be alive today if they'd had the money for the medical care."

"And when you get old?"

"I have my retirement fund. My 401(k)."

"What if your company ripped it off, or if it was all in stocks and the market crashed?"

He shook his head. "I'd be living on the streets, or in my kid's garage, assuming he could afford to have me. It wouldn't be pretty."

Even more than his words, his tone of voice and his eyes gave away his essential insecurity. If his employer went down, so would he. He was living—as was I at the time—on a tenuous thread of debt, workaday income, and hope that the government could somehow manage to keep the country's financial house of cards from crashing down as it had so many times in the past few centuries.

"If you could have anything at all," I asked him, "what would it be?"

"That's easy," he said, smiling. "More time. There aren't enough hours in the day, and I feel as though I'm on a continuous treadmill. There's never enough time to spend with my kids, my wife, our family and friends, or even to read a good book. Three nights out of the week I bring work home, and I know that if I'm going to make partner in the firm one day, it'll have to become five, and maybe even seven days a week. I have no time."

My friend, surrounded by a wealth of physical possessions, a fancy home with elegant carpeting and furniture, a new Mercedes, wearing an $1,800 suit, was steeped in the poverty that is unique to younger cultures—the poverty of spirit, of time, of security and support. His life had no safe foundation and seemed to have little meaning beyond achieving the next level of income and creature comforts.

As my Native American mentor said of me, "Boy, you think you're rich, but you're poor beyond your imaginings." So we must, as a culture, rediscover where the point of "enough" is, both materially and spiritually. By finding this point, you become infinitely richer.

PART IV
Earth and Edges

E DGES ARE WHERE ALL THE ACTION IS," THOM HARTMANN WROTE in his book *Threshold: The Crisis of Western Culture*. He was talking about natural edges—forests and seashores—as well as human edges like war zones and the borders between countries. In these kinds of places, he says, "we find the most visible truths about where we've been, where we are, and where we're going. When we look closely at our planet, we can easily see the truth about where we're going."

These days we are all living on the edge. A confluence of environmental breaking points—deforestation, the collapse of ocean fisheries, the depletion of ancient aquifers, mass extinctions, and the deterioration of our atmosphere—are leading us to the precipice of disaster. With the United Nations predicting that the world's peak population will reach 9 billion by 2050—an increase equal to the entire population of the world in 1950—it's vital that we confront the fact of our burgeoning human population, which is driving this ecological crisis. Truthfully, Planet Earth may survive all of these threats, but human civilization as we know it will not. All the signs point to the inescapable conclusion that we'd better change our ways and soon.

Despite what the climate deniers would have you believe, climate change is not a matter of opinion; it's hard science, as Hartmann persuasively shows in "The Atmosphere." It's going to take a collective effort to overcome our addiction to oil and rein in the corporations and the billionaires who are making fortunes pumping carbon into our atmosphere. We are so accustomed to thinking that for every problem, we can buy something to solve it; that technology, or some technology yet to be invented, will save us. While Hartmann doesn't believe that technology is the answer to our problems, he is no Luddite, and he is enthusiastic about wise uses of technology.

"Cool Our Fever" chronicles the remarkable German experiment in solar energy. Germany's investment in solar roof panels—in a country that is cloudy much of the year—has drastically reduced its reliance on fossil fuels and provided its citizens with a clean, renewable form of energy. More solar panels cover rooftops in Germany than in the US and Japan combined. If it can happen there, why not here?

Hartmann has long held that our attitudes are just as damaging to the world's ecosystems as our behavior. By disconnecting ourselves from the natural world, "shrinking into separateness" as we watch the glowing boxes in our living rooms, we have brought about our own destruction. The answer to our global dilemma is simple and obvious: If we want to change our world, we must change our worldview. We must return to an older-culture way of being, a perspective that has been buried and forgotten. As we reestablish the links to what we knew in the past, we can reclaim our future. We can live well without destroying the world around us.

The older-culture worldview is a close cousin to deep ecology and to the Buddhist principle of interdependence. It highlights the interconnectedness of human and nonhuman life, holding that all life forms have an inherent right to life and are not here on earth to serve and supply us. As Hartmann illustrates in "The Death of the Trees" and "Something Will Save Us," this is a powerfully transformative viewpoint.

People often hear that our way of life is unsustainable, but at the same time they must not really hear it because they don't change their behavior. That's because they are stuck in the rut of younger-culture thinking, a blindly adolescent mindset that feels it is entitled to everything it has and more. What Hartmann proposes is an evolution of consciousness, the collective awakening we so desperately need: "If we were to set aside our assumption of supremacy and instead adopt the older-culture view of all things having value and a sacred right to live on this planet, the odds of our unwittingly taking planet-scorching actions plummet."

The Atmosphere

From *Threshold: The Crisis of Western Culture*

O N FEBRUARY 24, 2007, AN EXPEDITION ACROSS THE POLAR NORTH
funded in part by the National Geographic Society and Sir Richard Branson set out on 78-day journey.[1] Guided by local Inuit hunters
and trackers, they found that the environment there was changing—
warming—at about twice the rate of the more temperate and equatorial regions of the world. The result was multifold.

Landmarks—usually giant mountains of ice that had been known
by the Inuit people (and even named and the subject of folklore) for
tens of thousands of years—are moving, changing, and in many cases
vanishing altogether. The open sea (which absorbs about 70 percent
of the solar radiation that hits it) is quickly replacing polar ice (which
reflects back out into space about 70 percent of the solar radiation that
hits it). Animals never before seen in the region—finches, dolphins,
and robins, for example—are moving farther north as their migratory
patterns are pushed by global climate change, while animals that have
lived in the region for tens of thousands of years (most notably the
polar bear) are facing extinction, as there is no place "farther north"
for them to go to find the environment to which millions of years of
evolution have adapted them.

Meanwhile, on the other side of the planet, the collapse of two
massive ice sheets, the Larsen A and B shelves, on the edge of the
Antarctic continent have provided National Geographic Society and
other scientists a glimpse of previously unknown species.[2] For millennia the Larsen A and B shelves provided a ceiling to a unique undersea
environment, and the loss of these two shelves, totaling more than
3,900 square miles of polar ice, has exposed this world to man for
the first time. Marine biologists found, for example, a poisonous sea
anemone that attaches itself to the back of a snail, protecting it from

predators; meanwhile the snail provides the movement necessary for the anemone to find food. Biologists also found a giant barnacle and a shrimplike crustacean.

It remains to be seen if the changes in the temperatures and the levels of light reaching the area will now also cause the extinction of these and other newly discovered species.

How Much Power Is a Watt?

When I was 13 years old, I got my novice and then my general amateur radio operator's license from the Federal Communications Commission. It required passing what was, in 1964, a pretty hefty test on electronics; and one of the formulas I remember from the test is that 1 *ampere* (a measure of the "volume" of electricity) passing through a wire at 1 *volt* (a measure of the "pressure" of electricity) can do the amount of "work" (e.g., heat a wire, turn a motor, light a bulb) of 1 *watt* (W). The math is pretty simple: $W = EI$, where W is watts, E is volts, and I is amperes.

One watt of "work," or "heat," may not seem like a lot. After all, a typical electric room heater runs between 1,000 W and 1,500 W (the maximum capacity of a typical American household electrical outlet is 110 volts at 20 amperes, or 2,200 W). A toaster may run as much as 1,800 W. And a 60 W light bulb, while it can throw enough light to illuminate a room, as well as get hot enough to burn your hand, doesn't seem like it's going to melt the seas or change the face of the earth.

Yet in June 2005, the top climate scientist for NASA's Goddard Institute for Space Studies, James Hansen, along with 14 other scientists representing the Jet Propulsion Laboratory, the Lawrence Berkeley National Laboratory, Columbia University's Department of Earth and Environmental Sciences and its Earth Institute, and SGT Incorporated published such a startling research paper[3] in the journal *Science* that it shook the scientific community of the entire world.

They were looking at how much more "power"—expressed in watts per square meter (W/m^2)—the surface of the earth was absorbing from the sun versus the amount it lost to radiation into outer space. Historically, the two numbers have been in balance, leaving the surface of the earth at a relatively even temperature over millions of years. Their concern was that if the earth began absorbing significantly more energy than in times past, this extra heat would drive a "climate forcing" that could produce radical changes in the world in which we live—changes that could even render it unfit for human habitation over a period as short as a few decades or centuries.

Looking at measurements of gases in the atmosphere, and thousands of temperature-measurement points, from 1880 to today, they found that during this time the "thermal inertia"—the movement toward global warming—is now about 1.8 W/m^2 over the entire surface of the earth. This means that every square meter—roughly the surface size of the desk I'm working on right now—of the planet is absorbing 1.8 W more energy than it was in 1880.

A quarter-acre house lot (a pretty good-sized lot these days) represents 1,012 square meters of planet surface. At 1.8 W per square meter, that's roughly 1,800 W of energy—about the same as is produced by the toaster referenced earlier—for every quarter acre of the planet.

As Hansen and his colleagues point out in the *Science* article, until recently (the past 150 years) the earth had largely been stable in the amount of heat it absorbed. The increase wasn't 1.8 W/m^2 over a 128-year period but 0 W/m^2 over at least a 10,000-year period. If the past 10,000 years had simply been 1 W/m^2 higher (not the *1.8 W/m^2* we're seeing today), the surface temperature of the world's oceans today would not be roughly 59 degrees Fahrenheit (F) but instead be 271 degrees F. Water boils at 212 degrees F, which means that much of our oceans would simply have boiled off into the atmosphere, increasing heat-trapping atmospheric moisture and thus increasing the temperature even more. Our planet would not be even remotely habitable by humans—or most life forms alive today.

Since 1880 we've been throwing greenhouse gases—particularly carbon dioxide and methane—into the atmosphere at rates the planet hasn't seen since the early, heavily volcanic days prior to the dinosaurs.

Thus the sea ice is melting, corals are dying/bleaching, sea life is dying/moving, and the ocean's currents are changing (which alters our weather—seen a good-sized tornado, cyclone, or hurricane recently?). And eventually—and maybe soon—that energy will begin to spill out of what Hansen refers to as the storage "pipeline" of the oceans, and the killing of life on land—the expanding deserts, vanishing glaciers, and drying rivers and lakes—will speed up to astonishing and human-life-threatening levels.

Back in 2005—before the massive ice sheet breakups and the open water of the Arctic were visible—Hansen suggested that we look at these effects as signs that the added wattage the planet was absorbing might be tipping us into a forward-crash of spiraling temperatures that would be impossible to stop. In the cold language of science, he and his colleagues wrote:[4]

> The destabilizing effect of comparable ocean and ice sheet response times is apparent. Assume that initial stages of ice sheet disintegration are detected. Before action to counter this trend could be effective, it would be necessary to eliminate the positive planetary energy imbalance, now 0.85 W/m^2, which exists as a result of the oceans' thermal inertia. Given energy infrastructure inertia and trends in energy use, that task could require on the order of a century to complete. If the time for a substantial ice response is as short as a century, the positive ice-climate feedbacks imply the possibility of a system out of our control.

Three years later, on April 7, 2008, in a statement that went way beyond anything even Al Gore was predicting in his 2005 book and movie *An Inconvenient Truth: The Planetary Emergency of Global Warming and What We Can Do About It*, Hansen and a group of scientists submitted a new article. While Gore was largely concerned with rising oceans and spreading deserts, Hansen and his colleagues were looking at the possibility of the extinction of most complex life forms on the planet if we don't quickly get our atmospheric CO_2 levels down below where they were 25 years ago. The article, "Target Atmospheric CO_2: Where Should Humanity Aim?," though written in dense scientific jargon, included two frighteningly important sentences, in language any average nonscientist could understand:[5]

> If humanity wishes to preserve a planet similar to that on which civilization developed and to which life on Earth is adapted, paleo-climate evidence and ongoing climate change suggest that CO_2 will need to be reduced from its current 385 ppm [parts per million] to at most 350 ppm . . . If the present overshoot of this target CO_2 is not brief, there is a possibility of seeding irreversible catastrophic effects.

We are, Hansen and his colleagues suggest, near the point where our use of carbon-based fossil fuels could throw the planet so out of balance that eventually the oceans will heat up to the point that they're uninhabitable for current complex life forms, and much of the complex life as we know it will vanish. If this drastic worst-case scenario event were to happen, it could take billions of years of evolution for the deep-sea and single-cell organisms that survived to evolve back into anything resembling the complex life forms we're familiar with (including ourselves).

The article concludes:[6]

> Present policies, with continued construction of coal-fired power plants without CO_2 capture, suggest that decision-makers do not appreciate the gravity of the situation. We must begin to move now toward the era beyond fossil fuels. Continued growth of greenhouse gas emissions, for just another decade, practically eliminates the possibility of near-term return of atmospheric composition beneath the tipping level for catastrophic effects.

> The most difficult task, phase-out over the next 20–25 years of coal use that does not capture CO_2, is Herculean, yet feasible when compared with the efforts that went into World War II. The stakes, for all life on the planet, surpass those of any previous crisis. The greatest danger is continued ignorance and denial, which could make tragic consequences unavoidable.

In 2000, according to the Intergovernmental Panel on Climate Change, 6.4 billion tons of CO_2 were poured into our atmosphere by human activity. Just five years later, that 6.4 billion tons had jumped to 7.2 billion tons, with about 5.5 billion tons coming from burning fossil fuels and 1.7 billion tons from the destruction of forests and rain forests worldwide. All along, the oceans and the land seem to be able to "sink out" or absorb only about 3.9 billion tons combined, leaving a net increase in CO_2 in 2005 of around 3.3 billion tons.

As Hansen and his colleagues point out in their 2008 article, unless we can *reverse* these numbers—turn them *negative*—long enough to go back down below 350 ppm, the human race (and most other mammals) may crash into a dead-end wall.

Other Greenhouse Gases

And that's just carbon dioxide. A methane molecule, like carbon dioxide, contains a single atom of carbon, but instead of attaching to it two atoms of oxygen (as with CO_2), it attaches to it four atoms of hydrogen (CH_4). The molecule is somewhat unstable: it will oxidize rapidly (burn) when exposed to high temperatures and will oxidize slowly (decompose into CO_2 and H_2O) in the atmosphere at a rate of about half of the total methane every seven years. (That's the good news: methane will eventually wring itself out if we stop pushing it into the atmosphere.)

Natural gas is about 78 percent methane. The biggest sources of it are decomposing vegetation and, literally, animal flatulence. And we have a lot of very flatulent animals that we grow for human food.

For example, while there are more than 6 billion humans, there are more than 20 billion livestock mammals (pigs, cows, goats, sheep) and about 16 billion chickens in the world—more than 99 percent of them grown by humans as food for humans. The Food and Agriculture Organization of the United Nations (FAO) in a 2007 report[7] noted that 37 percent of the world's total methane production (and 9 percent of all CO_2 and 65 percent of all nitrous oxide emissions) comes from our livestock. Because nitrous oxide is 296 times stronger than CO_2 at global warming, and methane is about 23 times as potent as CO_2, the combined greenhouse effect of our livestock worldwide is greater than the sum total of all our cars, trains, buses, trucks, ships, airplanes, and jets.

A sudden and worldwide shift to vegetarianism (or even close to vegetarianism—most indigenous societies historically have used meat as a flavoring rather than a staple, eating less than one-fifth of the meat and dairy products that Americans do) would have more impact on global warming than if every jet plane and car in the world were to fall silent forever.

University of Chicago research[8] found that simply going vegetarian would reduce the average American's carbon footprint by more than 1.5 tons of carbon per year. That's half again more than doubling the gas mileage of your car by moving from a big sedan to a small hybrid (which typically saves about 1 ton of carbon per year).

For hundreds of thousands of years, methane concentrations in the atmosphere were pretty stable (again, varying with solar cycles), at 715 parts per billion (ppb) around the time, for example, of the Civil War. Today they're more than 1,774 ppb. Nitrous oxide has also gone up, from 270 ppb in pre-industrial times to more than 320 ppb now. Almost all of both increases tie back to agriculture.

So, here we have four colliding "linear" systems, all pushing against the "circle" of our blue marble floating through space, Planet Earth: human population exploding; increasing levels of fossilized carbon being consumed, with its waste (mostly CO_2) put into our atmosphere; increasing numbers of food animals for all us humans, producing unsustainable levels of waste that is also altering our environment; and an atmosphere absorbing all of this about to tip over into an unstable state, which could render the planet uninhabitable for us and most other complex life forms.

Rebooting Evolution

The word *unsustainable* is vastly underrated, probably because it's so overused. But it's not a "maybe" word. It doesn't refer to a process. It refers directly to an end point and says that when that point is reached, whatever behavior or process it's referencing *must* change or end.

Our polluting our atmosphere is unsustainable. Our agricultural techniques are unsustainable. Our fossil fuel consumption is unsustainable. Our consumption of raw materials and our production of toxic waste that can't be eaten by anything else are unsustainable. Our consumption of water is unsustainable. Our population growth is unsustainable. *Our way of life is unsustainable.*

Many cultures and human societies before ours were unsustainable, and are now gone. In many cases, all of their members died out within a generation or two, and even their DNA has become as lost to us as are their languages, worldviews, religions, and cultures. Their cities are ruins, sometimes consumed by jungles, more often covered with sand, as their agricultural or forestry practices were unsustainable and created desertification and loss of topsoil.

You and I are descendants of successful cultures—ones that, at least over the past 165,000 years, were in one way or another sustainable at least through the next generation. But our ancestors knew people—or knew of people—who had no descendants; none of their progeny are among our peers. Their line died out.

The difference between us and them is one of scale. When they died out, other humans were largely unaffected. Most humans on the planet didn't even notice when the Incan and Mayan cultures collapsed and their languages and religions were lost, or when the Sumerians vanished and their language and religion were forgotten.

But if our culture goes, it will probably take all of humanity with it. It will probably take most of the large mammals on the planet—actually, it already has. We've already killed off 90 percent of the big fish that were in the world's oceans just 60 years ago. Since the first days of our culture, we've laid waste to more than half of the world's forests (3 billion of 7.5 billion hectares),[9] and we're burning and slashing through the world's rain forests at a current rate of 16 million hectares per year, meaning by the end of this century they could all be gone.[10] More than 50 percent of the world's topsoil[11] is already gone.

The Iroquois Confederacy had a law that every decision had to be made in the context of its impact on the seventh subsequent generation. Given the current velocity of our trend lines, if there is not a sea change in our cultural beliefs and actions within the current generation (that means you and me), there may no longer be humans on this planet in seven generations.

From *Threshold: The Crisis of Western Culture* by Thom Hartmann, © 2009, published by Viking Penguin, a division of Penguin Group (USA) Inc.

The Death of the Trees

From *The Last Hours of Ancient Sunlight:*
Waking Up to Personal and Global Transformation

The development of civilization and industry in general has
always shown itself so active in the destruction of forests
that everything that has been done for their conservation
and production is completely insignificant in comparison.

—KARL MARX (1818–1883), *DAS CAPITAL* (1867)

WHEN I WAS IN ELEMENTARY SCHOOL, WE WERE TAUGHT THAT
the oceans and the forests were the chief sources of oxygen for
the planet. It turns out that, at least for those animals that breathe air,
this is only partially correct. The oceans account for less than 8 percent of the atmosphere's oxygen, and that is dropping rapidly: there
are now millions of acres of ocean that are dying from the dumping of
toxic wastes or changes in water temperature, and they therefore have
become net *consumers* of oxygen.

Trees, it turns out, are *the* major source of recycled oxygen for
the atmosphere. They are our planet's lungs. A full-grown pine or
hardwood tree has a leaf surface area that can run from 0.25 acre to
more than 3 acres, depending on the species. Rain forest trees have
leaf surface areas that run as high as 40 acres per tree. Throughout
this enormous surface area, sunlight is used as an energy source to
drive the conversion of carbon dioxide into oxygen and plant matter (using the C, which is carbon). Trees literally breathe in the CO_2
through that enormous leaf area after we exhale it as biological waste,
and they exhale oxygen as their own waste. Without trees our atmosphere would most likely become toxic to us; and because rain forest
trees have such a massively larger leaf area than our common trees,

the rain forests of the world provide much of the oxygen that you are breathing as you read this page.

While this is common knowledge, it's really among the least important functions that trees play: other details about trees' role in our survival are less well known.

The Root System "Water Pump"

A rain forest tree will draw 3 million gallons of water up through its roots and release it into the atmosphere as water vapor during its lifetime. While it may seem that this would deplete the soil of water, actually the reverse is true: trees draw water *into* the soil, the first step in a complex cycle that prevents land from becoming desert.

Without forestland pumping millions of tons of water into an area's atmosphere, there's little moisture released into the air to condense into clouds and then fall again as rain. The result is that just downwind of the place that was once forest but is now denuded, the rains no longer fall and a process called *desertification* begins. This has happened over much of north and eastern Africa, leading to massive famines as the rains stop, crops fail, the topsoil is blown away, and what is left is desert.

Most rainfall on nonforestland is either absorbed and becomes surface ground water or is transported along culverts, ditches, sewers, streams, and rivers, eventually reaching the ocean. On our continental landmasses, only *trees* effectively cycle large quantities of water back into the atmosphere. For comparison, think about the evaporation from a 40-acre lake. That may seem like a lot of water to be evaporating into the atmosphere, but those 40 acres equal the evaporative leaf surface of a *single* large tree.

As of this writing, more than 1,500 acres of land are becoming desert worldwide every hour, largely because of the destruction of upwind forests. The total amount of rain forest left on the planet is about the size of the continental United States, and every year an area the size of Florida is cut down and permanently destroyed.

Reseeded Saplings Can't Pull the Water Down

The timber industry's ads that show loggers planting seedlings after stripping trees from a forest are utterly misleading with regard to water. They may well be replacing trees, but they're creating a decades-long gap in the water cycle.

Another problem is that they're setting up an ecological disaster by planting the same species throughout a deforested area. When an entire forest is all made of the same species of tree, and they're all the same age, it becomes an irresistible treat for tree-eating caterpillars, beetles, and fungi, as we've seen in numerous forests in North America and Europe.

Taking thousands of tons of biomass (fully grown trees and habitat) out of a forest and replacing it with saplings that weigh a few ounces will do little for the downwind areas that need the atmospheric moisture to produce rainfall. Even by the time the trees regenerate, the ecological diversity and the natural fauna and flora of the region have been decimated, as the diversity of numerous plant species are replaced by the single-species seedlings used by the loggers. But it's not just the timber companies who are responsible for the destruction of the planet's forests.

Trees for Beef: Slashing Rain Forests So Americans Can Have a 99-Cent Burger

According to a 1996 report by the Consultative Group on International Agricultural Research, funded by the World Bank and the United Nations, 72 acres of rain forest are destroyed every minute, mostly by impoverished people working for multinational corporations, who are cutting and burning the forest to create agricultural or pasturelands to grow beef for export to the United States.[1]

This 38-million-acres-per-year loss will wipe out the entire world's rain forests in our children's lifetimes if it continues at its current pace. The end, literally, is within sight.

A spokesman for the World Bank said that the study pointed out poverty and overpopulation as the primary factors leading to the destruction of these forests, which are so essential to maintaining human life on the planet. He conveniently overlooked the role of huge agricultural corporations.

Recently, a friend of my son's complained to me that one of the giant fast-food hamburger chains was responsible for the destruction of many of the rain forests in the Americas. I didn't understand what he meant: the assumption I'd always had was that the rain forests were cut by timber companies eager to sell rare woods to Japan and Scandinavia for manufacture of furniture and specialty items. If the fast-food chains were killing off the rain forests, I thought, it must be because they were buying cheap wood for paper to wrap their burgers in, or that their plastic packaging was somehow damaging to the rain forests.

It turns out, however, that I shared a common misconception, one that I'm sure the American fast-food industry is probably quite happy keeping intact.

While these rain forests that have taken centuries to grow are often logged and the wood is sold, they're just as often simply burned and not reseeded, particularly if they're in places where it's inconvenient to take the wood to market. The "free" wood is usually only an added bonus, a quick buck for a peasant farmer to use to buy some breeder cattle.

The most common reason why people are destroying most of the South and Central American rain forests is corporate greed: the American meat habit has provided an economic boom to multinational corporate ranchers, and it is the primary reason behind the destruction of the tropical rain forests of the Americas. Poor farmers and factory farmers alike engage in slash-and-burn agriculture, cutting ancient forests to plant a single crop: grass for cattle.

As John Robbins points out in his book *Diet for a New America,* "The United States imports 200 million pounds of beef every year from El Salvador, Guatemala, Nicaragua, Honduras, Costa Rica, and Panama—while the average citizen in those countries eats less meat each year than the average American house cat."[2]

This deforestation of Latin America for burgers is particularly distressing when you consider that this very fragile area contains

58 percent of the entire planet's rain forests (19 percent are in Africa and 23 percent in Oceania and Southeast Asia).

Deforesting Removes Roots, Affecting Groundwater and the Water Cycle

Another problem related to deforestation is the loss of drinkable groundwater.

Drinkable water falls from the skies as rain and soaks into the ground.

At deeper levels, the water has often acquired (from the soil) high concentrations of dissolved minerals, particularly salts. Trees reach deeply down into the earth and draw up moisture from just above this salty water and pump it up into the atmosphere, using the minerals to harden the wood of the tree. This removal of water from the soil creates a downward draw, into the soil, for the fresh water raining down from above. This circulation keeps the soil healthy.

When forests are cut, however, the more saline subterranean water begins to creep upward, infiltrating into higher and higher levels of soil. When this salty water hits a level a few yards below the surface, the remaining trees become immune damaged, just like an AIDS patient, vulnerable to parasitic infections. We see the result of this in beetle infestations and fungal infections such as "rust," which are wiping out trees around the world.

People often think that beetle, caterpillar, moth, and fungus infections are external agents that cause forests to die, so they react with mass sprayings of insecticides or fungicides or by shrugging their shoulders and saying that nothing can be done. But in a healthy forest, such infestations are rare, just as in a healthy human opportunistic infections are rare. One reason why even multispecied, varied-aged tracts of forest in Europe and the United States are dying from these conditions is because they've already been weakened by humans' pumping out much of the surface water, pouring down acid rain on them, and destroying surrounding forests.

In Europe the percentage of land that is forest has been reduced to 27 percent. In Asia it's 19 percent. In North America (including the vast forests of Canada), it's at 25 percent. The worldwide replacement of forests with pastureland for cows has become so pervasive that wood-poor England is now, in some communities, using charcoal made from burned cow bones instead of the traditional wood charcoal to filter city water supplies. Reacting to protests from vegetarians in Yorkshire, England, the Yorkshire Water company pointed out that the bones were imported from India because the company couldn't afford the cost of wood-made charcoal and, the Associated Press quoted an official as saying, "We can't undertake to supply water which meets individual dietary needs."[3] As of 1997 cow-bone charcoal, cheaper than wood charcoal even after including the cost of shipping it from India, was being used in 10 water treatment plants, and the company planned to add it to six more.

When the salty water continues higher and reaches a foot or two below the surface, crops begin to die. And when it hits the surface, the soil becomes incapable of sustaining vegetation and desertification sets in.

To deal with this growing soil salinity crisis, farmers from California to Europe to Australia have begun installing deep-water pumps to remove the salt-contaminated water that the trees would have once drawn down deep below the surface. While this works as a short-term solution, over the long term it only makes the problem worse because that undesirable water is not being cycled back up into the atmosphere, as it would be by a tree, but instead is dumped into waterways, which it poisons on its way to the sea. The result is further downwind desertification as well as the poisoning of rivers and lakes.

The loss of trees means not only the loss of current topsoil because of salination and desertification but also the loss of future soils. The roots of most plants anchor only into the topsoil, using it for mechanical support and as a medium from which to derive nutrients and water. Trees, however, have deep roots that break up lower levels of rock, slowly bringing them to the surface, and shallow roots that break up surface rock. They also draw minerals up into the tree itself to help make the plant matter. When the leaves are shed, they form an essential component of soil.

The result of this action by the roots of trees is the formation of new topsoil. It takes, on average, about 400 years for a forest to create a foot of topsoil that is capable of sustaining crops. Without a forest there is almost no topsoil being created at all. (Some sand is formed through air and water erosion of rock, but that is not soil.) This also shows how slash-and-burn agriculture, where a few feet of topsoil are exposed by burning a forest and then used up by agriculture over just a few years, is so shortsighted.

Given that without soil we can have no crops, it would seem that we'd be concerned about both the loss of our soil-creating trees and the loss of our current soil itself. Instead, more than 300 tons of topsoil are lost worldwide *every minute* as governments and the agricultural corporations that produce most of America's crops look the other way.

Because of rising average temperatures from global warming, the life cycle of the bark beetle in Alaska has been cut from two years to one for reproduction. This has led to a near doubling of the population of bark beetles, which have devastated several million acres of Alaskan forests.

Forests are imperiled worldwide.

Hardly anything illustrates the rich, complex, interdependent nature of our environment as well as trees do, but they continue to be cut and burned. The result aggravates our situation in these last hours of ancient sunlight: we have less oxygen-releasing leaf surface, less circulation in the water cycle, and increased desertification, while at the same time the burning puts more carbon into the atmosphere. These facts make it appear that humans (at least the humans who control such matters) have no concept of their role in the ecosystem.

From *The Last Hours of Ancient Sunlight* by Thom Hartmann, © 1998, 1999, 2004, published by Harmony Books, a division of Random House, Inc.

Cool Our Fever

From *Rebooting the American Dream: 11 Ways to Rebuild Our Country*

> We live in a democracy and policies represent our collective
> will. We cannot blame others. If we allow the planet to
> pass tipping points…it will be hard to explain our role to
> our children. We cannot claim…that "we didn't know."
>
> —Jim Hansen, director, NASA Goddard
> Institute for Space Studies[1]

I HAVE TAKEN THE FOUR-HOUR TRAIN RIDE FROM THE AIRPORT IN
Frankfurt, Germany, to the Bavarian town of Stadtsteinach in the
Frankenwald often enough to know it by heart. I look out the window
and see the familiar sights—the towns, the rivers, the houses.

I have visited Stadtsteinach many times over the past 30 years,
working with Salem International. At least once a year I've made it
back to Germany, and we lived there for a year in the mid-1980s. During the past decade, as the train rolls along eastward from Frankfurt,
I've seen a dramatic change in the scenery and the landscape. First
there were just a few: purplish-blue reflections, almost like deep, still
water, covering large parts of the south-facing roofs as I looked north
out the window of the train. Solar panels.

Then, over the next few years, the purplish-blue chunks began
to spread all over, so now when I travel that route it seems like about
a third—and in many towns even more—of all the roofs are covered
with photovoltaic solar panels.

Given that Germany is one of the cloudiest countries in Europe,
right up there with England—the sun shines for only about a third
of the year—it seems crazy that it would have more solar panels per
capita than any other country in the world and that it employs more

than 40,000 people in the solar power industry. But the Germans made it happen.

They figured out a way to use their existing banking and power systems to begin to shift from dependence on coal and nuclear power to solar. And all it took were pretty small tweaks in the grand scheme of things. A minor recalibration in the way money moves around in the energy and banking sectors has turned the country into a solar powerhouse. Within the past decade, Germany has gone from near zero to producing 8,000 megawatts (MW) of power from solar, the equivalent capacity of eight nuclear power plants in the United States.

We can and should do the same—begin to invest in solar and other renewable forms of energy in America. For far too long, we have been hooked on oil, and we continue to pay a terrible price for it economically, politically, militarily, and environmentally. We need to wean ourselves from it both for our own future survival and prosperity and because so often other countries of the world look to us as an example of what they can or should do.

Strip Oil of Its Strategic Value

Two hundred years ago—and for a thousand years before that—one of the most strategic substances on earth was salt. It was "strategic" because no army could travel without it—salt was necessary to preserve food in a pre-refrigeration era. Wars were fought over it, and countries that had lots of salt made out well, while land-locked countries with no salt reserves were forced to sell their natural resources in exchange for it.

Oil is the new salt. It is now the planet's number one strategic resource. And, as has been noted by numerous commentators since the first Gulf War in 1990–1991, if the primary export of Iraq were broccoli, we wouldn't have given a damn that Saddam Hussein was a tin-pot tyrant.

The unfortunate reality is that we have within and around our national boundaries about 3 percent of the world's oil, but we consume about 24 percent of the world's produced oil. So we buy what we don't produce. This dependence represents a massive transfer of wealth from us to oil-producing countries.

Countries like Saudi Arabia rake in billions from oil-dependent countries like the United States, and oil revenues fuel their economies. In 2008, for instance, Saudi oil revenues spiked to $281 billion, a quadrupling of revenues from 2002. In 2009 those fell sharply to $115 billion, still nothing to sneeze at.[2] Oil revenues fund much of the fundamentalist Wahhabi Movement within Saudi Arabia, and it's out of this movement that come the most virulent anti-American and anti-Semitic rhetoric, textbooks, and television and radio programming.

Thirty years ago the nations composing OPEC, the Organization of Petroleum Exporting Countries, were producing around 30 million barrels per day, nearly half of the world's oil consumption. Regardless of how much we buy from OPEC nations or instead buy from Mexico, their production will continue, because oil is a fungible commodity, and it will just go to others who are no longer buying from whomever we choose to buy from. The proof of this is that today OPEC production is still around 30 million barrels—even though world oil consumption has increased and is now around 85 million barrels per day. The OPEC nations don't adjust production to meet demand; they maintain it to control prices so they have relatively stable income.

The only way we can change this situation is by reducing the amount of oil we use. Oil is a strategic commodity, and we need to strip it of its strategic value.

So what do we use all that oil for that makes it a strategic resource? We certainly don't use it to produce electricity—only 2 percent of our electricity is generated by oil because we have huge domestic supplies of coal, which produce more than half of our electricity. Pretty much nobody is producing electricity with oil except the oil-rich countries of the Middle East; even rapidly growing countries like China and India, for example, are not producing oil-fired power plants.

Thus, moving to solar, wind, biomass, or even nuclear power to generate electricity in the United States will help tremendously with our CO_2 output and all the pollution "externalities" associated with coal, but it will *not* make us less oil dependent or strip oil of its *strategic* significance.

The simple fact is that oil accounts for roughly 95 percent of the energy used for *transportation* in the United States (and our military is the world's single largest consumer of oil), and that's what makes it strategic. If we want to strip oil of its strategic value, so it can't be used as a weapon against us and we can use our remaining oil supplies for rational things like producing plastics and medicines, we need to shift our transportation sector away from oil and do so quickly.

This has been the essence of T. Boone Pickens's rant, although the eccentric oil billionaire is now a natural-gas billionaire, and he's suggesting that we convert our truck fleet in this country from oil to natural gas, which is nearly as bad a source of greenhouse gases as is oil. He's right that such a change would make us stronger and safer, both militarily and strategically, but he misses the climate change part of the equation (which is also increasingly becoming a strategic issue, as global climate deterioration leads to crises both at home and abroad).

Europe, Japan, and China are moving fast to shift their transportation sectors from oil to electricity, mostly through the use of trains. Brazil did it over the past 20 years by mandating that all cars and trucks sold would have to be "flex-fuel"—capable of burning gasoline or ethanol, diesel, or biodiesel. The result is that Brazil now meets nearly half of its transportation needs with domestically grown ethanol made from sugarcane, and more than 80 percent of its cars and trucks are now flex-fuel. And the added cost to Brazilian drivers to buy a flex-fuel car instead of a gasoline- or diesel-only car? About $100.

China is similarly moving in the direction of flex-fuel cars and is doubling every year its methanol production (mostly derived from domestically produced coal).

Flex-fuel cars can also burn part-ethanol, part-gasoline. If, for example, we were to shift to only 20 percent of automotive fuel being gasoline (the remainder being ethanol or methanol), a single gallon of gas would go five times as far. A 40-miles-per-gallon (mpg) car would become a 200 mpg car in terms of the strategic resource of oil-derived gasoline.

Most significantly, in the United States fully half of all automobiles are driven fewer than 20 miles in any given day. This is an easy range for an electric-only or a plug-in-hybrid car. By moving to the latter immediately—mandating them—we could shift the entire US auto fleet to consuming 50 percent or more electricity instead of gas/diesel in less than a decade, stripping oil of half its strategic importance.

And our trade policies are *really* stupid on this. We have no import tariff whatsoever on oil, so there is nothing to discourage American drivers from using foreign-produced oil products to fuel their cars and trucks. But we charge an import tariff of more than $0.50 per gallon on ethanol, discouraging Americans from using the fuel and discouraging the more than 100 countries in the world where there's enough intense sunlight and sugarcane grows well from becoming net fuel exporters.

If we add to all of this some good scientific innovation in developing a mix of low-carbon energy resources (solar, biomass, geothermal, wind, tidal power) and can figure out a way to strip the carbon dioxide from our power plant smokestacks and turn it into a solid (calcium carbonate—which you can buy at the store under the brand name "Tums"—is a good candidate), it's not inconceivable that by 2050 we could cut our CO_2 emissions by more than 80 percent. And perhaps even decades sooner, if we begin now.[3] Plus we could strip oil of its strategic value and make our nation independent of Middle Eastern dictatorships.

So today we face a twofold crisis: First, the planet is getting warmer and it appears that our reliance on carbon-based fossil fuels is at the core of that trend. Second, the United States itself is more vulnerable to being held hostage by our reliance on imported fuel than we were in the early 1970s when the Arab oil embargo, triggered by our support of Israel in the Arab-Israeli War of 1973, nearly brought us to our knees.

Make Polluters Pay

In Denmark gasoline is taxed heavily and costs nearly $10 per gallon because the government—with the consent of its citizens, the result of a public information campaign that wasn't drowned out because there is no domestic oil industry to speak of—realized it was picking up about $3 per gallon of the real cost of gasoline.

Cars and trucks produce exhaust, which deteriorates buildings and statues, causes cancers and asthmas, and, when rain catches it on the way down, pollutes waterways and crops, with those poisons ending up in the food chain. With a national health-care system in addition to other public services, taxpayers in Denmark are picking up the cost of cleaning public areas and historic sites, treating the cancers and the asthmas, cleaning waterways, and restoring farmland that's been polluted by gas additives, like lead and MTBE (methyl tert-butyl ether).

So they decided to recover those "externalized costs" from gasoline with an increased gas tax.

Internalizing Profits while Externalizing Costs

Here in the United States, we allow businesses to externalize those costs and have government or consumers (in the case of cancers and asthma) pay for them, instead of incorporating that cost into the retail price of gas. The first imperative in business is to make a profit, and one of the effective ways to do so is to internalize profits while externalizing costs.

The internalizing-profits part is pretty easy to figure out: keep as much money as possible in the company, jack up prices to the maximum the market will bear, reduce expenses like labor and raw materials as much as possible, and increase efficiencies. All of these things constitute "the way of doing business" that most Americans understand.

But it's only half of the equation. "Externalizing costs" is a fancy way of saying, "Pass along the costs of doing business to consumers or to the government so that they don't affect profits."

Another part of this equation is the use of nature, which involves a bit of both internalizing to the company the "free" services of nature, including the presence of fossil fuels, and externalizing to nature the "costs" of pollution.

For example, a nuclear power plant must exhaust hundreds of millions of calories of "waste heat" every day. The way the nuclear industry does this is by building nuclear plants next to rivers or lakes and cycling the cold water from "nature" through the nuke's cooling towers. Not only do nuclear power plants *not* pay for this water but the heat that's added into the rivers or lakes (and the water that escapes as steam, evaporated in huge plumes from the cooling towers) has a real set of "costs" associated with it.

Fish die, ecosystems are altered, and less water is available downstream for uses like drinking and agriculture. The same is true of the lethal radioactive nuclear waste that is produced at every nuclear plant, which is temporarily kept on-site and eventually shipped off to government-run waste management sites.

Not one of these costs is paid by nuclear power plant operators: instead, where they're run for-profit (like in the USA), it's the taxpayers, the citizens, and nature itself that pay the externalized costs.

The result is that we're wiping out nature by our use of its "free" resources. In 2001, with support from the United Nations, 1,360 of the world's top scientists and experts convened to examine the consequence on nature of these externalized costs. Four years later, after exhaustive analysis of ecosystems around the world, the Millennium Ecosystem Assessment was explicit:[4]

> Nearly two-thirds of the services provided by nature to humankind are found to be in decline worldwide. In effect, the benefits reaped from our engineering of the planet have been achieved by running down natural capital assets.

> In many cases, it is literally a matter of living on borrowed time. By using up supplies of fresh ground water faster than can be recharged, for example, we are depleting assets at the expense of our children....

Unless we acknowledge the debt and prevent it from growing, we place in jeopardy the dreams of citizens everywhere to rid the world of hunger, extreme poverty, and avoidable disease—as well as increasing the risk of sudden changes to the planet's life-support systems from which even the wealthiest may not be shielded.

We also move into a world in which the variety of life becomes ever-more limited. The simpler, more uniform landscapes created by human activity have put thousands of species under the threat of extinction, affecting both the resilience of natural services and less tangible spiritual or cultural values.

We need to step back a bit from our oil, transportation, and energy policies and take a holistic view of the planet's ecology and how human actions affect it.

Earth as an Organism

Since the Gaia Hypothesis of James Lovelock, first popularized in his 1979 book,[5] the scientific and philosophical worlds are becoming increasingly aware that the planet is a single giant living organism, and all the living and "nonliving" parts of it are actually continually interacting in the dance we call life.

Our Aristotelian and Cartesian worldviews—that the world is actually a giant machine of sorts, and if we can just find the right lever to pull, we can fix everything—are being shown for the myths that they are, whether by climate change, the massive amount of oil that poured into the Gulf of Mexico in 2010, or the explosion of cancers and gender deformities in life forms worldwide (from frogs to humans) over the past 50 years as we've dumped huge amounts of hormone-mimicking plasticizers and other chemicals into our environment.

The simple reality is that I can take a car apart in my driveway, then put it back together, turn the key, and it'll run. But if I took a cow apart in my driveway, no matter how skilled a surgeon I am in reassembling it, it'll never moo again. Life is different from machines.

And our separation from life—whether by our worshiping gods in boxes every weekend, our belief in the supremacy of science, or our living, moving, and working in separated-from-life environments—has caused us to make personal and societal decisions that are destructive to life all around us for millennia. The tragic reality is that life is undergoing the sixth-biggest extinction in the history of the planet—an extinction that may one day include us if we don't quickly wake up.

What we need to do immediately is to start taking small, incremental steps while also raising societal awareness in preparation for taking bigger and more substantive steps toward more earth-friendly approaches and policies when it comes to energy use.

The good news is that we know what we need to do to help solve our energy and sustainability problems.

For example, about 10 percent of the electricity we generate in the United States is consumed by "vampire" appliances and power supplies that are not even turned on or in use.[6] Another 6.5 percent of the electricity we produce in this country is wasted through "line losses"—the resistance of copper wires to the passage of electricity through them over long-line high-power transmission lines.[7] If we used electricity at the point of generation—like running your house off your own solar power—that loss percentage would drop to zero. Instead, because it's profitable for large power companies to have centralized generating stations, we're losing all that electricity as heat from transmission lines and are burning enormous amounts of coal, natural gas, and oil to produce it.

Lessons from Abroad

These problems are huge but they're not insurmountable. Other countries are already showing the way. Just as America now faces an unsustainable thirst for energy, so too was Germany faced with a power crisis in the late 1990s. Growing demands for electricity collided with the reality that the country has no oil reserves and a strong bias among its people against building new nuclear power plants in the wake of the nearby Chernobyl meltdown in 1986.

Yet the government knew that the country needed the electricity equivalent of at least one or two nuclear reactors over the next decade. So, how was it to generate that much electricity without nuclear power?

Germany's Alternative to Nuclear

In 1999 progressives in Germany passed the 100,000 Roofs Program (Stromeinspeisungsgesetz),[8] which mandated that banks had to provide low-interest 10-year loans to homeowners sufficient for them to put solar panels on their houses. They then passed the Renewable Energies Law (Erneuerbare-Energien-Gesetz) and in 2004 integrated the 100,000 Roofs Program into it.[9] The Renewable Energies Law mandated that for the next 10 years the power company had to buy back power from those homeowners at a level substantially above the going rate so the homeowners' income from the solar panels would equal their loan payment on the panels and would also represent the actual cost to the power company to generate that amount of power had it built a new nuclear reactor.

At the end of the 10 years, the power company gets to buy solar power from its customers at its regular rate, and it now has a new source of power without having to pay to maintain (and eventually dismantle) a nuclear reactor. In fact, while the reactor would have had a 20- to 30-year lifespan, the solar panels typically have a lifespan of 50 years.

For the homeowners it was a no-brainer: they were getting low-interest loans from banks for the solar panels, and the power companies were paying for the power generated by those panels at a rate high enough to pay off the loans. It was like getting solar power panels for free.

If anything, the government underestimated how rapidly Germans would embrace the program and thus how much more power would be produced and how quickly. By 2007 Germany accounted for about half of the entire world's solar market. Just that one year, 2007, saw 1,300 MW of solar-generating capacity brought online across the country.[10]

For comparison, consider that the average generating capacity of each of the past five nuclear power plants brought online in the United States is 1,160 MW.[11]

In 2008 Germany added 2,000 MW of solar power to its grid, and in 2009 homeowners and businesses put onto their roofs enough solar panels to generate an additional 2,500 MW. Although the goal for the first decade of this century was to generate around 3,000 MW, eliminating the need to build two new nuclear power plants, this simple, no-risk program had instead added more than 8,500 MW of power.

And because the generation sources were scattered across the country, there was no need to run new high-tension power lines from central generating stations, making it more efficient and less expensive. Meanwhile, as dozens of German companies got into the business of manufacturing and installing solar power systems, the cost dropped by more than half between 1997 and 2007 and continues to plummet.[12]

The Germans expect that by 2050 more than 25 percent of their total electricity will come from solar (it's now just over 1 percent), adding to the roughly 12.5 percent of all German energy currently being produced by renewable sources (mostly hydro but also including wind, biomass, and geothermal).[13]

The solar panel program has been so successful that the German government is now thinking that it's time to back off and leave this to the marketplace. As the *New York Times* noted in May 2008:[14]

> Thanks to its aggressive push into renewable energies, cloud-wreathed Germany has become an unlikely leader in the race to harness the sun's energy. It has by far the largest market for photovoltaic systems, which convert sunlight into electricity, with roughly half of the world's total installations. . . .
>
> Now, though, with so many solar panels on so many rooftops, critics say Germany has too much of a good thing—even in a time of record oil prices. Conservative lawmakers, in particular, want to pare back generous government incentives that support solar development. They say solar generation is growing so fast that it threatens to overburden consumers with high electricity bills.

Translation: the solar panel manufacturers want the subsidies to stop so they can catch up with demand and then bump up the price— and the profits. Because of the subsidies, prices have been dropping faster than manufacturing costs.

Other Lessons from Europe

Germany is now considering incentives for its world-famous domestic auto industry to manufacture flex-fuel plug-in-hybrid automobiles that can get more than 500 mpg of (strategic) gasoline (boosted by domestically produced rooftop solar) with existing technology.

Meanwhile, Denmark has invested billions into having more than half of its entire auto fleet using only electricity by 2030.

Even China is no slouch when it comes to renewable energy. Although the Chinese continue to bring a dirty coal-fired power plant online about once a week, they surpassed every other nation in the world in 2010 in direct investment in the production of solar and wind power. As the *Los Angeles Times* reported in March 2010:[15]

> US clean energy investments hit $18.6 billion last year, a report from the Pew Charitable Trusts said, a little more than half the Chinese total of $34.6 billion. Five years ago, China's investments in clean energy totaled just $2.5 billion.

> The United States also slipped behind 10 other countries, including Canada and Mexico, in clean energy investments as a share of the national economy. . . .

> The Pew report pointed to another factor constraining US competitiveness: a lack of national mandates for renewable energy production or a surcharge on greenhouse gas emissions that would make fossil fuels more expensive.

Clearly, it is time for the United States to take action.

It's the Taxes, Stupid

Taxes do two things. First and most obviously, they fund the operations of government. But far more importantly, taxes have been used since the founding of this country to encourage behaviors that we deem good for the nation and to discourage behaviors we consider bad.

For example, in 1793 Congress passed much of Alexander Hamilton's plan to use taxes—tariffs—on imported goods to encourage Americans to start manufacturing companies to meet demand and needs here in this country. Those tariffs stood until the 1980s, and American jobs stayed here along with them.

Similarly, two presidents—Republican Herbert Hoover (1929 to 1933) and Democrat Franklin D. Roosevelt (1933 to 1945)—supported high taxes on the rich. They believed it's not a good thing for too much wealth to be concentrated in too few hands because it would lead the wealthy to influence government policy for their own good rather than the public good.

So they taxed incomes above approximately $3 million per year (in today's dollars) at around 90 percent, and the effect of that tax from the 1930s until it was repealed by Ronald Reagan in the 1980s was that CEO pay in the United States was about the same as in the rest of the world—around 30 times that of the lowest-paid employee—and few families of dynastic wealth rose up to try to seize political power.

Other examples of using tax policies to promote public policy are the home mortgage interest deduction (which encourages home ownership) and providing accelerated deductibility to companies for research and development.

Taxing Carbon

Now we need a new tax to encourage change that will help us kick our addiction to oil and spur us toward a clean-energy future. We need a tax on carbon. Other countries are already doing it in a variety of direct and indirect ways. This simple solution will address both the environmental problem of carbon-based fuels' fouling our atmosphere and the strategic problem of our transportation system's being the weakness that keeps us addicted to imported oil.

There are two pretty straightforward ways to tax carbon. The first is to simply assign a tariff or tax value to it at any particular point in its use cycle. The tax could be levied when it's used, for example, or when it's extracted. A tax on carbon that's imported would serve to really speed our change from gasoline-only cars to flex-fuel and plug-in-hybrid cars.

The second way to tax carbon is to tax the industrial emission of it but also "allow" a certain amount of carbon to be released into the atmosphere by "giving away" to polluters what are referred to as "carbon credits." A threshold is set for the total amount of carbon a country will allow to be emitted (a "cap"), and anything above that point is heavily taxed. Companies that don't want to pay the tax can instead pay to buy carbon-emitting credits from companies that have a surplus of them (presumably because they've reduced their levels of carbon pollution), thus "trading" the carbon credits.

This cap-and-trade program can work if the threshold is low enough, the number of credits "given away" is low enough, and the tax is high enough. On the other hand, if the thresholds are set high, the taxes are low, and the majority of the credits are given away, cap-and-trade policy becomes a windfall for Wall Street (the credits are traded via conventional commodity exchange mechanisms) but doesn't do much for reducing carbon emissions.

The European Union, for example, has instituted a cap-and-trade program, although many European countries (Denmark is the leader) have gone one better by instituting domestic carbon or oil taxes to further encourage conservation, innovation, and the development of domestic renewables.

We should do the same.

One problem with this is that, in the absence of tariffs, many companies will simply export more manufacturing jobs to the few countries in the world that are not taxing carbon so that they can continue to use carbon-based fuels (or electricity generated from them) *over there* instead of here.

But there is a way around this. We can extend our carbon tax throughout the chain of manufacture. Just like our tariffs used to be based, in part, on the relative cost of foreign labor, a carbon tax tariff could be based on the amount of carbon generated in the manufacture of goods overseas. A carbon-based value-added-tax, where a small tax is imposed at every stage of manufacture reflecting the carbon used to bring about that manufacture, would do the job quite nicely if it had the power to extend itself to imported goods.

Of course, this is what the oilmen who fund the right-wing protest movements fear the most. But their interests are not those of the United States of America. And the faster Americans realize that, the better.

From *Rebooting the American Dream: 11 Ways to Rebuild Our Country* by Thom Hartmann, © 2010, published by Berrett-Koehler.

Something Will Save Us

From *The Last Hours of Ancient Sunlight:*
Waking Up to Personal and Global Transformation

> But how did we do this? How could we drink up the sea? Who
> gave us the sponge to wipe away the entire horizon? What were
> we doing when we unchained this earth from its sun? Whither is
> it moving now? Whither are we moving? . . . *Do we hear nothing*
> *as yet of the noise of the gravediggers* who are burying God?
>
> —FRIEDRICH NIETZSCHE (1849–1900),
> THE GAY SCIENCE (1882)

WENDY KAMINER WROTE A BRILLIANT BOOK TITLED *I'M DYS-functional, You're Dysfunctional: The Recovery Movement and Other Self-Help.* In it she pointed to the pervasive assumptions of dysfunction inherent in the self-help movement and the increasing obsession with emotional and psychological pathology in our culture. She didn't offer any specific solutions; she only defined the problem. (Although one could say that her solution was really the most elegant of all: see the problem for what it is and refuse to dance the dance. In this she argued forcibly for people to reclaim their own inherent power and emotional health.)

Kaminer received numerous letters from people demanding solutions to the problems she had identified. She pointed out this irony in a later edition of the book: it was as if the people writing wanted her to suggest the creation of a self-help group or book to help those addicted to them.

Some of the initial responses to the early editions of *The Last Hours of Ancient Sunlight* were similar. I received letters, e-mails, and calls from people telling me with great certainty that the only solu- tion to the problems outlined in the first third of the book would be found in smaller families; cold fusion; coaxing the flying saucer people out of hiding; a worldwide conversion to Christianity (at least a half-dozen different people suggested that only their particular Christian sect could bring this about, and all other Christians must ultimately recognize the error of their ways), Islam, or some other religion; or the immediate institution of a benevolent one-world government. The letters ranged from amazement to outrage that I'd failed to see and support their perspective.

But these are all something-will-save-us solutions. This kind of thinking is a symptom of our younger culture—and fighting fire with fire is only rarely successful. Usually, it just produces more flames. As Jesus, Gandhi, and Martin Luther King Jr. demonstrated, often the most powerful and effective way to "fight back" against the pathological kings and kingdoms is to walk away from the kings, see the situation for what it is, and stop playing the dominator's game.

But that involves a shift of perspective that some people find very difficult. There are, for example, those who point to the foundational belief of our culture (and, particularly, to European-ancestry citizens of the United States) that we can solve any problem if we just put our minds to it. Some even argue that the exploding human population is a good thing because the more people there are, the greater the possibility we will find among them the next Thomas Jefferson, Albert Einstein, or Thomas Edison, who will figure out how to get us out of this mess. It is, of course, a simplistic, and ultimately cruel, notion but one that has been used for years, usually to advance a dominator religious or economic agenda.

In fact, it's somewhere between unlikely and impossible that children born into the contemporary slums of Islamabad or Haiti, or even Baltimore or East Los Angeles, will grow up to change the world or solve our problems. They may become very competent; any corrections officer can tell you there are geniuses among our cities' gang members and in our prisons. But grinding poverty and pervasive violence—born of overcrowding and a lack of resources and security—rarely produce more than a surfeit of ingenious criminals and competent jailhouse lawyers.

On the other hand, Jefferson was a member of the land-owning elite, what we would today call the very wealthy. Translated into today's dollars, nearly every signer of the Declaration of Independence was a millionaire or multimillionaire. Einstein was never truly poor, and he lived a life ranging from comfortable to wealthy. And even Edison, penniless when he ran away from home at age 15, entered a world with a total population that was a fifth of what it is today, rich with cheap natural resources, and almost limitless opportunity for ambitious white young men who spoke American English. If any of them were to be born into the modern-day sewers of Bogotá, they might end up being hunted for sport—but it's unlikely that they'd ever have access to the resources necessary to create lasting and meaningful changes in the world.

True Change Is Not a Simple Process

There is no shortage of do-this-and-everything-will-be-okay solutions proffered in books and the press. The more commonly touted include worldwide birth control, strong controls on corporate exploiters and polluters, $5-per-gallon (or more) taxes on gasoline and oil products, doubling or tripling of the cost of water and electricity by increased taxation, worldwide destruction of weapons of war, more money for environmental remediation, and the creation and the empowerment of new political parties not beholden to corporate powers.

The idea of cultural change is often unpalatable because any sort of real, individual, personal change in beliefs and behaviors is so difficult as to be one of the rarest events we ever experience in our own lives or witness among those we know. It's easy to send $10 off to the Sierra Club; it's infinitely more difficult to reconsider beliefs and behaviors held since childhood and then change your way of life to one based on that new understanding, new viewpoint, or new story. But if such deep change is what we really need, I see no point in pretending that something simpler will do it.

The Something-Will-Save-Us Viewpoint

We are members of a culture that asserts that humans are at the top of a pyramid of creation and evolution. In our modern techno naiveté, we reveal our fatal belief that anything we have done—for better or worse—can also be undone. We tend to think that every problem, including manmade ones, has a solution.

In the deus ex machina ending in Greek plays, the hero inevitably finds himself in an impossible situation. To close the show, a platform is cranked down from the ceiling with a god on it, who waves his staff and makes everything well again. Similarly, we have faith that somehow things will turn out okay. "Don't worry," our sitcom culture tells us, "human ingenuity will save us."

We envision that our salvation will come from new technologies, or perhaps the rise of a new leader or political party, or the return/appearance of ancient founders of our largest religions. The more esoteric among us suggest that people from outer space will show up and either share their planet-saving technology or take us to a less polluted and more paradisiacal planet. The Christian "rapture" envisions the world's "good people" being removed from this mess we've created and relocated to a paradise created just for them. Among the New Age movement, a popular notion is that just in the nick of time the Ancient Ones, now available only in channeled form through our mediums and psychics, will make themselves known and tell us how to solve our problems. And, of course, there is no shortage of "just follow me, worship me, do as I say, and you'll be happy forever" gurus.

Whatever form it takes, our culture whispers in our ears daily, "Something or someone will save us. Just continue your life as it was, and keep on consuming, because you couldn't possibly save the world, but somebody else will."

This is what I refer to as something-will-save-us thinking.

It's built into our culture, at the foundation of our certainty about how life should be lived, how the world works, and our role in it. It most likely originated as a way for dominators in emerging younger cultures to control their slaves: "Just keep picking that cotton and praying, and you'll eventually be saved. It may be after you die, but it'll happen; don't worry about that. In the meantime, don't stop picking that cotton!"

Far from being the solution, something-will-save-us thinking is at the root of our problems.

Younger Cultures and Something-Will-Save-Us Beliefs

Something-will-save-us beliefs are at the core of younger cultures but are startlingly rare among older ones. This is not to say that older cultures don't have spirituality, belief in deities or spirits, elaborate rituals, offerings or oblations to gods or spirits, personal mystical experience, and so on. But younger-culture beliefs require two essential elements that are lacking from most older cultures:

- The belief that there is, to paraphrase Daniel Quinn, only One Right Way to Live (which, of course, is "our" way) and that when everybody on the planet figures this out and lives our way, things will be good. Conversely, this belief says that if we fail to convert everybody to our way of life, the deity (or, for secularists, the science/technology) who defined this One Right Way to Live will punish us. This punishment may be personal, or it may involve the destruction of the entire planet; but, in either case, those who fail to conform to the dominator culture's way will suffer, and the only way to be saved from doom is to conform.

- The belief that humans are essentially flawed, sinful, damned by a specific deity, or intrinsically destructive and, therefore, they (we) can and must be "saved." According to this belief, this personal (and thus worldwide) salvation process can happen only by intense personal effort and devotion to a particular program (yoga, rosary, prostrations, good deeds, psychotherapy, jihad, Prozac, evangelism) or through the intervention of a divine being or beings who reside in a nonearthly realm (aliens from space) or nonphysical realm (gods, saviors, angels, prophets, gurus, channeled Wise Ones).

The most secular among us believe that we will find, among our own human race, people who will save us from ourselves. Historically, this was the basis of the rule of dominator kings: they had to have absolute power over their people, they said, to save the people from themselves. This is also a core belief among modern people who treat either politics or science as a something-will-save-us religion.

Because members of older cultures assume that there are Many Right Ways to Live, each unique to a particular time, place, and people, they avoid evangelism. Instead they respect other cultures and beliefs, carefully protecting their own ways and beliefs from outsiders and accepting "converts" in only the rarest of circumstances.

Believing in the flawed or "fallen" nature of humanity allows people to rationalize the various genocides, past and present, committed against humans and nonhumans. According to this worldview, some of us will act out "human nature" (whether it's biologically caused as the neo-Darwinians suggest or a curse from an upset god as some religions suggest) and commit all sorts of crimes against the human and natural world.

But if evil is fundamental to human nature, how could it be that it doesn't exist in all cultures? Few ever pause to question whether the evil or dysfunction may be in the nature of our culture rather than in the humans our culture comprises.

If We Could Just Find the Right Lever

Something-will-save-us beliefs—whether rooted in technology or religion—suggest that our problems are always solvable by new and improved human actions: they're things we can control and manipulate if only we have the right science or can figure out the right prayers to motivate the right god(s) or space aliens.

The technological something-will-save-us believers say that we haven't yet mastered the technology of efficient and nonpolluting energy use, equitable economic and political systems, simple and widespread methods of food and birth control (and their distribution), better medicines, and efficient communications. Their refrain always begins, "If only there were more of . . ." or "If only everybody would. . ." and is then followed by the doxology of the particular solution being recommended.

Religionists say we just haven't yet mastered the technology of pleasing the particular god of their sect: if every last tribe is found and converted to a particular institutionalized religion, or if all the ancient prophecies are fulfilled, or if enough people would meditate with the right technique or say the right magic words or the right magical name, we'll be saved from doom. We haven't yet gotten that system perfect, they feel, so we need to work harder on it.

Older Cultures and the Synergist Worldview

The true problem we're facing is a natural and predictable result of this way of viewing the world. The problem is the stories we tell ourselves, what we see and hear and feel as we move through the world, our disconnection from the sacred natural world, and our insistence on quick-fix/external-to-us solutions to natural-world crises that we ourselves created.

Most of us can't even imagine what it would be like to live with a different worldview from our own. (We do, though, keep getting glimpses—most often in the words of our "enlightened ones"—and we usually ignore those glimpses because, being older-culture wisdom, they're so inconsistent with our way of life.)

The younger culture says, "Who cares what our children's children will inherit: that's their problem, and they can work out their own salvation just as we must work out ours."

The older-culture perspective says, "We're here, now, and must deal with the practical realities of this life. Any decisions we make must consider the impact on our grandchildren seven or more generations from now."

I find value in many of the technological suggestions people are exploring and promoting worldwide, and many must ultimately play a role in the transformation of our world if we are to avoid utter disaster. But none attacks the problem at its core. We must begin to live a sustainable, egalitarian, peaceful way of life. This can happen through political or religious transformation, but at its core its *cultural* transformation.

This is not a secret: Older-culture people have been shouting it at us since we first began our genocide against them 7,000 years ago. Most of them are still trying as hard as they can, but we're not capable of hearing because our culture has plugged our ears to their message. Here it is:

> *Return to the ancient and honest ways in which humans participated*
> *in the web of life on the earth, seeing yourselves and all things as sacred*
> *and interpenetrated. Listen to the voice of all life, and feel the heartbeat*
> *of Mother Earth.*

Living from this place, all other decisions we make will be appropriate.

The good news is that this is a very clear solution, embodying, as it does, only a single issue and a single change in a single culture (ours). The bad news is that that single issue is the most difficult and wrenching change I can envision—but we must begin, now, to take the first steps.

It's the same problem with which the prophets of old wrestled: their message was most often *Change your way of seeing and living in the world because the path you're currently walking will lead to disaster.* As secular and Bible history show, such prophets were almost always ignored, at least until the predicted (and inevitable) disasters struck, and even then the responses to the disasters were reactive: more animal sacrifices, building bigger temples, developing new medicines, drilling deeper wells, seizing distant and more-fertile lands, and so on.

The worldview of older cultures rarely brought them to the inevitable and cyclic crises that younger cultures have faced since their first eruption 5,000 to 7,000 years ago. Because people in these older cultures assumed that humans were intrinsically good, emphasis was on nurturing and healing rather than controlling and punishing. Because they believed that humans and natural systems were not separate but rather interpenetrated and interdependent—synergistic—they developed cultural, religious, and economic systems that preserved the abundance of their natural environment and provided for their descendants generation after generation.

So What Are the Easy Answers to Difficult Problems?

Unlike many of our self-assured gurus, ecologists, and technologist something-will-save-us believers, I don't claim to know the exact details of our future. What I do know is that if we are to save some part of this world for our children and all other life, the answers won't simply rest in just the application of technology, economy, government, messianic figures, or new religions, sects, and cults.

True and lasting solutions will require that a critical mass of people achieve an older-culture way of viewing the world—the perspective that successfully and sustainably maintained human populations for hundreds of thousands of years.

Because I'm convinced that our problem is rooted in our worldview, the solutions I offer derive from ways we can change that, which will then naturally transform the technological/political/economic details that emerge from that new perspective. For example:

- History demonstrates that the deepest and most meaningful cultural/social/political changes began with individuals, not organizations, governments, or institutions.

- In helping "save the world," the most important work you and I face is to help individuals transform their ability to perceive reality and control the stories they believe because people do tend to live out what they believe is true. This has to do with people's taking back personal spirituality, finding their own personal power, and realizing that most of our religious, political, and economic institutions are younger-culture dominators that must be transformed if we are to prevent them from destroying us.

■ Then, out of this new perspective, we ourselves will come up with the solutions in ways that you and I right now probably can't even imagine.

In the reality and the experience of an older-culture perspective— a life-connected worldview—we find a life rich and deep with wisdom, love, and the very real experience of the presence of the sacred in all things and all humans. It is a world that works for every living thing, including our children's children's children.

PART V
Journeys

Thom Hartmann's travels alone could fill a volume. He has circled the globe many times over on humanitarian missions, journalism assignments, or doing research for a book. An inventory of the countries he's visited, and the timing of his visits, invites the observation that he should consider traveling with a bulletproof vest: He was in the Philippines when Ferdinand Marcos fled the country, in Egypt the week Anwar Sadat was shot, and in Germany when the Berlin wall came down. He was on the Czech border the week Chernobyl melted down, in Venezuela during one of the 1992 coup attempts, and in Beijing during the first student demonstrations. And that's just the beginning of a long list linking Hartmann's name to revolution and general mayhem around the world. In one sense the timing is coincidental, but in another it gets to the core of what drives Hartmann. He is drawn to turbulence, to "places fermenting with change"—those edges, again—because that's where the action is, that's where one has the opportunity to confront reality, whether it's a shining beacon or an intolerable glare.

In 1980, following the ouster of dictator Idi Amin, Hartmann went to Uganda with Gottfried Müller to negotiate with the provisional government for land to build a Salem refugee center. Uganda during that era was in violent confusion, and Hartmann said the experience, related here in "Uganda Sojourn," was both "shattering and strengthening." "I'd been in the slums of America and much of the developing world but had never experienced children dying in my arms or people starving to death as I watched." He realized he had to accept the reality of Uganda as it was and do the best he could. The refugee center he helped start on the site of a former prison farm evolved into a comprehensive community center that today provides health and social welfare services and conservation education to scores of people in eastern Uganda. It confirms Hartmann's philosophy that even when something seems impossible, one must still "Do what's right, without regard for the seemingly overwhelming odds."

Russia in 1991 was also a country in turmoil, though for different reasons and with different results. Notebook in hand, Hartmann confronts the ineptitude, lack of motivation, and learned helplessness that was so pervasive in post-communist Russia, and the resulting essay, "Russia: A New Seed Planted among Thorns," is an almost surreal portrait of a society in the midst of a painful yet extraordinary transition.

In 2009 Hartmann went on a very different sort of expedition— a research trip to the excavation of an ancient city, as told in "Caral, Peru: A Thousand Years of Peace." He'd been contemplating questions stirred up by his travels. A year earlier he'd gone to Darfur, where he found the same kinds of crises he'd seen in Uganda nearly three decades earlier: starvation, disease, and ethnic violence. What was driving all this human wretchedness? What causes such breakdowns? Are we doomed to repeat our mistakes again and again? In the ancient city of Caral, Hartmann found his answers. Caral is a "mother city," the remnant of a stable civilization that existed peacefully for a thousand years with no evidence of warfare or conflict. It defies conventional wisdom that cities are really citadels, meant to defend their residents from attack from other societies. Hartmann shows how the lessons of Caral can help nurture our own young democracy.

The last piece in this section, "After the Crash," is a journey not of miles but of imagination, as Hartmann invites us to share his dramatic vision of one possible future after the world's oil runs dry. Take this journey if you want to see how an American community might look if we were to abandon our addiction to oil, bring corporations to heel, and reconnect to our families, our communities, nature, and ourselves. This essay puts a human face on some of Hartmann's most closely held beliefs and theories, depicting a way of life that some may find idealistic but which he proves is actually utterly practical.

Uganda Sojourn

From *The Prophet's Way: A Guide to Living in the Now*

You can't say, "Civilization don't advance," however,
for in every war they kill you a new way.

—WILL ROGERS, *AUTOBIOGRAPHY*

KAMPALA, THE CAPITAL OF UGANDA, COVERING SEVERAL SQUARE miles, is built on seven hilltops. Before its destruction it must have been one of the world's most beautiful cities. Now everywhere are burned-out buildings, broken glass, and tens of thousands of hungry, haunted faces.

Young boys urgently cry out "cigarettes" among the thick crowd. Burlap bags lay empty upon the ground, with small piles of tobacco and salt upon them. They are part of sales in the vast, teeming black market. Corrugated metal and cardboard shacks house thousands of people in endless rows of fetid squalor. Urine and rotted waste clog the dirt paths of the market, as we gingerly navigate through the crowd, avoiding mud and pools of overwhelming stench. There has been no running water in this city for more than two years. Young children everywhere stagger about in dazed desperation, their parents brought to death by famine, disease, war, and the insane, random murders by soldiers and associates of the former president, Idi Amin.

Night is approaching. We must flee the market before the eight o'clock curfew falls and an army of young Tanzanian soldiers, their rifles puncturing the night sky with staccato bursts of machine-gun fire, fans through the city. Two years ago, when Amin was overthrown and his brutal dictatorship ended, Ugandans welcomed the Tanzanian liberators from the south. But the combination of an unprecedented drought in this area, as in other parts of East Africa, and an escalating civil war by factions still loyal to Amin and other dissidents have plunged this once-peaceful and fertile land into another round of fear and chaos.

In the morning we find the bodies of those who could not find shelter before the night descended. During a short walk, Herr Müller counts nine corpses, huddled in death next to buildings or sprawling naked in the streets.

Everywhere we come upon razed buildings, bullet holes, and the devastated ruins of a once-beautiful country. The first night we stay in a church dormitory with no water or electricity. The only food is white rice and stale white bread. Boiled rainwater is served on request, caught from the gutters, runoff from the roofs. We sleep on small steel cots in concrete-block rooms. There are half-inch steel bars on the windows, and the massive gray door of our cell has only a small glass-with-embedded-wire window. We are locked in for the night.

In the morning we rise early and leave by eight o'clock for Mbale, a small town on the fringe of the famine district and the site of a large refugee camp. Our route will take us through miles of jungle and over the waterfall that is the source of the Nile.

We arrive at the Mbale camp just as the sun begins to set, a heavy grayness covering the jungle. Approaching the first cluster of mud huts, we are surrounded by perhaps a hundred people: children, adults, enfeebled elders at the end of their lives. Sweat, urine, and the smoke of hundreds of small twig fires make the air bite and cut into my nose and lungs. The earth is as hard as stone, a red clay, and all about us are littered small bodies—crying, moaning, yelling for food or water, staggering about or sitting, staring emptily. Hunger haunts us as we walk about, incessantly tapping us on the shoulder as every-where we are brought face to face, hand to hand, skin to skin with the hollow pain of empty bodies and frightened souls.

A toothless, graying old woman makes her way slowly through the crowd toward us. Her shuffle is slow, and she seems to wince with every step. Her breasts lie flat and dry, hanging down to a wrinkled and shriveled stomach. She cries out softly to us in Swahili. Rev. James Mbonga, a government official who is accompanying us, interprets:

"I am a widow with eight young children. As my husband is dead, no one will help or care for me and my children. We shall die. Will you please help us?" A lump fills my throat.

"Soon," says Herr Müller gently. "Soon, I promise, we shall return with some food for you."

As we walk back to our car through the makeshift village, night descends. The air becomes cold, and people retreat into their huts. Outside one deserted hut we find three young children lying on a mat, naked to the approaching chill. Two of them are nearly dead. Their bodies look like skeletons, swollen heads on shrunken skin, too weak to even lift up or to make a sound. The third, a bit older, lifts himself up with obvious pain and tells his story. Their father is dead, their mother has never returned from a trip looking for food. Tears choke my eyes as we turn and walk away from these dying children. Forcing down the trembling in my throat, I whisper a silent prayer. I recall that back home in the United States today is Thanksgiving.

Tonight Sanford Ungar of National Public Radio's *All Things Considered* show has arranged a satellite call to us, routed to our hotel. He interviews me about the situation in the camps and the bush, and I later learned that the interview ran that night in the United States as *ATC*'s Thanksgiving special. Twice while we're talking to NPR, we're cut off by the military when Ungar asks me questions about troops and the dangers of being shot.

The next morning we leave for the northern region of Karamoja, where starvation and disease are reportedly at their worst. We load into an aging Mercedes and pull out of town. The sky is a vast expanse of blue, the sun burning down, scorching both earth and people alike. As we travel north on the dusty, broken road, the terrain gradually becomes more and more desertlike. We pass through expanses of scattered grass-covered plains dotted with occasional mesquitelike trees. A game preserve, this area was once home to herds of lion, buffalo, zebra, elephant, and other African mammals. Now all are gone, the victims of poachers and hungry, fleeing troops and refugees.

As noon approaches, the air becomes painfully hot and dry, the plains pregnant with death. Reverend Mbonga points out some skeletons by the side of the road, those who couldn't make the 81-mile march to Mbale. Their bones were picked clean by buzzards and ants. Empty eye sockets stare at us as we pass.

About 1:00 p.m. we come to a huge, barbed-wire-enclosed compound with concrete and corrugated-iron buildings: the Namalu Prison Farm, scene of countless atrocities under the reign of Idi Amin, now a hospital and feeding station for the Karamoja refugees. As we pull into the compound, I see several hundred naked children huddled around one large building. From inside I can hear shouting and crying—this is the feeding center. The United Nations has been trucking in food recently, and each child is allotted one bowl of ground corn and powdered milk per day.

We stiffly climb out of the car and walk up to the building. Hundreds of sparkling, expectant eyes and outstretched hands greet us. My hands are grabbed and shaken over and over as we walk in. All around us, pressing against me, are huge bellies, festering sores, malaria, tuberculosis, yellow fever, worms, lice, leprosy. At first I recoil, trying not to touch these sick and dying children. Then I remember Jesus's words, "I was hungry and you fed me, I was naked and you clothed me, I was sick . . ." Looking into these innocent, helpless faces, I lean forward and meet their handshakes and hugs.

Inside the feeding room, we meet Ann, a thin Irish woman with brown hair, green eyes, and freckles, who supervises the feeding. The floor of the large building is covered with tattered little bodies, some obviously near death. Ann directs us to the medical station next door. There we are met by hundreds of disfigured and nearly dead people. Dr. Jacques from the French Red Cross shows us around the tuberculosis (TB) wards, the malaria area, and the "emergency" area. All are large, empty, concrete rooms—smashed-out windows, no furniture, and with sleeping, unconscious, and moaning people lying on the hard dirt floors. The human suffering is more than I could have ever imagined.

We spend a few hours walking about and talking with the medical staff—all French nationals. We learn that they are out of medicine, that nearly everyone has malaria, and that TB is rampant. Herr Müller promises to send emergency medicine from Europe.

A mother carrying a baby approaches me. There are tears in her eyes, and her tone is pleading as she lifts her child to show me two large holes in the skin of his buttocks, areas about the size of quarters, where the skin and the flesh have been eaten away, revealing the muscle beneath. The child makes no sound or movement as the mother continues to stare hopefully into my eyes and cries to me in Swahili. He is the same age as my young son back in New Hampshire, and I wonder what I would be saying if I were her, what I would be thinking, if I would be able to endure the agony of watching my son die as I hold him in my arms.

"She is asking for food," Reverend Mbonga says. "And she wants you to heal her child."

My eyes fill with tears and I have to turn away. Herr Müller says, a crack in his voice, "Tell her we will send food and medication as soon as we can."

Reverend Mbonga translates, as I look back at the woman. When she hears his words, she looks at me for a long moment, as if trying to decide if we are telling the truth, and then she silently turns and shuffles away.

On the way back to town and our "hotel," we stop at another refugee camp in Sirocco. A native ceremony is under way, and I take out my pocket recorder to tape it. Children start clustering around, and I play back a bit of their own voices. Shrieking with delight, hundreds of them crowd about me. Meanwhile Reverend Mbonga and Herr Müller sneak back to the car to get out several hundred loaves of organic whole wheat and sesame flatbread, which we have brought from the bakery of the Salem Children's Village in West Germany. The ruse works only for a moment. We had hoped to give the small amount of food we were able to "smuggle" into the country in our suitcases only to the most needy, those unable to come out and beg for it. But as soon as the food is out of the car, Reverend Mbonga and Herr Müller are attacked by the mob of children and teenagers. A sea of screaming, hungry bodies descends on my friends, threatening to trample them. Within seconds all the food is devoured; we frantically pile into the car and drive off.

In a town between Sirocco and our hotel, we visit another refugee camp. They have some food, although there are hundreds of people on the edge of town who are starving. The village elders invite us to an evening ritual.

Twelve old African men sit around a fire, with Herr Müller, Reverend Mbonga, and me spaced at every fourth man. Near the fire is a brown clay pot about 2 feet in diameter: it's filled with a frothy brown liquid, and the men each have a long straw made from a reed of some sort that goes from the pot to their mouths.

The man to my right, toothless and shriveled, clad only in a wraparound that was once half a bedsheet, says something to me in Swahili and offers me his straw.

"What is it?" I ask Reverend Mbonga.

"It's the local brew," he says with a faint smile. "The women chew up a few different roots and herbs, then spit it into the pot. Water is added, and it ferments for about a week. The herbs are supposed to connect you to their gods: they're probably mild hallucinogens. It's probably alcoholic enough that you won't get sick from it, but you can refuse without hurting his feelings."

"Are you going to drink any?" I say.

He shakes his head. "I don't drink alcohol."

The old man says something to me.

"He said that it will open a door to the future for you," Reverend Mbonga tells me.

I look at Herr Müller with a question in my eyes. The man next to him offers him his reed, and Herr Müller, without a moment's hesitation, takes a long draw on the straw.

I turn to the man next to me and do the same. It tastes bitter and thick, like a milkshake with wormwood, and the bite of alcohol is unmistakable. The other men around the fire all murmur and drink from their straws.

The men begin to talk to us. Reverend Mbonga translates.

The oldest man of the group, long white hair, probably about 60 pounds, all skin and bones, wearing a cloth around his waist and sitting on the hard dirt cross-legged, says, "The world is fragile. Your American companies, sugar and coffee, they have raped our land. Now the earth will no longer give us food because it is angry with what we have allowed you to do here."

He is starting to shimmer. His face looks younger, and his features are changing, becoming clearer. I can see the details of the wrinkles in the skin of his face although he is sitting 6 feet from me, and now the wrinkles are starting to go away. His skin is getting slightly lighter in color, and it's tightening.

"What can be done?" I ask.

He shakes his head. There is a little visual echo left in the air by the motion. "It has gone too far," he says, and now I can understand his Swahili even as Reverend Mbonga continues to translate. The men around the fire murmur their agreement. "The earth cannot be saved by man: this is stupidity. The earth will save itself, by killing off the men. Perhaps some of mankind can be saved, but the earth will protect itself."

Another man interjects. He is younger, perhaps in his sixties, and I can see through his skin. A moment earlier it was black and solid; now it's transparent, and I can see his veins and arteries, red and blue, and his muscles, as if looking through a thin film of dark gauze. His face looks compassionate. "This is the future you are seeing," he says, waving his hand around him at the refugee camp, the bare ground, the dead trees, the big-bellied children squatting and watching us from a respectful distance. "One day it will be the white man's future, too."

I shiver, believing his words.

We sit and talk for another hour about the spirit of the earth, the future, and the role Americans and Europeans have played in the rape of the developing world. The drug wears off, and I'm left with a dull headache. We leave, and each man shakes my hand in a grave gesture, as if he knows we will never again meet.

Back at the hotel, it's a dark night, and sounds of the African wilds fill the air through the open window. We discuss ways to help; we decide to begin a Salem "baby home" nearby and to try to start with the three starving children we saw the night before in Mbale.

The following morning, our fourth day in the country, we leave the hotel at seven o'clock to visit the camp just about a mile outside of Mbale. The sun is just rising, the ground and the grass are wet with dew, and the air has a penetrating chill. This is the camp where we found the starving widows and the three babies lying on the hard ground. We take with us special food, as we had promised. Most of the people are still in their huts, although a few are wandering about when we arrive. Reverend Mbonga leads us through the maze of huts and stinking mud to where the two widows live. One has eight children, the other seven. We leave them all our flatbread, about 30 pieces. The three children are nowhere to be found. It has been two days.

Driving back to Kampala in the afternoon, we stop in Jinja to meet with Mother Jane, a remarkable African lady who has started a "baby home" for 35 to 40 children in her own residence. About five years ago, she rescued the first one, a baby boy, whom she found on a folded up newspaper at the edge of the river. The baby's fate reminded her of the story of the infant Moses in the Bible, and so her home became known as Center Moses. Since then she has rescued countless other babies and children from garbage cans, burned-out buildings, and parched fields. Those we meet this afternoon range in age from a tiny, fragile six-month old (whose twin sister and mother died when she was born) to a young teenager who appears to be about seven because of malnutrition. They have no toilet, no medicine, no water, and only two more days of food.

"Only God knows how much longer we shall survive," Mother Jane says. Despite the great anguish around her and in her eyes, she manages to smile and display a refreshing sense of humor. She tells us that her 24-hour-a-day, seven-day-a-week work keeps her physically and spiritually strong. Her main concern, besides the omnipresent risk of disease and starvation, is people stealing her children for forced labor. We leave her six cans of powdered soymilk for the infants, some whole-wheat bread and sesame, and a little chamomile for tea to calm upset or ill children.

One little parentless boy, about three years old, his head barely reaching above my knees, runs up and warmly embraces my legs, holding me immobile. He looks up into my face and smiles. I reach down and rub his back and head, and we stand together like this for a minute or so. Then our party moves on, and I have to break his grip. I leave him sadly holding his face in his hands, and a lump forms in my throat.

It is about a two-hour drive from Jinja to Kampala. Having stared down the barrels of hundreds of machine guns this past week, we found the many roadblocks to be almost normal. We arrive in Kampala and are driven to the International Hotel, a modern high-rise in the center of town, where we are invited to a reception in our honor by the commissioner of the Ministry of Rehabilitation. The building has obviously been the scene of fighting in the recent war.

I haven't had a bath in four days nor changed my clothes, which are now rank with body odor and red Karamoja dust. As we sit down to a lunch of white rice and potatoes, I apologize to the commissioner for my condition. He says not to worry, that he hasn't had water (or, presumably, a bath) for more than two years and that, in times like these, we needn't stand on formality. I notice that the clothing of his staff is old and tattered and recall that the factories and the local importers haven't been open for more than two years either.

The commissioner is excited about our plans to help the French medical team and to start a children's village in Uganda. He comments several times about the problems of temporary relief programs and says he hopes we will become a permanent part of Uganda.

That night we leave for Entebbe and, after a 1,000-shilling "payment" at gunpoint to a police officer to pass through customs, we then depart for Nairobi, the capital of neighboring Kenya. From there we will fly to London. I realize that I've contracted some sort of dysentery, as I have awful diarrhea and every muscle in my body aches. Yet my discomfort is minuscule compared with those thousands of sick and dying people with whom we've spent the past week. My thoughts keep wandering back to Mother Jane in Jinja, with her 30 or 40 babies. With a cloth wrapped around her head and the copper gleam of her face in the hot Ugandan sun, she appears as firm as a rock. Her love and faith are as timeless as the bones of humanity's earliest ancestors, which have been found in East Africa not far from here. I am reminded of the words of the psalmist: "I have been young and now am old; yet have I not seen the righteous forsaken."

First published in *East/West Journal*, July 1981

From *The Prophet's Way* by Thom Hartmann,
© 1997, published by Inner Traditions International.

Russia: A New Seed Planted among Thorns

From *The Prophet's Way: A Guide to Living in the Now*

> Every second of existence is a new miracle. Consider the
> countless variations and possibilities that await us every
> second—avenues into the future. We take only one of these;
> the others—who knows where they go? This is the eternal
> marvel, the magnificent uncertainty of the next second to
> come, with the past a steady unfolding carpet of denouement.

—JACK VANCE, *THE HOUSES OF ISZM*

I WAS IN THE SCANDINAVIAN AIRLINES TWIN-PROP PLANE THAT
landed at about noon on a gray, blustery, raw-cold December day
in Kaliningrad, Russia. The airport is about 20 miles outside the town,
surrounded by now-unused barbed-wire fences and empty guard stations. Inside the terminal there was no heat, and only about half the
overhead lights worked. Remembering the lengthy interrogations I'd
been through when entering and leaving East Berlin years earlier, I
was expecting rigid formalities on entering, particularly because
Kaliningrad was a "special zone," an area of secret military installa-
tions and one of the former Soviet Union's most sensitive places. Even
normal Russians aren't allowed to travel into the region, but on this
day the immigration inspector just looked at my visa, stamped my
passport, smiled, and said, "Welcome to Russia." Nobody was even
checking luggage for contraband in the customs area: I just walked
outside, carrying my shoulder bag and the 5 liters of water I'd brought
from Copenhagen.

Outside, Gerhard Lipfert waited with the blue Volkswagen bus
he'd driven from Germany. He greeted me with a huge hug, saying,
"Welcome to Russia!"

Inside the bus was a man named Herr Burkhardt, who'd been a foot-soldier in Hitler's army, captured by the Russians, and spent decades as a prisoner of war in Russia. He was finally released and returned to Germany, where he now worked for Salem as a Russian/German translator. His face creased in a wide smile as he welcomed me.

The next morning we set out for an area about 200 kilometers from Kaliningrad, near the Polish border, where Salem has undertaken a project in Russia. It was bitterly cold, and the sky was so dim, the clouds so thick, that the world looked like an old black-and-white movie from the forties.

As we drove through the countryside, I watched the passing parade of fallen-down fences, broken-down houses, ancient cars, potholed pavement, and the steady stream of old men and women hitchhiking. (Horst Von Heyer, a Salem colleague, once remarked to me that you can tell the poverty of a nation by the age of the hitchhikers. I've found this to be so very true, all over the world.)

It was close to 10:00 p.m. when we arrived in a little town whose name I never managed to get straight. In the midst of rolling fields and gentle hills, the Russian farmlands, was this little collection of box-square houses, each identical to the other, each just a bit larger than a double-wide trailer home. There were perhaps 60 houses that made up the town, maybe five streets.

We stopped first at Erika's house. It was her mother's birthday, a little old lady with a scarf over her white hair, her face wrinkled with age and weather, and a birthday celebration was in full swing. Twenty people packed the house, 15 or so of them in the living room, where a long makeshift table that had been set up was covered with food and drink. There were potatoes and carrots next to a bottle of vodka. Beans and some sort of meat were next to another bottle of vodka. Several piles of Salem bread from Germany sat by a bottle of peach schnapps. Red beet soup and sauerkraut were next to the bottle of wine.

People were laughing; the women were singing long songs, rocking from side to side together, hugging each other. Each person wanted to shake my hand, and every time anybody walked by me, they put their hand on my shoulder or back. At first it struck me, a rather reserved American, as overly demonstrative, but I then saw that this was how everybody was with everybody. Here was the soul of Russia, the heart of the people: touching, laughing, kissing, hugging, singing maudlin songs while holding hands.

We were given places of honor at the table, and Lipfert gestured for me to eat the food. "This is a rare occasion," he said. "And most of the food is what we've brought here recently. You can eat it safely, but don't drink the water."

I didn't have to worry about drinking the water. First a glass of sangria was put in front of me; we all toasted, and everybody downed his or hers in one gulp. Next was a tumbler of straight vodka. Then the schnapps. Then back to the vodka. I was accumulating half-full glasses in front of me, to the great amusement of my hosts, but my explanation that I was sick from the airplane seemed to soften the blow of my lack of participation.

There was another surprise at the party: it was Horst Von Heyer, the Salem employee who had been shot in the Kurdistan region of northern Iraq two years earlier, when Salem was trying to set up a program to help the Kurds there. Von Heyer, having survived the loss of his assistant in Namibia to a crocodile, and five bullets in his body in Iraq, was again up and around, a distinguished man in his late fifties who stands well over 6 feet tall and speaks perfect British English (and a half dozen other languages). It was great to see him. He'd taken me into Uganda the second time I'd gone to Africa, and we'd spent many an evening together talking long into the nights the year our family lived at Salem in Stadtsteinach. Now he was helping the Salem project here in Russia.

Around midnight the party broke up, people bundling up to trudge out into the cold, black night (no streetlights, dirt streets) back to their homes. Several liters of vodka had been consumed, along with the schnapps and the wine. I was amazed anybody could stand up much less walk home. Later, Lipfert told me that alcohol was a major problem in Russia. In this small town of 400 people, 22 have died in the past year from alcoholism. Two deaths a month in a town of 400! Vodka is cheaper and more readily available than bottled water; and, as Von Heyer said, with the "morale of the people so utterly destroyed, with nothing to do or strive for," all they do is drink. Lipfert blames it on communism, Burkhardt says it's part of the Russian psyche, and I just watched, observing it and trying not to judge it.

Herr Burkhardt and I spent the night in the house next door to Erika's, inhabited by Olga; her husband, Sergei; and their two children, a boy about 13 and a girl around seven. The two kids share a room with a small bed on either side, and Olga moved them onto a mattress in the kitchen and gave Burkhardt and me their beds. I went to sleep, exhausted.

Saturday

The next morning I woke up around 10 o'clock, still a bit jet-lagged. I dressed and joined Olga's family in the kitchen. They all sat on little stools around a small metal table with a new German-made tablecloth, and there was bread from the bakeries at Salem in Germany on the table, along with tea so dark it looked like coffee; homemade plum preserves were filled with large pits that you scooped around. I brought a liter of Danish bottled water and shared it with the table.

Twenty minutes later Lipfert and Von Heyer arrived from next door, where they'd been sleeping, and told Burkhardt and me to get dressed up to go out. In my jet-lag daze, I forgot to put on my long underwear and just pulled on a jacket, hat, gloves, and boots. Outside it was snowing so hard I couldn't see more than 100 feet, and the wind was howling. We bundled into the bus along with an old woman who I soon learned was the "bookkeeper" for the Salem Russia operation, and we drove off along frozen, pitted dirt roads.

We drove for an hour or so through the countryside. For about a half mile, there was a high double barbed-wire fence on our right. "It's the border with Poland," Lipfert said. I tried to place it on the map in my mind but was lost.

The heater in the Volkswagen microbus was effective enough only to melt the snow that had covered my clothes, and I was now both cold and wet, shivering. We crested a hill and, pitching wildly from side to side, came down into an area in the midst of desolate miles of empty land, punctuated only by two houses under construction and a small wooden shed.

"This is the beginning of Salem here," Lipfert said, turning off the bus.

We all climbed out and walked through foot-deep snow to the first of the two houses. They were two-story brick-and-wood homes with steeply pitched roofs. The outsides were covered with scaffolding, no windows or doors were yet in place, and the wind hooted mournfully as it whipped through the skeletal buildings.

In the first house we found four men bundled against the cold in heavy coats, Cossack hats, and thick black boots. One was listlessly driving nails into a wall; the other three were smoking cigarettes and apparently supervising the first man. All four were mostly toothless, with aged and lined faces, wind-burned skin, and thick and cracked hands—men in their thirties who looked like they were in their sixties, their bones and teeth ravaged by malnutrition, their livers and skin devoured by vodka and cigarettes.

Von Heyer became very upset when he saw their work. The wood boards didn't fit together: you could see outdoors through the cracks in the walls. The carpentry looked like a kid's tree house constructed of scrap wood. The electrical wires weren't recessed into the brickwork or the walls but stapled haphazardly across walls and ceilings. And the chimney (as with most all the brickwork) had no mortar vertically between the bricks, only above and below them (and they were uneven at that). As I stood on one side of the chimney, I could see between the bricks clear through to the other side and get a glimpse of Von Heyer.

I shook my head and started to say something; Von Heyer put a finger to his lips. "You be the silent one," he said, "and try to look upset."

Lipfert and Von Heyer brought over Burkhardt and, with loud and angry tones, pointed out the deficiencies, waving their arms and hitting the flimsy walls with their fists. The workers yelled back, and it seemed that the winner wouldn't be the person with the greatest logic but the loudest voice. Then Burkhardt pointed to me and said something in a low and menacing voice, and they all got quiet.

We marched out of the first house and walked through the snow, leaning into the wind, to the second house, where the scene was repeated, although this time the workers kept glancing furtively at me and didn't yell back so much. I looked around, wondering if I'd been cast in the role of some sort of building inspector.

There was the same central heating with no room controls in each room as at Olga's house. The walls were a crazy quilt of fiberboard, pine board, and plywood. The window and door frames were obviously prefabricated and put into place, and the wood was uneven, showing big gaps. In some places, where a piece of wood wasn't long enough to complete a seal, smaller pieces were nailed into place, willy-nilly.

After the showing was over, we stood by the old stove and I said, "What's going on with the houses?"

Von Heyer snorted. "The materials are pathetic. We have to buy them as prefab houses, because everything in this country is made in huge central factories. You wouldn't believe the size of the factories or the ancient machinery they have in them. It's pitiful."

"So the walls and the doors are prefabricated?"

"And the concrete for the foundation—those big slabs of concrete out there with the holes running lengthwise through them."

"But what about the assembly? The men putting the houses together? They don't seem like happy workers."

He shook his head. "They don't know how to work. And even when you can get them to work, they don't know how to do the job."

"What do you mean?"

"The brickwork is all wrong; you saw that."

"Yes," I said. "Looked to me like the house would burn down the first time somebody started a fire in the furnace."

"Exactly," he said. "But when we pointed it out to them, they said that we should hire somebody else to redo it. And still pay them!"

"They don't know how to lay bricks?"

"They said they did, but their work gives the lie to that. Same with the carpentry and the electrical work. One's drunk and the other three are incompetent."

"Why not fire them?"

"I already did that once. They work for a local contractor, and I fired him the last time I was here, last month. We hired another contractor, and he brought out these same men. They don't care. The work ethic here has been totally destroyed. That's the doom of this country. They've been ruled by kings, czars, or communist dictators for a thousand years; they have no understanding of individual initiative, of pride in workmanship, of climbing up through hard work.

"I suggested to the bricklayer that we could bring a master mason from Germany, or send him there for an apprenticeship. He asked how long it takes to become a master mason in Germany; and when I told him it's a three-year apprenticeship, he told me I was crazy. 'That's impossible,' he said. 'Anybody can learn how to lay bricks in a few days.' I tried to tell him that he doesn't know about the subtleties of mortar, how to plan the bricks, how to select them, what tools to use, how temperature affects the way the mortar sets, and on and on. He just shrugged. There are no apprenticeship programs left here, there's no status to being a craftsman, and they don't care!"

Over in the corner, another argument had erupted. I moved a step closer to the stove, which Von Heyer eyed with consternation. "So, what do you do?" I asked.

"Well, first we yell and scream and jump up and down. That gets their attention. We threaten to not pay them, but they know that's an empty threat because the government will back them up in their claim for wages. And finally we brought you in."

"Me?"

"Traditionally in Russia, particularly under the communists, the 'big boss' was the guy who stood quietly in the back and said nothing. If he didn't like things, he was very quiet, which is a very dangerous sign to the workers. They can't imagine that somebody like Lipfert or me—who is out working with the people, helping plant the fields, getting his hands dirty, living in the houses with the farmers—could possibly be 'big bosses.' But you, you're quiet. You stand in the back. You wear nice clothes and stay for only a day or two. And you're from America. They know that Yeltsin has many friends in America. Maybe you have influence with the government, and that could be dangerous to them. We're hoping your presence will encourage them to do the job right."

I looked over at the workmen, who were again shouting and waving their fists, and saw now the fear in the way they glanced at me.

"Seems like a pretty damn poor way to have to get things done," I said, feeling resentful about the role I'd been cast in without consultation.

"This is a pretty damn poor country," Von Heyer said, his voice thick with frustration. "I had an easier time getting the native people in Uganda to help build our hospital. Straight from the bush, never a day's school in their lives, but they were eager to learn and to work. But not these people. Their spirit has been totally broken."

We went back out into the snow. My clothes were now soaking wet, the sky had darkened, and the wind had picked up. The snow had let up. Perhaps it was too cold to snow.

We piled into the bus, and Von Heyer put me in the front by the heater. Back on the rural roads, the windows closed and the heat on, I asked Lipfert to explain to me exactly what the Salem work in this area was.

"As you've seen, many skills have been lost," he said. "These include not only construction skills but also agricultural skills. As when you went with us into Africa in 1980, you know that if people are starving, we will feed them, but our goal is to leave, to make them self-sufficient. We built the children's village, the hospital, and the farm in

Uganda, and now we're turning it over to the people who live there. Here we'll start with the farm, because in this climate that's the first basic of survival."

"You're teaching farming?"

"Small-scale, organic, low-tech agriculture—what will work in a country like this with so little infrastructure. Seven families back in the village where we are staying are being helped by us. Herr Müller heard about their plight from one of their relatives, who wrote to him about them. When we arrived here, they had no food, no work, only the clothes on their backs. There was the very real risk that first winter that they might die of illnesses related to malnutrition. So we brought in food, blankets, clothing, and cooking utensils and helped them rent the houses they're living in back in the village.

"Then we rented some land, and they farmed it last summer, using our techniques. The result was such a huge harvest, the largest in this entire state, that they could make a profit selling it, and the government came in and honored them with an award. In the past few months, 120 families have formally applied to us to 'join' our project. They still have this collective-type thinking, and we're trying to tell them to just imitate what we're doing, on a small scale, with only a few families at a time. It's re-creating the family farm, which built Europe and America. Now Herr Müller has committed to build them seven houses on land that they're buying and some land that we've gotten from the government to teach agricultural methods, and you saw the first two just now. We'd hoped to have all seven finished by now, but things take very, very long in this country."

"I think I'm beginning to understand why."

"It's not just the workers," Lipfert said. "It's also the materials. If we could just truck materials in from Germany, it would be easy, but the government won't let us do that. You saw what we went through just trying to bring in a busload of household goods. So we have to buy locally, with hard currencies, and what we get is so substandard it's almost impossible to build with."

"So what do you do?"

He looked at me with a grin. "We persist, of course. Nobody ever said doing a good work is easy."

Back at Olga's house, the TV was on in the living room. She moved a rug and raised part of the hallway floor, then lifted up a jar of pickles from the dirt crawlspace under the house. She brought out some bread and wine, I got one of my bottles of water, and we sat with the old woman and Herr Burkhardt and watched the TV. They were absorbed in the show; I was trying to warm up—and to pick up a few words of Russian.

When the show ended, a man's face filled the screen. He was giving some sort of speech, and his face was twisted with an insane anger. He pounded his fist and shook his finger at the camera, then became soft and soothing in his voice, then began shouting again. He was followed by a news anchorwoman, sitting behind a desk, making commentary.

"What's that?" I said to the room in general.

"Vladimir Zhiranovski," said Olga. "He's a candidate in tomorrow's election, and he said that if he's elected, we should work more closely with Germany, reestablish our old border with them."

"Isn't Poland in between you and Germany?"

"That's what he means," Olga said, shaking her head in disbelief. "Get rid of Poland."

I shivered.

An hour later Lipfert and Von Heyer came over, having changed their clothes. "Tonight is another birthday party," Lipfert announced. "Not one of the Salem families but another family down the street, and they've invited us to come. It'll be very high status for them if we drop in, so we really should."

So we set off through the absolutely black night to a house a few blocks away.

There a family was gathered: Mom and Dad and two sons just short of their teenage years. Von Heyer, Lipfert, Burkhardt, and I were the guests. Mom put a liter bottle of vodka on the table and poured shots for all of us, then gave a toast and downed hers in one gulp, as did her husband. The boys, who weren't invited to sit at the table but only watched from the couch, observed the ritual with sad eyes.

The conversation over dinner, punctuated by rounds of the vodka (Mom was now drinking it out of a water glass), was mostly about the election. I got up to use the bathroom and discovered that, unlike in the houses of the families Salem was supporting, there was no toilet paper in this house. Instead next to the toilet was a pile of computer paper torn into four-inch-square scraps, and next to that was a basket for the used paper. When I tried to raise the toilet seat, it fell off.

Sunday

The next morning was Election Day. When I woke up, Olga's family was clustered around the TV, watching Zhiranovski make another speech. "What's he saying?" I asked.

Olga turned, shaking her head with an amazed look on her face. "He says that everybody who votes for him will get a liter of vodka and a turkey after the election."

"People fall for that?" I asked.

She nodded. "Remember, Russia has been here nearly a thousand years. And this is the first democratic election ever—*ever!* People have no idea what to do, how to do it, or what to believe."

I went into the kitchen and made myself some rice and lentils and finished off a bottle of Danish water. Around noon Von Heyer and Lipfert came by to collect me, and, my bag packed and a final water bottle under my arm, I said good-bye to my hosts. The 10 Danish chocolate bars I left for Olga and the small airport-bought toys for her kids brought tears to their eyes.

We drove through a blizzard for six hours to Kaliningrad, finally arriving back at the ship, Hotel Hanza.

We went out into the city, which was unnaturally dark. All the "official" stores were closed, but in the area around Lenin's Square, a central park in the city, was a series of kiosks the size of New York City newsstands. All were open and doing brisk business. "These are the stores the Mafia runs," Burkhardt explained as we parked the car. "Therefore this is the safest part of town."

At the first kiosk was every imaginable type of chocolate—Swiss, Danish, German, French, Austrian . . . but nothing Russian.

The second kiosk had booze and cigarettes—Johnny Walker, Marlboro, Winston; again there was nothing Russian, except vodka. Even the maps and the souvenirs that they had were printed in German and referred to the town as Königsberg.

And on down the line we found toys, gum, candy, more chocolate, more booze, but nothing Russian. "The country is dead," Burkhardt said as we climbed into the bus without having found a Russian souvenir of any sort. "Their only product is vodka."

Monday

At six o'clock the next morning, we drove out to the airport. The airport gate was closed, but the guard station and the machine-gun turret were empty, so I got out of the bus and opened what was once the high-security gate myself; we drove through.

The building was unlocked. An old woman with a homemade broom of straw tied to a stick with wire was stooped over nearly to her knees, sweeping the floor. No heat, nothing open. There was nothing open except a small café off to one side.

A few minutes before the scheduled departure time, the flight crew arrived. Lipfert and Von Heyer left, and I went through security. The metal on my jacket fired off the metal detector, but the people at security just waved me through anyway. They didn't even bother to watch the screen as my bag went through the X-ray machine: perhaps it didn't work.

We walked out across the frozen and slick ramp to the plane and climbed ice-covered stairs. A de-icing truck came out, and two men began to listlessly spray something on the plane, blowing off the accumulation of snow and ice from the previous night. It took them an hour, and I cringed as I watched one of them walking on the wing, one foot on the flaps, walking all over areas that, on US planes, are clearly marked "NO STEP" and, on this plane, had a similar-looking marking in Cyrillic.

Finally, we took off for Berlin. The plane smelled musty and my seat kept falling back into the lap of the man behind me, but we wobbled up into the air and two hours later landed in Berlin during one of the heaviest blizzards I've flown through in years. Stepping into the Berlin airport, with all its shops and signs and products and well-dressed people going one place or another, I remembered the people back in Russia. How long would it take them to rebuild their country? Von Heyer thought it would be at least two generations; Olga was more optimistic and thought 10 to 15 years. And the politicians, of course, are promising to do it in two.

Traveling to Russia for Salem taught me an important lesson. I saw how the communist concept—once embraced by the Russians as the solution to the problems of the West—destroyed the human spirit because it detached people's actions from any response. What happened in the Soviet Union, for generations, is that although people acted (did their jobs), it made no difference in how their lives went; whether they worked hard or not, there was no change in their standard of living. With no connection between initiative and outcome, their productive spirit died.

On my visit I'd seen people whose spirit was destroyed by centuries of repression, by alcohol, and by a total lack of hope. I'd also seen and come to know those who believed change was possible, that there could be a future for Russia if only the "older" wisdom of the peasants could be brought back and enough people could see and sense the possibility of success.

Salem is a start. The impact we've had on a small region is already startling, with 120 families going from being suspicious and skeptical to enthusiastically wanting to jump on the bandwagon. Because the media is so centralized and pervasive in Russia, it's possible that once the Salem program is up and running at full speed it could be a model that will quickly spread across the country, teaching the basics of free enterprise, agriculture, food storage, and nutrition.

The next step, Lipfert says, is to help upgrade the local hospitals and change the way the orphanages are run, moving them to the Salem family model. With enough help, and if the government doesn't turn in on itself or experience a total economic collapse like the one that in part led to World War II, I believe it just may work.

From *The Prophet's Way* by Thom Hartmann,
© 1997, published by Inner Traditions International.

Caral, Peru: A Thousand Years of Peace

From *Threshold: The Crisis of Western Culture*

> Mankind must put an end to war, or war will put an
> end to mankind. . . . War will exist until that distant
> day when the conscientious objector enjoys the same
> reputation and prestige that the warrior does today.
>
> —JOHN F. KENNEDY

> When you realize how small the earth is in relation to the
> cosmos, and how small we are in relation to the earth, then you
> can understand the appropriate place of humans in relation to
> the earth. These people looked up at the stars and understood
> this. We look at the earth too much and miss the big picture,
> the stars. We must see a larger view if we are to live in peace.
>
> —DR. RUTH SHADY

THROUGHOUT HUMANITY'S 160,000-PLUS-YEAR HISTORY, CUL-tures ranging from tribes to city-states have undergone a three-stage process. They start out (stage one) immature: exploitative of one another and of the world around them. Like children, as a society they think they're the center of the universe, the only "real people" and thus unique from all other forms of life (and other cultures), so they think they have the (often divinely ordained) right to dominate and exploit everything around them. This exploitation inevitably leads to stage two: environmental and cultural disaster. Cultures then disappear, disperse, or reach stage three: maturity.

Ecological disasters—in most cases manmade—are at the root of virtually every historic disappearance or dispersal of cultures. (Even Rome fell because of deforestation: the felling of the last forests in Italy led to a currency crisis when there wasn't enough wood to fuel the furnaces to smelt silver; this provoked Rome's outward expansion across the rest of Europe—which led to the fall of the Roman Empire.)

Similarly, the American Empire—and arguably many others (Chinese, Russian, Japanese, and European)—is setting up ecological disasters that are already producing catastrophic consequences. From deforestation to global warming to changing ocean currents (which could plunge the world into a new ice age in a period as short as two years) to massive species loss, the planet is dying. Duke University professor Dr. Stuart Pimm documents how about a quarter of all species alive just 200 years ago are now extinct; and if current trends continue, half of all species will be extinct within 30 years.[1]

The planet is a living organism, and the species on it are parts of an interconnected whole, a grand web of life. Just as a person can live and function without a few body parts—an eye, a kidney, a limb, or even an entire hemisphere of the brain—when a certain critical mass of body parts or blood is gone or damaged, the entire body will cease to function.

What is driving all this is our culture and the core cultural assumption that we are born to dominate one another, primarily through the instrument of war. Thus one of the great debates among those who study the arc of human history has been whether maturity is based on war or whether war is an aberration in a mature society. And it's not just war of one human against another, one society against another, but also war against nature, humans behaving in ways that destroy the natural world.

Is the natural state of humans warlike? Is that why we naturally organize into clans, tribes, cities, states, and nations—to protect ourselves from other naturally warlike humans?

Or is the natural state of humans peaceful, and war an aberration? Do we organize ourselves into cities to achieve our highest potential instead of to defend ourselves from our lowest nature? Is the purpose of "society" supportive, nurturing, and ennobling?

These are critical questions for us for two reasons. The first is that we today stand at the precipice of environmental and war-driven disaster. The second is that the United States and most other modern liberal democracies were founded out of the Enlightenment notion that the true natural state of humankind is peace, not war; enlightenment, not hatred; integration with "natural law," not defiance of it.

For a significant majority of tribal societies around the world, the question was settled tens of thousands of years ago: the natural state of humankind is peaceful. Hundreds of examples are easily found extant today among historically stable aboriginal peoples on all continents and detailed by anthropologists such as Robert Wolff and Peter Farb— and extensively by Thomas Jefferson.

But what about "modern civilizations"—cities and nations?

For most of the 7,000-year history of city-states, conventional wisdom has held that they were created to defend people from nearby warriors. Castles are essentially defensive institutions, developed to protect their inhabitants from instruments of warfare. In Europe, Asia, the Middle East, and South America, the largest early cities were essentially giant castles, and evidence of warfare is everywhere, from ancient instruments of war to ancient murals of warriors at battle.

But is this why these cities were started, as defensive fortifications? Until now nobody has known because the ancient cities we've excavated so far around the world are built layer upon layer over themselves, one conquering group after another; so, after a few thousand years, some are hundreds of feet higher than they were when they were first built and a dozen to a hundred layers of successive cultures deep. Excavating all the way down to the "mother city"—the first city, with its original artifacts and clues to its original purpose and way of life intact—has never been done successfully. The evidence of the mother city, in every one of our known ancient civilizations, is gone, destroyed by the ravages of time and the builders of subsequent layers upon the foundation of the original.

Until 1994.

That's when Dr. Ruth Shady of the University of San Marcos at Lima, Peru, began excavation of a site spreading over hundreds of acres that for 1,000 years or more had simply appeared to be a series of seven huge sand-covered mounds. By 2002 she realized she had found an ancient city; in 2004 she found artifacts that could be carbon-dated, and she discovered she had uncovered the oldest known intact city in the world—the world's first excavatable mother city.

This city, called Caral, predated not only the Bronze and Iron Ages but even the Ceramic Age, yet it had huge plazas, giant pyramids, elaborate homes, and the remains of art, music, and a complex culture. The citizens of this city lived in peace for more than 1,000 years before climate change covered their city over and they abandoned it. There is absolutely no evidence whatsoever of war or the instruments of war. Instead everything, from the art to the musical instruments to the burial sites, indicates that the people of Caral lived in peace and harmony.

In September 2008 I made the trek to Peru to meet Dr. Shady and hear and see for myself what could be learned from a human culture that, though ancient, existed in harmony within its environment and in peace with neighboring societies.

It was a cold, gray morning in Lima as Renan, my interpreter, and two large, tough-looking guys picked me up at the hotel. Renan had lived in the United States and was fluent and well spoken in English; our two bodyguards, Lucho and Gilberto, spoke only Spanish.

We drove for miles past squatter slums along a highway that runs up the west coast of South America. Renan said you can follow this highway all the way to the United States. Much of the road was empty and barren—sand-covered hills stretching into the distance, the product of millions of years of sand blowing in from the Pacific Ocean coast.

The slums rolled up and over the hillsides along the highway, shacks made of scrap materials but located close enough to the road that their residents could catch a bus ride into Lima to work. Raw sewage ran in open gutters along the dirt "streets" of the slums, and the odor occasionally reached our car. The sky was gunmetal gray and the air chilly when we left Lima, but as we traveled north up along the coast, climbing steadily, the sky opened up and the air became warm.

This long stretch of highway was where Renan said that bandits will sometimes roll large boulders out onto the road, and when you stop to move them you find yourself with an AK-47 in your face. Our bodyguards, Lucho and Gilberto, were former SEALs in the Peruvian navy. I asked Renan if they were armed, and he said, "Yes, and so am I." I hoped the guns would not be needed.

After traveling almost two hours north, we came to a large truckstop-style gas station with an attached restaurant. Here we met Dr. Shady with her driver/bodyguard and shared some breakfast and coffee. Dr. Shady is a pleasant-looking woman of middle years, with a broad smile and a contagious enthusiasm for archeology and for Caral, the city she is largely responsible for excavating.

As we sat and ate, I asked her what was most significant about Caral.

"Here the civilization was different," she said, contrasting the Caral of 5,000 years ago with the city-states that were emerging in Egypt, India, and Asia. "The focus [of the culture] was different. When this civilization was formed here, peace was very important. There was no war." She paused and looked at me with a glint in her eye. "Why? Why was there no war?" she asked, as if quizzing me.

I shrugged. "Many people think that the only reason cities were originally created was to provide fortifications for war."

But that was not the case in Caral, Dr. Shady said. There were no fortifications built at any time during the city's 1,000 years of continuous, peaceful occupation.

"I think it is very important for the people in the world to ask [how Caral could live without war] because it is different in the modern world. I think the Caral civilization has a very important message to the world about how societies can live in peace."

Dr. Shady noted that Caral was a complex society and had complex interactions with many other societies in the region, many of which lived in radically different ways. "Caral had state or political authorities because this civilization had interactions with societies that lived on the coast, the highlands, and the lowlands—all different environments," she said. "They were interacting because they were very different. Different resources. The religion was very important. I think most important was that the political authorities used religion for social cohesion and political coercion rather than using violence and war."

But was it just religion, I asked, that made for peace?

"We had information that women were very important," she said. "In Caral we found two figures, a man and a woman together. The woman had a dress very similar to the white of the Incas, and I think she was a very important person. She had two necklaces made of a very special material with an important design of a cross. Her face had tattoos and holes for earrings—the symbol of political importance until the Incas. The man had only one necklace, and his eyes were looking at her."

Dr. Shady added that the figurines were consistent with other ancient artifacts from peaceful societies and that even among the much later Incan Empire—a warlike empire—"the wife of the Inca, as the Spanish chronicled, had the special role of diplomat and negotiated peace."

An hour later, after driving into an incredibly remote valley through miles of dense scrub and then miles of desertlike dust, and then through a valley where the road was only barely discernable, we came to the site where the city of Caral was being excavated. The sun was bright and so intense at this elevation and latitude that by day's end my face was bright red. Dr. Shady put on a scarf and a hat to protect herself from the sun. We walked among ruins and hills concealing ruins that were from two to 10 (modern building) stories tall, and we talked.

"We began to work in the valley in 1994," Dr. Shady said. "Soon we were working all the valley. We found a site with monumental buildings. But nobody knew the age of the site. After the first month,

I could see that there weren't any ceramics, only textiles [among the remains], and the techniques of these textiles were similar [to those of] another very old site that we know of in this country from the Archaic period."

"Pre-Ceramic?" I asked. This would have made the city a transition point from Stone Age cultures to city-living cultures, dating it from about 5,000 years ago—long before iron or bronze or any other metal was refined, long before glass was made, before even kiln-based pottery techniques were developed.

"Yes," she said. "This was pre-Ceramic. But here the difference [from most pre-Ceramic societies] was the very big buildings—the human design."

We walked along a pathway that was defined on both sides by small stones, to keep people from wandering randomly around the site. We passed a place where the sandy soil had been dug deeply, revealing stone buildings that looked like the rooms of a house. "Under all this sand are homes?" I asked.

Dr. Shady pointed to the excavation and said, "One group here." We stood along a long ridge, a flat area with bare, sand-covered hills in the far distance. A mile or two behind us, a few hundred feet below in elevation, was a lush valley with a river that had been running through it for tens of thousands of years or more. She pointed to 30 acres or so of hillside. "Another group here. And I think all these people lived here because it's so near to the valley."

She explained that the people were agriculturalists who worked the valley but that their primary crop was cotton, which was formed into fishing nets and then traded with coastal-living people in exchange for everything from anchovies (primarily) to whales. The societies were interdependent and symbiotic rather than competitive.

There was also a strong emphasis on the family unit, she said, as shown by the way the housing was organized. Even today the local people of the Caral area continue with traditions that Dr. Shady believes trace back thousands of years ago to when the ancient city of Caral was occupied.

She described to me how the locals she'd hired for excavation asked her every year to bring a shaman into the community to keep the site sacred and thus keep them safe. "Each year I have to do a religious event here," she said, "because the people think that if I don't, they can have accidents because they work in this sacred site. So every October I have to do this ceremony of the *Pago a la Tierra*—I have to pay the earth."

I asked her about the shamans (sometimes a woman) she brought in every October. Where did they conduct the ceremony?

She noted that there were two parts or sides to Caral, one on a slightly higher plain, with large administrative buildings and plazas, all square or rectangular and with all the public areas laid out in straight lines. And then there was another site, essentially on the other side of a slight hill and road that bisected the area, where the public areas were round, including a dramatic round public amphitheater that was dug 20 or more feet into the ground. Its acoustics were perfect—you could stand in the middle of it and speak and then hear a perfect echo of your voice—and this was the area where, Dr. Shady said, they had found most of the musical instruments. And it was the only area where the shamans were willing to perform their sacred ceremonies.

Dr. Shady noted that a colleague, Dr. R. Tom Zuidema, professor of anthropology emeritus at the University of Illinois, suggested to her that the "round" areas were probably under the control of women rather than men, an idea that made sense to her.

And, apparently, it made sense to the shamans. "When the person who conducts the religious ceremonies comes here, she won't make them here," Dr. Shady said as we stood in the "square" part of town.

"Why?" I asked.

"Because she said she heard people crying here."

I looked at the hills around us—many of them still unexcavated pyramids and buildings—and tried to imagine what life must have been like here 5,000 years ago. As I looked at the excavated houses, it wasn't hard to imagine the spirits of the people who lived here so long ago as still being around.

Further reinforcing Dr. Shady's idea that the square buildings were administrative or governmental and the round areas ceremonial, she and her helpers had found 32 flutes and 38 *antaras* (a type of carved-bone panpipe) in the round areas, particularly around the amphitheater.

"I think the social organization was complex for the music also," she said. "These instruments weren't for solo performances; they were for groups of people to play."

"And this was another way in which Caral was a mother city? The music? The instruments indicated social complexity?"

"I think the first complex society was born here and was the mother of political organizations that were copied for later civilizations."

I asked her how a 5,000-year-old city could have been successfully hidden for 4,000 years so it wouldn't be looted or torn down and built over, as all other mother cities had been.

"When I came here all the pyramids were like this," she said, waving her arms at what seemed like 30 or so rolling, sand-covered hills—under which her archeologists were discovering pyramids, buildings, and dense housing complexes. "The people in this valley thought they were hills, only hills."

The reason, she explained, was that around 4,000 years ago there was a change in the climate—a major El Niño–type of event off the Pacific coast, 15 miles away—that produced a multigenerational drought. People couldn't grow anything, so they moved away. The plants holding the soil died, leaving the sandy soil from the ocean to the west all the way to this valley to the mercy of the continuous winds, which brought, over the years, foot after foot of sand, which covered the buildings and the pyramids and filled in the amphitheater. Whereas Pompeii was covered by several feet of ash overnight, Caral was covered by yards of sand and micro-fine soil in just a few hundred years. The sand became so deep that nobody ever tried settling here again because the soil was too unstable to build anything on and too sandy (and salty) to grow anything in.

The city of Caral had been sealed into such a perfect time capsule that when one of Dr. Shady's archeologists took me on a tour of the pyramids, he showed me nets filled with stones used to fill in spaces between walls, and the nets—made of 5,000-year-old handspun cotton—were still intact, still holding the stones in place. Seeds and food were found in storage rooms, along with clothing, figurines, and musical instruments—it was all there. *Quipus*—knotted cords used to record events and transactions—were intact. And all could be radiocarbon-dated to accurately prove that this was the most ancient mother city ever discovered intact. A city filled with music. A city with an amphitheater strewn with musical instruments and the remnants of games. A city that lived for 1,000 years in peace.

Are we innately evil or good, warlike or peaceful?

In 1634 in his book *Leviathan,* Thomas Hobbes stated our culture's assumption of the essentially evil nature of humans, saying that life without the iron fist of church or state would be "war of every man against every man," resulting in a society where life is "poor, nasty, brutish, and short."

A generation later Jean-Jacques Rousseau and John Locke challenged Hobbes, suggesting that evidence from tribes being discovered across Africa and the Americas by European explorers demonstrated that, instead, the natural state of humankind was good, egalitarian, and peaceful.

The thinking of Rousseau and Locke explicitly and overtly influenced the Founders of the United States, particularly Thomas Jefferson, who saw verification of it in their own contact with Native Americans.

Thus began America as an egalitarian experiment, an experiment that has been expanded and developed by nearly 100 other nations in the world that claim democracy, particularly the countries of northern Europe, where once-feared and warlike people—most notably the Vikings of Norway and Sweden—are now among the happiest and most peaceful and self-sufficient people in the world.

Yet the Hobbeses of the world are currently ascendant, in terms of both war on humans and war on the environment.

But what should be done?

As I said in Leonardo DiCaprio's environmental documentary *The 11th Hour:*

> The problem is not a problem of technology. The problem is not a problem of too much carbon dioxide. The problem is not a problem of global warming. The problem is not a problem of waste. All of those things are symptoms of the problem. The problem is the way that we are thinking. The problem is fundamentally a cultural problem. It's at the level of our culture that this illness is happening.

In my books I have shared stories from all around the world of cultures that have matured, awakened, and found ways to live in peace, harmony, and ecological balance, and the fate of others that have not. Some are pre-city aboriginal and tribal cultures, some are modern communities, and some are fully developed city-states moving quickly in the direction of peace. All offer us a new vision of how life can be in a world where the core assumptions of modern culture are challenged and modified.

This is not a radical or New Age or easily dismissed concept. It started with the Enlightenment of the seventeenth century.

Its first experiment was the founding of the United States of America in the eighteenth century.

It flowered around the world throughout the nineteenth century, as nation after nation flipped from warrior-king states to democracies.

It found global acceptance in the twentieth century with the foundation of the United Nations, the first international organization whose single explicit purpose for existence was to create, promote, and maintain worldwide peace.

And now, in the twenty-first century, as war (against humans and against nature) is increasingly being viewed with horror by people around the world, movements are springing up all over the planet to reject the immature cultural paradigms of the past and move us into a postcarbon, postwarfare, egalitarian, and peaceful world where there is room both for humans and for all other life.

Why and When Did War Begin?

If it's true, as scientists from Peter Farb to Riane Eisler to Ruth Shady point out, that a prime differentiator between warrior societies and peaceful societies is the role of power relationships between men and women, the question is raised: *Why and when does war begin, and how is it related to the relationship between the sexes?*

Most preliterate cultures, from those in the Arctic to those in the southernmost tips of South America and Africa, were largely peaceful before contact with modern technology and culture. While there was conflict, and often violent conflict, it rarely reached the proportion of organized, sustained, legally sanctioned mass murder that today we call war.

As anthropologist Peter Farb has documented, some Native American societies—for example, the Shoshone—didn't even have a word for war in their vocabulary. Others used organized games to resolve conflicts.

Many theories have been put forward for how and why the warrior mentality took over. Marija Gimbutas and others suggest it was associated with the beginning of animal husbandry—herding and pastoralism. When we began to domesticate large mammals that share the limbic, or "emotional," brain with us (something birds and reptiles don't have), we developed emotional ties to them. In some cases these ties became so strong that people have been known to die to protect animals (many of the people who didn't leave New Orleans during Hurricane Katrina stayed behind because they were unwilling to abandon their pets).

Building these emotional bonds with cows, goats, sheep, pigs (smarter than dogs!), and camels and then killing those same animals for food required a certain type of disconnected thinking, a breaking of the bond between emotion and intellect, between seeing another living thing as a fellow-feeling being and objectifying it as an "it," seeing it as "just an animal."

The learned ability to disconnect oneself from the product of mammal-to-mammal killing was, suggested Gimbutas, the emotional/

psychosocial disconnect that then led people to more easily objectify and then kill one another, starting around 7,000 years ago with early pastoralism.

One objection to this theory of how war began and the men took over, though, is that there are numerous pastoralist tribes throughout the world that don't routinely engage in genocidal wars.

Another theory about the emergence of non-food-based warfare and the male dominance that seems to accompany it, first advanced by Walter J. Ong and Robert K. Logan, and later popularized by Leonard Shlain, is that the development of abstract alphabets and the literacy based on them fundamentally rewired our brains as children in such a way as to make us all potential killers.

Broadly speaking, the right hemisphere of our brain is nonverbal and processes music, relationship-based behaviors, and what have been broadly (and with terrible overgeneralization) described as "creative" efforts. This hemisphere is sometimes described as the "feminine" part of our brain. (The left/right male/female brain notion is a pop-culture generalization that makes neurologists cringe, but, like with so many clichés, it also contains a large grain of truth, particularly when viewed in a modern cultural context.)

While most thinking originates in the evolutionarily more ancient right brain (which controls the left side of our bodies), it then passes into the left hemisphere of the brain for final processing. Our left hemisphere is verbal, spatial, and abstract. While the right hemisphere experiences things in a more holistic sense, the left hemisphere makes distinctions, separations, and logical partitions. While the right hemisphere is filled with music or silence, the left hemisphere is filled with words. It is linear, methodical, unemotional, and broadly (again, often too broadly) described as the "masculine" part of our brain.

The left hemisphere is where abstractions—such as alphabets— are processed. Shlain, Ong, Logan, and others suggest that the coup by men (as opposed to balanced egalitarianism) came about when children learned to read at an early age. This over-exercises the left hemisphere; as a result, instead of its behaving cooperatively with the right hemisphere, it rises up and "takes over" the rest of the brain. The result is a colder and less emotional form of thinking and behaving and a feeling of disconnection from all life around us (or, more accurately, a lack of a feeling of connection, as that's the province of the right hemisphere). This disconnect, Shlain argues, has led directly to centuries of war and even to the Nazi horrors of the Holocaust.

The critical age, it turns out, is around seven years old, when the brain "demylenates," or prunes away unused cells; if one hemisphere has become dominant, it is "fixed," or neurologically "burned in," for life. In support of the idea of teaching children abstractions such as reading only after the age of seven, Shlain points out how during the several hundred years of European Dark Ages, not only was there a boringly consistent (relatively speaking) lack of war in Europe but the major object of worship was a female goddess deity, Mary.

Once the Catholic Church's ban on literacy was lifted and young people began to learn to read at an early age, Shlain notes, more than a million women were tortured and murdered within a few generations, and shrines to Mary were torn down and replaced with images of Jesus.

A remnant of the language of Caral is still spoken in a few remote nearby towns today, a language with no other clear root from nearby peoples or countries. But the people who lived in Caral were not literate (although they did use textiles and knotted ropes to record events and transactions). This may be one of the keys to their thousand years of peace—that children under the age of seven weren't taught an alphabet, and so the men and women lived in a relatively equal balance of power.

Is There a Normal Cycle to Cultures?

Most aboriginal/indigenous/tribal peoples around the world live in relative peace and homeostasis with their environment, the result of thousands (and in some cases tens of thousands) of years of trial-and-error cultural development adapted to local conditions. Caral shows that the first transition to city living was also peaceful, further suggesting that war may well be the cultural equivalent of a mental illness.

Given these assumptions (which much, but not all, history suggests are simply facts), the question arises: *How do we create city-state cultures that live in peace?* Is it even possible, or are we all doomed to cycles of boom and bust, of empire and subsequent crash/poverty? Britain's former prime minister Tony Blair pointed out one of the most interesting—and little noted—modern realities to Jon Stewart on *The Daily Show* in September 2008: "No two democracies," Blair said, "have ever gone to war with each other."

This point—that people in a true democracy will never empower their leaders to attack another democracy—is such an absolute article of faith among neoconservatives that it was one of the rationales used to invade Iraq in 2003, to "turn it into a democracy." Unfortunately, they failed to realize its corollary: that democracies that don't grow organically from within rarely survive as democracies. As comedian Dick Gregory commented to me when we were traveling to Uganda in 1981, "You don't have to shove our way of life down people's throats with the barrel of a gun. If it's that good, they will steal it themselves!" And in the 30 years since then, country after country has done just that, from South Africa to Ukraine to East Germany to Argentina. (Although Iraq is still in a state of crisis because of the neocon belief that they could bomb a nation into democracy, it appears that the road to hell really is paved with good intentions.)

Cultural history—from what clearly appears to be a self-governing (small-*d* democratic in the context of that day) Caral to today—and biology tell us that democracy is the normal and homeostatic anchor of peoples who have had enough time to work it out by trial and error. A landscape littered with nondemocratic cultures and civilizations that have risen and fallen and a planet covered on five continents with living or remnant tribal cultures that have been stable democracies for thousands or tens of thousands of years show us the inevitability of culturally egalitarian democracy.

The difference between us today and those who lived in previous times is that we have the luxury of looking back across the whole sweep of world history and "prehistory" to see how it works (and what prevents it from working) and, it is hoped, to finally get it right.

From *Threshold: The Crisis of Western Culture* by Thom Hartmann, © 2009, published by Viking Penguin, a division of Penguin Group (USA) Inc.

After the Crash

From *Imagine: What America Could Be in the 21st Century,* ed. Marianne Williamson

URING THE TIME YOU SPEND READING THIS ESSAY, 500 PEO-
ple—300 of them children—will die of starvation. Two or three
species will vanish forever. A quarter million pounds of toxic and
cancer-causing waste from corporate polluters will pour into our air,
soil, and water. More than 2,000 acres of rain forest will be burned,
cut, or bulldozed. In America alone, guns will kill two or three people,
and at least one teenager will commit suicide.

It doesn't have to be this way.

Imagine a future America where these problems are part of a bitter past. Imagine an America where people care for one another and
life is rich and meaningful, where we actually know the names of our
neighbors because we talk, eat, and laugh with them regularly. Imagine
America a generation from now—if we make the right choices today.

The resurgence of community imagined in this essay would be
brought about by an oil crisis. Nonetheless it would improve the quality of Americans' lives.

In the ideal America of the future, neighborhoods are again
places where people live as neighbors. When one family is in need,
it becomes the business of the entire community to fill that need. If
one family has a sick child, everybody says a prayer for her or babysits
or brings over soup or medicine—often a mixture made from herbs
grown in the garden. If one person's house burns down, everyone else
opens their homes to that person and the community mobilizes to
erect a new home.

Nearly every neighborhood has a community building, often
part of the power station or the place of worship, where people gather
during the day to converse and during the evening to share potluck

dinners and entertain one another with music, storytelling, dancing, games, and reading aloud. Some communities have saunas or sweat lodges attached to their community buildings, or hallowed groves, stone circles, labyrinths, public crucifixes, or other sacred sites. These are important for prayer and meditation and for the rites of passage that communities conduct as children grow up and adults grow older.

Families tend to stay in the area where they were living at the time of the Crash, so cousins now play together and children are raised with their grandparents' help.

People walk everywhere, for exercise as well as for social interaction. Extensive systems of hiking trails are set up in the forests. In the cities, historic and other interesting sites are well marked, and residents who would enjoy hosting visitors leave their front doors open. People spend evenings on their porches, simply rocking in chairs or chatting with family and neighbors and offering tea, snacks, or music.

Most goods and resources are locally produced and locally consumed. Lawns—anachronistic twentieth-century imitations of the greenswards of the medieval British aristocracy—are long forgotten; people now grow vegetables and grains in the soil around their homes. Fruit and nut trees are popular both for decoration and for shade. Families grow much of their own food, while the community garden supplies most of the rest.

Electricity and heat are produced by small local stations the size of garages, each one serving its own community of 12 to 20 homes. The fuel sources vary, depending on the climate, from solar to wind to biomass to trash. The community stations supplement home power stations—rooftop photovoltaic collectors and basement fuel cells—which supply most of the power that families need. Each central station also purifies water for the community and processes its liquid and solid wastes.

Even though resources are primarily produced and used locally, there is considerable trade among neighborhoods. Some communities specialize in growing particular types of food or in making unique clothing. One may have a healer with special talents. Others might have brilliant technical specialists who help maintain the power plants or who mentor youngsters in the upkeep of homes and gardens. Trade is almost always done by means of barter; goods may be exchanged for labor and vice versa. Food, however, is considered sacred and is never traded for anything except other food. The free giving of food is one of the highest social obligations and one of the fastest ways to achieve status in the community.

Laws and cultural norms are mostly determined locally. Neighborhoods have names and can seem a bit tribal: Residents of a particular neighborhood are often related by blood and usually share lifestyles and religious values. Although most are racially homogenous, some communities have chosen to go the full tribal route, particularly those who still have historic tribal roots.

Tribalism is no longer considered racist—as it was before the Crash—because "other" no longer means "inferior," "competitor," or "to be conquered." Physical and cultural differences are respected and even celebrated. People living in a community understand that their neighborhood is theirs, that they are who they were born to be, and that every other neighborhood has an equal right to be itself.

Each community administers its own justice. The concepts of sin and punishment, which grew out of the king-based religions of ancient Samaria, with their idea that human nature is evil, have been rejected. People have returned to the concepts of harmony and disharmony, balance and imbalance, reflecting how humans had lived for millions of years before the Younger-Culture Eruption from 6000 BCE to 2012 CE. The assumption is that people are essentially good and their misbehavior is an aberration, not the converse.

When a person's behavior steps outside the standards of the community, everybody feels it as a ripple of imbalance within the neighborhood. People gather in the community center to discuss with the out-of-balance person and those he may have harmed ideas about how to come back into harmony and restore balance. When Americans figured out that having the world's fastest-growing prison population was a sign of cultural failure and noticed that tribal people had never had police or prisons, we relearned the ancient ways of valuing every member of the community and working as a group to restore harmony. Only rarely is a person so far out of balance that he must travel to a refuge or an outside community of healers.

Teaching is done by groups of families, who take turns hosting schools of 5 to 10 children. The goal is to make sure that all children grow up with strong self-esteem, a sense of personal power, and certainty about their options and passions. Each teenager chooses a career based on his own passions; then an appropriate mentor in that trade or profession teaches the teenager during an apprenticeship, whether in power-plant maintenance, sewing, or surgery.

Negative labels such as *attention deficit disordered* and *learning disabled* are recognized as vestiges of the Bad Old Days, also known as the Era of the Corporate Kings, when schools were run like factories, with children as standardized products on a conveyor belt. These negative labels simply described children whose gifts weren't useful to corporations, children who wouldn't work well in factories or cubicles. (People woke up when they noticed that there were no diagnostic categories, therapies, or medications being developed or sold by the big drug companies for "art disabled" or "creativity disordered" or "music deficient" children because these were disorders of talents that the corporations did not care about.) Instead of trying to determine what's wrong with children, the goal of education now is to determine their individual gifts and help them develop these into both vocations and avocations.

There are still universities, but they're no longer beholden to corporate interests to fund their research or determine their curricula. Americans awakened to realize that "government of, by, and for the people" meant that the government wasn't the enemy and its function was, first and foremost, to make sure that basic human needs were met and human rights respected. When multinational corporations tried to usurp this function, attempting to control human needs such as those for health care and food and to limit human rights by placing themselves above living, breathing people in the legal hierarchy, the laws that Thomas Jefferson first put into place to restrain corporations were restored. Corporate charters now must be renewed annually, and the first obligation of a corporation is to its community; the profit it makes for its shareholders comes second, as was the case for the first 100 years of American history.

Even if this image of a future America sounds unrealistic or idealistic, it's not. It's simply a practical way to live. Americans have used all aspects of it at various times over the past 300 years. Even if it sounds nostalgic, it's not. It's based on the way most stable human cultures have functioned for 200,000 years or more, the way most Native American cultures have functioned for 10,000 years, and the way a dwindling number of tribal, intentional, and remote small-town communities function in America today.

It's quite different, however, from the way typical Americans experience daily life at the dawn of the twenty-first century. Instead of a life filled with family and friends, in the past 30 years we've entered a time of hyper-competition, fear of HMOs and insurance companies, and the frenetic struggle to earn more, more, more and buy more, more, more. We wake up to nightmares of downsizing and stock market crashes, and we try not to wonder what will happen when the world's oil runs dry sometime in the twenty-first century. We pretend that it's normal that suicide is the second-leading cause of death among schoolchildren and that it is merely unfortunate that the majority of America's lakes, streams, and coastal areas are measurably polluted with toxic waste and human pathogens.

The same industry that brought us DDT now brings us bio-engineered foods that may well usher in the silent spring that Rachel Carson warned us about, but we consider it impolite to discuss in the media the millions of dollars that chemical companies and agribusiness give our politicians, the employment revolving door between these corporations and the governmental agencies that regulate them, and the growing stranglehold that corporations have on the funding and the publication of university research.

What happened?

Somewhere along the way—many would say between the development of the advertising industry in the 1920s and the time in the 1960s when, for the first time, more than half of all American households owned televisions—we lost our bearings. We became confused and disoriented, shifting our attention from our communities, neighbors, and families to an electronic neurological drug delivered hourly by multinational corporations.

In our collective mythic identity, we moved from the truly middle-class life of Ralph Kramden's and Lucy Ricardo's 1950s apartments to Frasier's multimillion-dollar penthouse, complete with a beautiful maid and expensive furniture. The Joneses with whom we tried to keep up shifted from the neighbors we actually knew to those we watched on television, where the average home cost more than $1 million.

A national explosion of upscaling brought us a country studded with child-care facilities for our preschoolers and TV sets in every bedroom of our school-age children. Fully half of all American children at the beginning of the twenty-first century come home to a house silent but for the television.

Within two generations we have become the most voracious consumers on earth, using 30 times the planetary resources per capita consumed by a typical resident of India. As we slid from an American culture based on community into one based on consumerism, we turned this nation from a rich garden into a giant mall.

Although feel-good evangelists for a consumer culture preach that there's enough for everybody, the fact is that if every human on earth adopted the lifestyle of a poverty-level American, we would need the natural resources of at least four earths to sustain that level of consumption. We turned the poor of the world into our slaves: Peasants in China work for $1 a day so that we can buy cheap jeans, faux Tiffany lamps, and inexpensive area rugs. We didn't end slavery; we simply exported it.

This wasn't lost on the rest of the world. Planetwide, people watching American television began to demand the standard of living they saw on *Beverly Hills 90210* and *Baywatch,* a standard of living their governments could never deliver because the planet simply doesn't have the resources for 6 billion people to live that way.

Some of the world's poor believed in the American Dream that if they worked hard and long enough in sweatshops, they could lift themselves out of poverty. A few did reach a local version of the middle-class life in countries such as Korea and Thailand. But when labor became expensive in those places because of this upward mobility, post-GATT multinational corporations simply moved their factories from one nation to another, leaving economic and environmental disasters in their wakes.*

As a result, the developing world began to revolt. From Chiapas, Mexico, to Nicaragua to Indonesia to the Congo, people rebelled against governments aligned with multinational corporate interests that used the people of these countries as cheap labor to supply America's stores. From the outback of Australia to the tribal lands of North America, indigenous people protested the strip-mining and the destruction of their environments to provide cheap metals for a throwaway American culture. From the rain forests of Borneo to the jungles of Colombia to the forests of California, local residents protested with increasing noise and violence the theft of their trees to feed the junk mail avalanche and the furniture fads of Americans, Japanese, and western Europeans.

Throughout the 1980s and 1990s, the more loudly people protested, the more repressive governments became. Intelligence agencies

---

*The Clinton administration's ratification of the North American Free Trade Agreement (NAFTA) and the General Agreement on Tariffs and Trade (GATT) (as well as numerous other "trade agreements" since then) made it possible to shift manufacturing and production jobs from the United States to the developing world. The American situation is mirrored throughout the world, as industrialized nations lose manufacturing jobs and developing countries become spotted with sweatshops like a child with measles. Humans require passports and visas to travel from nation to nation, but corporations can now move anywhere with virtually no restrictions.

were omnipresent, and America trained the armies of the developing world's governments in the subtle and coarse arts of brainwashing and torture, the tools for which were provided by multinational weapons companies. By the year 2000, the world's food supplies were so poisoned that Inuit people were told not to eat seal blubber, their traditional delicacy, because of dioxins; fishermen from California to Michigan to Georgia were warned about mercury contamination of seafood; and red-tide algal, bacterial, and viral contamination was wiping out shellfish and coral around the planet.

Then things got really bad in the first two decades of the twenty-first century.

We Americans first realized that change was necessary when poor countries began to withhold their oil from us. Some, such as Myanmar (Burma), were down to just two- or three-year oil reserves. They couldn't pump cheap oil to sell to us any longer even if they wanted to. We could no longer just send in the Marines to protect our "vital national interest" in $1-per-gallon gasoline; we had to change the way we lived.

But we were facing this problem in the twenty-first century—the age of the automobile and the airplane. The shock of skyrocketing gasoline prices came first, and it toppled our stock markets, collapsing a worldwide economic house of cards. But we had to recover: there were simply too many humans on the planet to ignore.

It took from the time of the earliest fossils of fully modern humans, 200,000 years ago, until the year 1800 for us to produce the first 1 billion members of the species *Homo sapiens*. That 200,000-year-long feat was then repeated in only 130 years, as we hit a population of 2 billion in 1930. Our population grew to 3 billion in only 30 years (1960). We added the fourth billion in 14 years (1974), the fifth billion in 13 years (1987), and the sixth billion in 12 years (1999).

By the year 2000, humans outnumbered rats as the most numerous mammalian species on earth and had gone from consuming about 3 percent of the planet's total resources and 5 percent of its fresh water in 1800 (when there were 1 billion of us) to more than 50 percent of each. This left all other plants and animals to fight among themselves for the remaining half of the planet's resources, and they didn't do it particularly well: in the year 2000, species were becoming extinct at a rate of more than 120 a day.

We entered what Richard Leaky called the Sixth Extinction about the same time that the climate became violently unstable and butterflies nearly vanished from North America. Droughts and floods swept the land; tornadoes, frosts, and killer heatwaves occurred in places that had never seen them before; insect and rodent populations exploded in some areas, and wildlife and forests died off on a massive scale in others. We realized that not only was plant and animal life on the planet in crisis but, for the first time in history, so was human life.

At first we told ourselves that this was a predictable result of human nature. We believed that we were created defective, accursed sinners and that it was human nature to murder, ignore the environment, and stockpile personal wealth while ignoring other people's poverty. We thought that this was how it had always been, and we even guessed that it was because of a stupid mistake a woman had made millennia ago—a deal with a snake that justified 6,000 years of the oppression of women worldwide.

And then we noticed that there were other peoples who were not this way. We'd always called them "primitive" and "stupid" because we found it easy to kill them, to steal their lands, and to take their people as slaves. Our technological superiority was, in our minds, the proof of our cultural superiority. Some of us had even organized groups to evangelize them and convert them to our way of living because we were so certain that we represented the pinnacle of human evolution.

But they lived sustainably. Their populations were stable. Many didn't even have words for war in their vocabularies, and genocide was a totally alien concept to them. They didn't build prisons, and withholding health care or food from people was unthinkable. Their children didn't commit suicide.

What we found when we boiled it down was that our ways of acting and living were not as destructive to the world's ecosystems and our own future as our way of *thinking* was. Our behavior over the long term always derives from our beliefs, and the toxic beliefs we held in our culture—that people are inherently evil, that humans are meant to live hierarchically, that women are responsible for the "fall" of humankind, that happiness comes from having more toys, that nature is something different and separate from us, and that God or divinity or spirit is distant and is to be put in a box or a building and visited only once a week—are what brought us to the brink of destruction. Even our initial attempted solutions were grounded in the belief that the world is a machine and that we need only find the right levers: salvation through action.

So, the difficult reality of the end of the era of cheap oil and fabulous American wealth in the midst of a poverty-struck world caused us, in the first decades of the twenty-first century, to begin systematically reinventing our culture by changing our core assumptions about what is real and true and meaningful.

At first it seemed impossible; the bad news was that it is exceedingly difficult for a culture to change its foundational beliefs. But we made it happen. The good news was that we'd already made several very radical belief-shifts in just the previous few generations (resulting in the enfranchisement of women, the abolition of slavery, and the outlawing of segregation) and that we didn't need to invent new stories from scratch—we only needed to borrow them from the older cultures that still inhabited our planet.

The voluntary simplicity movement had already gained a number of adherents by 2000, but by 2020, eight years after the Crash, it was a national way of life. Americans awakened from their drugged stupor and disconnected their cable TVs, preferring only local news and programming. It became fashionable to wear clothes until they were threadbare, to live in smaller and simpler houses, and to use things until they were totally worn out. *New* meant "to replace something that is no longer useable" instead of "to make you happy just because of the novelty"; it ceased to be a useful word for advertising. People recycled not because it was fashionable or even because it was mandated; there just weren't very many disposable things around anymore. Folks saved jars and string and wire, and they handed down or passed around clothes their children had outgrown. A way of life that had once seemed quite normal but then was derided by the corporate-driven consumerism religion of the late twentieth century, returned. It fit Americans comfortably, like an old shoe.

As we reconnected with family, community, nature, and spirit, we discovered the deepest meanings of life in ways that were often startling to those who had been raised on a diet of shock television, dysfunctional schools, and violent movies. Those who believed that the fastest route to happiness was to go shopping discovered the shallowness of their previous lives and the richness of family, friends, and personal communication. In the late twentieth century, only those who worked with the dying and heard their final regrets knew that at the ends of their lives people never wished they had bought more things or worked more hours. By the mid-twenty-first century, it was common knowledge that true happiness and a meaningful day-to-day life come through creative work, gentle play, and connection with others.

Out of this new way of life, we naturally began to take better care of our environment, to live more lightly on the earth, and to reverse the toxic slide that seemed so irreversible during the Era of the Corporate Kings.

Can you imagine this new America? Will you help us build it?

I know you can.

From *Imagine: What America Could Be in the 21st Century,*
ed. Marianne Williamson, © 2001, published by NAL Trade.

PART VI

America the Corporatocracy

F
EW MODERN WRITERS HAVE DOCUMENTED THE CORPORATE
stranglehold on our lives more convincingly than Thom Hartmann. From the debacle of our privatized health care system in "Medicine for Health, Not for Profit," to the takeover of our natural resources
in "Privatizing the Commons," to the ruthlessly predatory worldview
in "Sociopathic Paychecks," Hartmann shows how corporate powers
have seized control of most of the details of our daily lives, down to the
air we breathe and the water we drink. Corporate-funded think tanks
and corporate lobbyists have twisted and perverted our democracy.
Corporations influence our elections by giving millions of dollars to
political candidates (a practice, Hartmann points out, that used to be
called bribery). At a time when we have the highest unemployment in
decades and safety net programs are struggling, corporate profits in
the third quarter of 2010 were $1.6 trillion, the highest on record.

How did we get here? How did American corporations insinu-
ate themselves into the US Constitution and claim for themselves the
rights of human beings? Curious, Hartmann visited the old Vermont
State Supreme Court law library and dug up an original copy of the
court proceedings from the 1886 US Supreme Court case, *Santa Clara
County v. Southern Pacific Railroad Company.* He discovered that
"corporate personhood"—the concept that a corporation has all the
rights of a person under the Constitution—was based on a mistaken
interpretation of a corrupt court reporter's notes in the case. "It was
like running down a detective mystery," he said. "That was when the

foundations for corporate power were laid in the United States, and they were laid on the basis of a lie."

While this erroneous notion has done immeasurable damage to our country, we face an even greater threat from the *Citizens United* decision, as Hartmann writes in "Wal-Mart Is *Not* a Person." This 2010 Supreme Court ruling asserted that because corporations are people, they have First Amendment rights to free speech and may spend unlimited money supporting the politicians and the ballot initiatives of their choice. The consequences, Hartmann writes, will be "the complete transformation of this country from a democracy into a corporate plutocracy."

He also investigated "The True Story of the Boston Tea Party," overturning centuries-old misconceptions and discovering that "that incident in Boston Harbor" was actually a revolutionary protest over a corporate tax break. "It was a real shock to me to discover that the event that kicked over the first domino leading directly to the American Revolution was a direct-action protest against multinational corporate power," he said. By going back to the beginnings of our nation, Hartmann shows how corporate personhood is incompatible with democracy. Thomas Jefferson and the other Founders were acutely aware of the dangers of unlimited corporate power and worked hard to ensure that a small group of affluent people would never dominate the United States.

Despite grave setbacks, it's not too late to protect our public institutions and our commons. There is a growing movement to rescind corporate personhood and amend the Constitution to say that only humans are living people, relegating corporations to their rightful place—as nonliving, nonbreathing entities.* Many communities have passed resolutions saying they will not recognize corporations as persons. We can all join this movement and work to abolish the corporate

---

*Community Environmental Legal Defense Fund (www.celdf.org); Reclaim Democracy (www.reclaimdemocracy.org); Move to Amend (www.moveto amend.org).

takeover of our politics and our culture. When you envision a world in which mega-corporations can pollute our air and water with impunity, cut down our forests, dodge taxes, control our media, buy and sell our elected officials, break laws at will, and even kill people without being held accountable, you begin to see that bringing an end to what Hartmann calls "the cancer of corporate personhood" is truly a life-or-death matter. "Rescinding corporate personhood is the first step toward a larger vision of reclaiming and reinvigorating democracy around the world," he writes.

It's always been Hartmann's deepest aspiration that his audience do more than just passively listen or read—that they become active, awakened, agents of change. That's why he wraps up each episode of his radio show with the slogan "Activism begins with you, democracy begins with you, get out there, get active! Tag, you're it!" Many listeners proudly share stories on Hartmann's blog of how they've become involved in local politics or grassroots organizing after listening to his radio program and becoming informed. In book after book, in articles and talks, on television and radio, Thom Hartmann constantly underscores the fact that a better, more sustainable, more equitable world begins with *you*. No special skills are required; just being a citizen of the United States gives you instant membership and a potent voice in our democracy. The rest is up to you. "Tag, you're it!"

The True Story of the Boston Tea Party

Adapted from Unequal Protection: How Corporations Became "People"—and How You Can Fight Back

O
N A COLD NOVEMBER EVENING, ACTIVISTS GATHERED IN A COASTAL town. The corporation had gone too far, and the 2,000 people who'd jammed into the meeting hall were torn as to what to do about it. Unemployment was exploding, and the economic crisis was deepening; corporate crime, governmental corruption spawned by corporate cash, and an ethos of greed were blamed. "Why do we wait?" demanded one at the meeting, a fisherman named George Hewes. "The more we delay, the more strength is acquired" by the company and its puppets in the government. "Now is the time to prove our courage," he said. Soon the moment came when the crowd decided for direct action and rushed into the streets.

That is how I tell the story of the Boston Tea Party, now that I have read a first-person account of it. While striving to understand my nation's struggles against corporations, I came upon a first edition of *A Retrospect of the Boston Tea-Party with a Memoir of George R. T. Hewes, a Survivor of the Little Band of Patriots Who Drowned the Tea in Boston Harbour in 1773*,[1] and I jumped at the chance to buy it. Because the identities of the Boston Tea Party participants were hidden (other than Samuel Adams) and all were sworn to secrecy for the next 50 years, this volume (published 61 years later) is the only first-person account of the event by a participant that exists, so far as I can find. As I read I began to understand the true causes of the American Revolution.

I learned that the Boston Tea Party resembled in many ways the growing modern-day protests against transnational corporations and

266

the small-town efforts to protect themselves from chain-store retailers and factory farms. The Boston Tea Party's participants thought of themselves as protesters against the actions of the multinational East India Company.

Although schoolchildren are usually taught that the American Revolution was a rebellion against "taxation without representation," akin to modern-day conservative taxpayer revolts, in fact what led to the revolution was rage against a transnational corporation that, by the 1760s, dominated trade from China to India to the Caribbean and controlled nearly all commerce to and from North America, with subsidies and special dispensation from the British Crown.

Hewes notes: "The [East India] Company received permission to transport tea, free of all duty, from Great Britain to America," enabling it to wipe out New England–based tea wholesalers and mom-and-pop stores and take over the tea business in all of America. "Hence," he told his biographer, "it was no longer the small vessels of private merchants, who went to vend tea for their own account in the ports of the colonies, but, on the contrary, ships of an enormous burthen, that transported immense quantities of this commodity . . . The colonies were now arrived at the decisive moment when they must cast the dye, and determine their course . . ."

A pamphlet called *The Alarm* was circulated through the colonies and signed by the enigmatic "Rusticus." One issue made clear the feelings of colonial Americans about England's largest transnational corporation and its behavior around the world:

> Their Conduct in Asia, for some Years past, has given simple Proof, how little they regard the Laws of Nations, the Rights, Liberties, or Lives of Men. They have levied War, excited Rebellions, dethroned lawful Princes, and sacrificed Millions for the Sake of Gain. The Revenues of Mighty Kingdoms have entered their Coffers. And these not being sufficient to glut their Avarice, they have, by the most unparalleled Barbarities, Extortions, and Monopolies, stripped the miserable Inhabitants of their Property, and reduced whole Provinces to Indigence and Ruin. Fifteen hundred Thousands, it is said, perished by Famine in one Year, not because the Earth denied its Fruits; but

[because] this Company and their Servants engulfed all the Neces-
saries of Life, and set them at so high a Rate that the poor could not
purchase them.

After protesters had turned back the company's ships in Phila-
delphia and New York, Hewes writes, "In Boston the general voice
declared the time was come to face the storm."

The citizens of the colonies were preparing to throw off one of the
corporations that for almost 200 years had determined nearly every
aspect of their lives through its economic and political power. They
were planning to destroy the goods of the world's largest multinational
corporation, intimidate its employees, and face down the guns of the
government that supported it.

The Queen's Corporation

The East India Company's influence had always been pervasive in the
colonies. Indeed it was not the Puritans but the East India Company
that founded America. The Puritans traveled to America on ships
owned by the East India Company, which had already established the
first colony in North America, at Jamestown, in the company-owned
Commonwealth of Virginia, stretching from the Atlantic Ocean to the
Mississippi. The commonwealth was named after the "virgin queen,"
Elizabeth I, who had chartered the corporation.

Elizabeth was trying to make England a player in the new global
trade sparked by the European "discovery" of the Americas. The wealth
that Spain began extracting from the New World caught the attention
of the European powers. In many European countries, particularly
Holland and France, consortiums were put together to finance ships to
sail the seas. In 1580 Queen Elizabeth became the largest shareholder
in the *Golden Hind,* a ship owned by Sir Francis Drake.

The investment worked out well for Queen Elizabeth. There's no
record of exactly how much she made when Drake paid her share of
the *Hind*'s dividends, but it was undoubtedly vast, since Drake himself
and the other minor shareholders all received a 5,000 percent return
on their investment. Plus, because the queen placed a maximum loss

to the initial investors of their investment amount only, it was a low-risk investment (low-risk for the investors at least; creditors, such as suppliers of provisions for the voyages or wood for the ships, and employees, for example, would be left unpaid if the venture failed, just as in a modern-day corporation). She was endorsing an investment model that led to the modern limited-liability corporation.

After making a fortune on Drake's expeditions, Elizabeth started looking for a more permanent arrangement. She authorized a group of 218 London merchants and noblemen to form a corporation. The East India Company was born on December 31, 1600.

By the 1760s the East India Company's power had grown massively and globally. This rapid expansion, however, was a mixed blessing, as the company went deep in debt trying to keep ahead of the Dutch trading companies; by 1770 it found itself nearly bankrupt.

The company turned to a strategy that multinational corporations follow to this day: they lobbied for laws that would make it easy for them to put their small-business competitors out of business.

Most of the members of the British government and royalty (including the king) were stockholders in the East India Company, so it was easy to get laws passed in its interests. Among the company's biggest and most vexing problems were American colonial entrepreneurs, who ran their own small ships to bring tea and other goods directly into America without routing them through Britain or through the company. Between 1681 and 1773, a series of laws were passed, granting the company a monopoly on tea sold in the American colonies and exempting it from tea taxes. Thus the company was able to lower its tea prices to undercut those of the local importers and the small teahouses in every town in America. But the colonists were unappreciative of their colonies being used as a profit center for the multinational corporation.

Boston's Million-Dollar Tea Party

And so, Hewes says, on a cold November evening in 1773, the first of the East India Company's ships of tax-free tea arrived in Boston

Harbor. The next morning a pamphlet was widely circulated, calling on patriots to meet at Faneuil Hall to discuss resistance to the East India Company and its tea. "Things thus appeared to be hastening to a disastrous issue," wrote Hewes. "The people of the country arrived in great numbers, the inhabitants of the town assembled. This assembly, on the 16th of December 1773, was the most numerous ever known, there being more than 2,000 from the country present."

The group called for a vote on whether to oppose the landing of the tea. The vote was unanimously affirmative, and it is related by one historian of that scene "that a person disguised after the manner of the Indians, who was in the gallery, shouted at this juncture, the cry of war; and that the meeting dissolved in the twinkling of an eye, and the multitude rushed in a mass to Griffin's wharf."

That night Hewes, blackening his face with coal dust, dressed as an Indian and joined crowds of other men in hacking apart the chests of tea and throwing them into the harbor. In all, the 342 chests of tea—more than 90,000 pounds—thrown overboard that night were enough to make 24 million cups of tea and were valued by the East India Company at 9,659 Pounds Sterling or, in today's currency, just over $1 million.

In response the British Parliament immediately passed the Boston Port Act of 1774, stating that the port of Boston would be closed until its citizens reimbursed the East India Company for the tea they had destroyed. The colonists refused. A year and a half later, the colonists would again state their defiance of the East India Company and Great Britain by taking on British troops in an armed conflict at Lexington and Concord (the "shots heard 'round the world") on April 19, 1775.

That war—finally triggered by a transnational corporation and its government patrons trying to deny American colonists a fair and competitive local marketplace—would end with independence for the colonies.

The revolutionaries had put the East India Company in its place with the Boston Tea Party, and that, they thought, was the end of that.

Unfortunately, the Boston Tea Party was not the end of that. It was only the beginning of corporate power in America.

The Birth of the Corporate "Person"

Fast-forward 225 years.

The American war over the power of corporations is heating up again. A current struggle centers on the question of whether corporations should be "people" in the eyes of the law.

In October 2002, Nike appealed a lawsuit against it to the US Supreme Court, asking the Court to rule that Nike's letters to newspapers about the treatment of its workers in Indonesia and Vietnam are protected by the First Amendment.

In Pennsylvania several townships recently passed laws banning corporate-owned farms. In response, agribusiness corporations threatened to sue the townships for violation of their civil rights—just as if these corporations were persons.

Imagine. In today's America, when a new human is born, the child is instantly protected by the full weight and power of the US Constitution and the Bill of Rights. Similarly, when papers called articles of incorporation are submitted to governments in America (and most other nations of the world), another type of new "person" is brought forth into the nation.

The new corporate person is instantly endowed with many of the rights and the protections of personhood. It doesn't breathe or eat, can't be enslaved, can live forever, doesn't fear prison, and can't be executed if found guilty of misdoings. It is not a human but a creation of humans. Nonetheless, the new corporation gets many of the constitutional protections America's Founders gave humans to protect them against governments or other potential oppressors. How did corporations become persons?

After the Revolutionary War, Thomas Jefferson proposed a Bill of Rights with 12 amendments, one of which would "ban commercial monopolies," forever making it illegal for corporations to own other corporations and to do business in more than one specific product or market. This legislation would forever prevent another oppressive commercial juggernaut like the East India Company from arising again in North America to threaten democracy and oppress the people.

But Jefferson's amendment failed, and the corporations fought back. Now those corporations use the club of the amendments that did pass to influence elections and legislation favoring them—in the name of their rights as persons.

A Historic Goof?

What most people don't realize is that this is a recent agreement—and it is based on a historic error. Only since 1886 have the Bill of Rights and the Fourteenth Amendment been applied explicitly to corporations. For 100 years people have believed that the 1886 case *Santa Clara County v. Southern Pacific Railroad Company* included the statement *Corporations are persons.* But looking at the actual case documents, I found that this was never stated by the Court, and indeed the chief justice explicitly ruled that matter out of consideration in the case.

The claim that corporations are persons was added by the court reporter, who wrote the introduction to the decision, called a "headnote." Headnotes have no legal standing.

It appears that corporations acquired personhood by persuading a court reporter and a Supreme Court judge to make a notation in the headnote of an unrelated law case. In *Everyman's Constitution* legal historian Howard Jay Graham documents scores of previous attempts by Supreme Court Justice Stephen J. Field to influence the legal process to the benefit of his open patrons, the railroad corporations.[2] Field, as judge on the Ninth Circuit in California, had repeatedly ruled that corporations were persons under the Fourteenth Amendment, so it doesn't take much imagination to guess what Field might have suggested court reporter J. C. Bancroft Davis include in the transcript, perhaps even offering the language, which happened to match his own language in previous lower-court cases.

Alternatively, Davis may have acted on his own initiative. This was no ordinary court reporter. He was well connected to the levers of power in his world, which in 1880s America were principally the railroads, and he himself had served as president of the board of a railroad company.

Regardless of how it happened, an amendment to the Constitution, designed to protect the rights of African Americans after the Civil War, passed by Congress, voted on and ratified by the states, and signed into law by the president, was reinterpreted in 1886 for the benefit of corporations. The notion that corporations are persons has never been voted into law by the people or by Congress, and all the court decisions endorsing it derive from the precedent of the 1886 case—from Davis's error.

Other legal errors have been corrected with time. The notions that women aren't persons under the law (affirmed, for example, in the 1873 *Bradwell v. Illinois* case) and that blacks aren't entitled to equal protection (decided in the *Dred Scott v. Sanford* and *Plessy v. Ferguson* cases) were superseded by court cases affirming the full rights of women and African Americans under the law. The establishment of corporate personhood, on the flimsy foundation of a court reporter's insertion of a phrase into a legal summary, may be the next mistake to be corrected, particularly if grassroots efforts continue to challenge the legitimacy of corporate personhood.

Adapted from *Unequal Protection: How Corporations Became "People"—and How You Can Fight Back* by Thom Hartmann, © 2010, published by Berrett-Koehler.

Wal-Mart Is *Not* a Person

From *Rebooting the American Dream: 11 Ways to Rebuild Our Country*

> The peculiar evil of silencing the expression of an opinion is that it is robbing the human race; posterity as well as the existing generation; those who dissent from the opinion, still more than those who hold it. If the opinion is right, they are deprived of the opportunity of exchanging error for truth: if wrong, they lose, what is almost as great a benefit, the clearer perception and livelier impression of truth, produced by its collision with error.
>
> —JOHN STUART MILL

IN 2003, AFTER MY BOOK *UNEQUAL PROTECTION* WAS FIRST PUB-lished, I gave a talk at one of the larger law schools in Vermont. Around 300 people showed up, mostly students, with a few dozen faculty and some local lawyers. I started by asking, "Please raise your hand if you know that in 1886, in the *Santa Clara County v. Southern Pacific Railroad Company* case, the Supreme Court ruled that corporations are persons and therefore entitled to rights under the Constitution and the Bill of Rights."

Almost everyone in the room raised their hand, and the few who didn't probably were new enough to the law that they hadn't gotten to study that case yet. Nobody questioned the basic premise of the statement.

And all of them were wrong.

We the People are the first three words of the Preamble to the Constitution; and from its adoption until the Robber Baron Era in the late nineteenth century, *people* meant human beings. In the 1886 *Santa Clara* case, however, the court reporter of the Supreme Court proclaimed in a "headnote"—a summary or statement added at the top of the court decision, which is separate from the decision and has no legal force whatsoever—that the word *person* in law and, particularly, in the Constitution, meant both humans *and* corporations.

Thus began in a big way (it actually started a half century earlier in a much smaller way with a case involving Dartmouth University) the corruption of American democracy and the shift, over the 125 years since then, to our modern corporate oligarchy.

Most recently, in a January 2010 ruling in *Citizens United v. Federal Election Commission,* the Supreme Court, under Chief Justice John G. Roberts, took the radical step of overturning more than a hundred years of laws passed by elected legislatures and signed by elected presidents and declared that not only are corporations "persons" but that they have constitutional rights such as the First Amendment right to free speech.

This decision is clear evidence of how far we have drifted away as a nation from our foundational principles and values. Particularly since the presidency of Ronald Reagan, over the past three decades our country and its democratic ideals have been hijacked by what Joseph Pulitzer a hundred years ago famously called "predatory plutocracy."

The *Citizens United* decision, which empowers and elevates corporations above citizens, is not just a symbolic but a *real* threat to our democracy, and only the will of We the People, exercised through a constitutional amendment to deny personhood to corporations, can slay the dragon the Court has unleashed.

The "Disadvantaged" Corporation

In 2008 a right-wing group named *Citizens United* put together a 90-minute "documentary," a flat-out hit-job on Hillary Clinton (then a senator and presidential aspirant) and wanted to run commercials promoting it on TV stations in strategic states. The Federal Election Commission (FEC) ruled that the movie and the television advertisements promoting it were really "campaign ads" and stopped them from airing because they violated McCain-Feingold (aka the Bipartisan Campaign Reform Act of 2002), which bars "independent expenditures" by corporations, unions, or other organizations 30 days before a primary election or 60 days before a general election. (Direct corporate contributions to campaigns of candidates have been banned repeatedly and in various ways since 1907, when Theodore Roosevelt pushed through the Tillman Act, which made it a felony for a corporation to give money to a politician for federal office; in 1947 the Taft-Hartley Act extended this ban to unions.)

McCain-Feingold was a good bipartisan achievement by conservative senator John McCain and liberal senator Russ Feingold to limit the ability of corporations to interfere around the edges of campaigns. The law required the "I'm John McCain and I approve this message" disclaimer and limited the amount of money that could be spent on any federal politician's behalf in campaign advertising. It also limited the ability of multimillionaires to finance their own elections.

But the law offended the members of the economic elite in this country who call themselves "conservatives" and believe that they should be able to spend vast amounts of money to influence electoral and legislative outcomes.

The Conservative Worldview

In part, this belief is derived from a more fundamental—and insidious—belief that political power in the hands of average working people is dangerous and destabilizing to America; this is the source of the antipathy of such conservatives to both democracy and labor unions. They believe in "original sin"—that we're all essentially evil and corruptible—and therefore it's necessary for a noble, well-educated, and wealthy (male) elite, working behind the scenes, to make the rules for and run our society.

Among the chief proponents of this Bible-based view of the errancy of average working people are the five right-wing members of the current US Supreme Court—John Roberts, Samuel Alito, Clarence Thomas, Antonin Scalia, and Anthony Kennedy—who have consistently worked to make America more hierarchical, only with a small, wealthy "conservative/corporate" elite in charge instead of a divinely ordained Pope.

And even though the *Citizens United* case—which landed in the Supreme Court's lap after the federal court in Washington, DC, ruled in favor of the FEC ban—was only about a small slice of the McCain-Feingold law, the Republican Five used it as an opportunity to make a monumental change to constitutionally empower corporations and undo a century of legal precedents.

After listening to oral arguments in early 2009, the Roberts Court chose to ignore those arguments and the originally narrow pleadings in the case, expanded the scope of the case, and scheduled hearings for September of that year, asking that the breadth of the arguments include reexamining the rationales for Congress to have *any* power to regulate corporate "free speech."

In this they were going along with a request from Theodore B. "Ted" Olson, the solicitor general under George W. Bush, and would now go back to reexamine and perhaps overturn the Court's own precedent in the *Austin v. Michigan Chamber of Commerce* case of 1990. In that case the Court held that it was constitutional for Congress to place limits on corporate political activities; and in a 2003 case, the Court (before the additions of Alito and Roberts) had already upheld McCain-Feingold as constitutional.[1]

Thus, on January 21, 2010, in a 5-to-4 decision, the Supreme Court ruled in the *Citizens United* case that it is unconstitutional for Congress to approve, or the president to sign into law, most restrictions on the "right" of a corporate "person" to heavily influence political campaigns so long as they don't directly donate to the politicians' campaign or party.

The majority decision, written by Justice Kennedy at the direction of Chief Justice Roberts, explicitly states that the government has virtually no right to limit corporate power when it comes to corporate "free speech."[2]

Kennedy began this line of reasoning by positing, "Premised on mistrust of governmental power, the First Amendment stands against attempts to disfavor certain subjects or viewpoints."

It sounds reasonable. He even noted, sounding almost like Martin Luther King Jr. or John F. Kennedy, that:

> By taking the right to speak from some and giving it to others, the Government deprives the disadvantaged person or class of the right to use speech to strive to establish worth, standing, and respect for the speaker's voice. The Government may not by these means deprive the public of the right and privilege to determine for itself what speech and speakers are worthy of consideration.

But who is that "disadvantaged person or class" of whom Kennedy was speaking? His answer is quite blunt (the parts in single quotation marks are where he is quoting from previous Supreme Court decisions): "The Court has recognized that First Amendment protection extends to corporations. . . . Under that rationale of these precedents, political speech does not lose First Amendment protection 'simply because its source is a corporation.'"

Two sentences later he nails it home: "The Court has thus rejected the argument that political speech of corporations or other associations should be treated differently under the First Amendment simply because such associations are not 'natural persons.'" (Historically, *natural persons* has been the term for humans under both British common law and American constitutional law; corporations, churches, and governments are referred to as *artificial persons*.)

Bemoaning how badly corporations and their trade associations (like the US Chamber of Commerce, the nation's leading front-group player in both national and local politics for decades and the number one lobbyist in terms of spending) had been treated by the Congress of the United States for more than a hundred years, Kennedy stuck up for the "disadvantaged" corporate "persons" the Roberts Court was seeking to protect:

> The censorship we now confront is vast in its reach. The Government has "muffled the voices that best represent the most significant segments of the economy." And "the electorate has been deprived of information, knowledge, and opinion vital to its function." By suppressing the speech of manifold corporations, both for-profit and

non-profit, the Government prevents their voices and viewpoints from reaching the public and advising voters on which persons or entities are hostile to their interests.

By reinterpreting the Fourteenth Amendment, which says that no "person" (the amendment's authors didn't add the word *natural* because it was written to free the slaves after the Civil War, so they figured *person* was sufficient) shall be denied equal protection under the law, the Roberts Court turned American democracy inside out. "We the People" now explicitly means "We the Citizens, Corporations, and Churches" with a few of the richest humans who run them thrown in.

Such a view is antithetical to how the Framers of our Constitution viewed corporations.

A Historical Perspective

The Founders of this nation were so wary of corporate power that when the British Parliament voted to give a massive tax break—through the Tea Act of 1773—to the East India Company on thousands of tons of tea it had in stock so that the company could wipe out its small, entrepreneurial colonial competitors, the colonists staged the Boston Tea Party.

This act of vandalism against the world's largest transnational corporation, destroying more than a million dollars' worth (in today's money) of corporate property, led the British to pass the Boston Port Act of 1774, which declared the Port of Boston closed to commerce until the city paid back the East India Company for its spoiled tea. It was an economic embargo like we declared against Cuba, Iraq, and Iran, and it led the colonists straight into open rebellion and the Revolutionary War.

Thus the Framers of our Constitution intentionally chose to not even use the word *corporation* in that document, as they wanted business entities and churches to be legally established at the state level, where local governments could keep an eye on them.

Throughout most of the first 100 years of our nation, corporations were severely restricted so that they could not gain too much power or wealth. It was illegal for a corporation to buy or own stock in another corporation, to engage in more than one type of business, to participate in politics, and to even exist for more than 40 years (so that the corporate form couldn't be used by wealthy and powerful families to amass great wealth in an intergenerational way and avoid paying an estate tax).

All of that came to an end during the "chartermongering" era of the 1890s when, after Ohio prepared to charge John D. Rockefeller with antitrust and other violations of the corporate laws of that state, he challenged other states to broaden and loosen their laws regarding corporate charters. A competition broke out among, primarily, Connecticut, New Jersey, New York, and Delaware, which Delaware ultimately won by enacting laws that were the most corporate-friendly in the nation. This is the reason why today more than half of the NYSE-listed companies are Delaware corporations.

In addition, the largest corporations of the era—the railroads—began a relentless campaign in the 1870s that reached its zenith in 1886, claiming that as "corporate persons" they should have "rights" under the Bill of Rights in the Constitution. That zenith was the *Santa Clara County v. Southern Pacific Railroad Company* case, where the Supreme Court did *not* rule that corporations are persons, but the court reporter claimed it had, establishing language that was cited repeatedly in subsequent Court decisions ratifying this newly found "corporate personhood" doctrine and cementing it into law.

A Patriotic Dissent

When the Republican Five on the Supreme Court ruled in the *Citizens United* case and handed to corporations nearly full human rights of free speech, it didn't come out of the blue. Although no bill in Congress from the time of George Washington to Barack Obama had declared that corporations should have these "human rights" (to the contrary, multiple laws had said the opposite), and no president had ever spoken in favor of corporate human rights, the five men in the majority on the Supreme Court took it upon themselves to hand our country over to the tender mercies of the world's largest transnational corporations.

The Court's Minority Pushes Back

This didn't sit well with the other four members of the Supreme Court.

Justice John Paul Stevens, with the concurrence of Justices Ruth Bader Ginsburg, Stephen Breyer, and Sonia Sotomayor, wrote the dissenting opinion in the *Citizens United* case.

Calling the decision "misguided" in the first paragraph of the 90-page dissent, Stevens (and his colleagues) pointed out that the Court majority had just effectively handed our country over to any foreign interest willing to incorporate here and spend money on political TV ads.

> If taken seriously, our colleagues' assumption that the identity of a speaker has no relevance to the Government's ability to regulate political speech would lead to some remarkable conclusions. Such an assumption would have accorded the propaganda broadcasts to our troops by "Tokyo Rose" during World War II the same protection as speech by Allied commanders. More pertinently, it would appear to afford the same protection to multinational corporations controlled by foreigners as to individual Americans: To do otherwise, after all, could "'enhance the relative voice'" of some (i.e., humans) over others (i.e., corporations).

In the same paragraph, Stevens further points out the absurdity of granting corporations what are essentially citizenship rights under the Constitution, suggesting that perhaps the next Court decision will be to give corporations the right to vote: "Under the majority's view, I suppose it may be a First Amendment problem that corporations are not permitted to vote, given that voting is, among other things, a form of speech."

Quoting earlier Supreme Court cases and the Founders, Stevens wrote: "The word 'soulless' constantly recurs in debates over corporations . . . Corporations, it was feared, could concentrate the worst urges of whole groups of men." Thomas Jefferson famously fretted that corporations would subvert the republic.

And, Stevens reasoned, the Founders could not have possibly meant to confer First Amendment rights on corporations when they adopted the Constitution in 1787 and proposed the Bill of Rights in 1789 because, "All general business corporation statutes appear to date from well after 1800":

> The Framers thus took it as a given that corporations could be comprehensively regulated in the service of the public welfare. Unlike our colleagues, they had little trouble distinguishing corporations from human beings, and when they constitutionalized the right to free speech in the First Amendment, it was the free speech of individual Americans they had in mind.

To make his point, Stevens even quoted Chief Justice John Marshall, who served from his appointment by President John Adams in 1800 until 1835, making him one of America's longest-serving chief justices. Sometimes referred to as the "father of the Supreme Court," Marshall had written in an early-nineteenth-century decision some text Stevens quoted in his *Citizen's United* dissent: "A corporation is an artificial being, invisible, intangible, and existing only in contemplation of law. Being a mere creature of law, it possesses only those properties which the charter of its creation confers upon it."

Stevens's dissent called out Roberts, Alito, Scalia, Thomas, and Kennedy for their behavior in the *Citizen's United* ruling, which he said was "the height of recklessness to dismiss Congress' years of bipartisan deliberation and its reasoned judgment . . .":

> The fact that corporations are different from human beings might seem to need no elaboration, except that the majority opinion almost completely elides it. . . . Unlike natural persons, corporations have "limited liability" for their owners and managers, "perpetual life," separation of ownership and control, "and favorable treatment of the accumulation of assets . . . that enhance their ability to attract capital and to deploy their resources in ways that maximize the return

on their shareholders' investments." Unlike voters in US elections, corporations may be foreign controlled.

Noting that "they inescapably structure the life of every citizen," Stevens continued:

> It might be added that corporations have no consciences, no beliefs, no feelings, no thoughts, no desires. Corporations help structure and facilitate the activities of human beings, to be sure, and their "personhood" often serves as a useful legal fiction. But they are not themselves members of "We the People" by whom and for whom our Constitution was established.

In this very eloquent and pointed dissent, Stevens even waxed philosophical, asking a series of questions for which there couldn't possibly be any clear or obvious answers if the Court were to maintain the "logic" of its *Citizens United* ruling:

> It is an interesting question "who" is even speaking when a business corporation places an advertisement that endorses or attacks a particular candidate. Presumably it is not the customers or employees, who typically have no say in such matters. It cannot realistically be said to be the shareholders, who tend to be far removed from the day-to-day decisions of the firm and whose political preferences may be opaque to management. Perhaps the officers or directors of the corporation have the best claim to be the ones speaking, except their fiduciary duties generally prohibit them from using corporate funds for personal ends. Some individuals associated with the corporation must make the decision to place the ad, but the idea that these individuals are thereby fostering their self-expression or cultivating their critical faculties is fanciful.

The dissenting justices argued that the majority's ruling wasn't merely wrong, both in a contemporary and a historical sense, but that it was *dangerous*. The dissent was explicit, clear, and shocking in how bluntly the three most senior members of the Court (along with the newbie, Sotomayor) called out their colleagues, two of whom (Roberts and Alito) had been just recently appointed by George W. Bush.

The dissenters noted that it was their five colleagues (and their friends in high places) who were clamoring for corporations to have personhood and free-speech rights, *not* the American people who were the "listeners" of such speech: "It is only certain Members of this Court, not the listeners themselves, who have agitated for more corporate electioneering."

They continued, noting that corporate interests are inherently different from the public (and human) interests:*

> [The] *Austin* [Supreme Court decision that upheld McCain/Feingold in 2003] recognized that there are substantial reasons why a legislature might conclude that unregulated general treasury expenditures will give corporations "unfair influence" in the electoral process, and distort public debate in ways that undermine rather than advance the interests of listeners. The legal structure of corporations allows them to amass and deploy financial resources on a scale few natural persons can match. The structure of a business corporation, furthermore, draws a line between the corporation's economic interests and the political preferences of the individuals associated with the corporation; the corporation must engage the electoral process with the aim "to enhance the profitability of the company, no matter how persuasive the arguments for a broader or conflicting set of priorities."

By having free-speech rights equal with people, Stevens argued, corporations will actually harm the "competition among ideas" that the Framers envisioned when they wrote the First Amendment:

> "[A] corporation . . . should have as its objective the conduct of business activities with a view to enhancing corporate profit and shareholder gain." In a state election . . . the interests of nonresident corporations may be fundamentally adverse to the interests of local voters. Consequently, when corporations grab up the prime

---

*Again, the words in quotation marks are where, in the dissent, the justices themselves are quoting from previous Supreme Court rulings. I've removed all the reference citations, as they make it hard to read; anybody wanting to dive deeper into this 90-page dissent can read it online at www.supremecourt.gov/opinions/09pdf/08-205.pdf.

broadcasting slots on the eve of an election, they can flood the market with advocacy that bears little or no correlation to the ideas of natural persons or to any broader notion of the public good. The opinions of real people may be marginalized.

Moreover, just the fact that corporations can participate on an unlimited basis as actors in the political process will, inevitably, cause average working Americans—the 99 percent who make less than $300,000 per year—to conclude that their "democracy" is now rigged.

The result will be that more and more people will simply stop participating in politics (it's interesting to note how many politicians announced within weeks of this decision that they would not run for reelection), stop being informed about politics, and stop voting. Our democracy will wither and could even die.

> When citizens turn on their televisions and radios before an election and hear only corporate electioneering, they may lose faith in their capacity, as citizens, to influence public policy. A Government captured by corporate interests, they may come to believe, will be neither responsive to their needs nor willing to give their views a fair hearing.
>
> The predictable result is cynicism and disenchantment: an increased perception that large spenders "call the tune" and a reduced "willingness of voters to take part in democratic governance."

And even if humans were willing to try to take on corporations (maybe a billionaire or two with good ethics would run for office?), virtually every single person who tries to run for office will have to dance to the corporate tune or risk being totally destroyed by the huge and now-unlimited amounts of cash that corporations can rain down on our heads.

> The majority's unwillingness to distinguish between corporations and humans similarly blinds it to the possibility that corporations' "war chests" and their special "advantages" in the legal realm may translate into special advantages in the market for legislation.

Scalia Is Offended

Horrified by the blunt language of the dissent and of being called "misguided," "dangerous," and "reckless" by his colleagues, Justice Scalia wrote a short concurring opinion in an attempt to once more speak up for the "disadvantaged" corporations:

> Despite the corporation-hating quotations the dissent has dredged up, it is far from clear that by the end of the 18th century corporations were despised. If so, how came there to be so many of them?
> . . . Indeed, to exclude or impede corporate speech is to muzzle the principal agents of the modern free economy. We should celebrate rather than condemn the addition of this [corporate] speech to the public debate.

Justice Roberts offered his own short concurring opinion, in self-defense, saying that for "our democracy" to work, the voices in the public arena shouldn't just be a human on a soapbox but *must* include massive transnational corporations:

> First Amendment rights could be confined to individuals, subverting the vibrant public discourse that is at the foundation of our democracy.

> The Court properly rejects that theory, and I join its opinion in full. The First Amendment protects more than just the individual on a soapbox and the lonely pamphleteer.

In other words, if a single corporation spends $700 million in television advertising to tell you that, for example, Senator Bernie Sanders is a "bad person" because he sponsored legislation that limits its profitability, and Sanders can raise only $3 million to defend himself with a few local TV spots, that's just the reality of "the vibrant public discourse that is at the foundation of our democracy."

The Decision and the Damage Done

There is no better evidence of the harm that the *Citizens United* decision poses to our democracy than to see the immediate reaction from the corporations—or, more accurately, the persons who run the corporations.

Two weeks after the decision, a headline in the *New York Times* said: "In a Message to Democrats, Wall St. Sends Cash to G.O.P." The article quoted banking industry sources (who now knew that they could use their considerable financial power politically) as saying that they were experiencing "buyer's remorse" over having given Obama and the Democrats $89 million in 2008: "Republicans are rushing to capitalize on what they call Wall Street's 'buyer's remorse' with the Democrats. And industry executives and lobbyists are warning Democrats that if Mr. Obama keeps attacking Wall Street 'fat cats,' they may fight back by withholding their cash."[3]

The article quoted several banking sources as saying they were outraged that the president had criticized their industry for the financial meltdown of 2008 or their big bonuses. It wrapped up with a quote from John Cornyn, the senator from Texas tasked with raising money for the National Republican Senatorial Committee, noting that he was now making regular visits to Wall Street in New York City. Speaking of the Democrats who dared challenge the banksters, he crowed: "I just don't know how long you can expect people to contribute money to a political party whose main plank of their platform is to punish you."

It was a loud shot across Obama's bow, and within two weeks the president had changed his tune on a wide variety of initiatives, ranging from taxes on the wealthy to backing away from truly strong regulations on the banking, insurance, and pharmaceutical industries and instead embracing more-cosmetic "reforms."

The fact is that about $5 billion was spent in *all* the political campaigns from coast to coast in the elections of 2008, a bit less than $2 billion of that on the presidential race. Compare that with January 2010, when a small cadre of senior executives and employees of the nation's top banks on Wall Street split up among themselves more than $145 billion in *personal bonus* money.

If those few thousand people had decided to take just 3 percent of their bonus and redirect it into a political campaign, no politician in

America could stand against them. And now none do. And that's just the banksters! Profits in the tens and hundreds of billions of dollars were reported in 2009 by the oil, pharmaceutical, insurance, agriculture, and retailing industries—all now considering how to use a small part of their profits to influence political races.

While WellPoint's Anthem Blue Cross division was raising insurance rates in California by up to 36 percent, the company declared a quarterly profit of well over $2 billion. And the six largest oil companies were making more than $1 billion dollars in *profits* per week. Even the smallest coalition, funneling their money through the US Chamber of Commerce, now has the ability to promote or destroy any politician.

There are now no limits to what corporations (or rich individuals using a corporation as a front) can spend to influence elections or ballot measures. Every member of Congress will now know before he or she votes in favor of any legislation that is opposed by a particular industry, or votes against a bill that is favored by that industry, that it will have consequences come reelection time.

Anyone concerned with the integrity of the political system should note that this decision affects the legitimacy of elections not only of the legislative and executive branches but also of judges. As Bill Moyers and Michael Winship wrote in the *Huffington Post* in February 2010,[4]

> Ninety-eight percent of all the lawsuits in this country take place in the state courts. In 39 states, judges have to run for election—that's more than 80 percent of the state judges in America.

> The *Citizens United* decision made those judges who are elected even more susceptible to the corrupting influence of cash, for many of their decisions in civil cases directly affect corporate America, and a significant amount of the money judges raise for their campaigns comes from lobbyists and lawyers.

Those inclined to underestimate the influence of cash on judicial elections should be reminded of some basic facts that Moyers and Winship provided:

During the 1990s, candidates for high court judgeships in states around the country and the parties that supported them raised $85 million . . . for their campaigns. Since the year 2000, the numbers have more than doubled to over $200 million.

The nine justices currently serving on the Texas Supreme Court have raised nearly $12 million in campaign contributions. The race for a seat on the Pennsylvania Supreme Court last year was the most expensive judicial race in the country, with more than four and a half million dollars spent by the Democrats and Republicans. With the Supreme Court's *Citizens United* decision, corporate money's muscle got a big hypodermic needle full of steroids.

This decision was a naked handoff of raw political power to corporate forces by five unelected judges; and as we saw earlier, the other four members of the Court said so in the plainest and most blunt terms.

Indeed, the First Amendment now protects the "free speech" rights of the presidents of Russia and China and Iran to form corporations in the United States and pour millions of dollars toward supporting or defeating members of Congress or presidential aspirants who favor trade policies or a foreign policy that suits their interests.

This decision also protects the "right" of the largest polluting corporations on earth to politically destroy any politician who wants to give any more authority to the Environmental Protection Agency (EPA) or to elevate to elected status any politician who is willing to dismantle the EPA.

This Supreme Court decision has vested power in already-powerful corporations that they never had before: to directly affect the outcome of elections for public office and of ballot measures.

So what's to be done?

Such a radical decision requires an equally radical response that must be both far-reaching and permanent.

Move to Amend

There are only three ways to undo a bad Supreme Court decision. All three have been used at various times.

The first is to wait until the composition of the Court changes—one or more of the bad judges retires or dies and is replaced by others more competent. (It's worth noting that even former Justice Sandra Day O'Connor, a Ronald Reagan appointee and longtime Republican activist, condemned the *Citizens United* ruling.) Then the Court takes on a case that involves the same issues and, like with *Brown v. Board of Education* and *Roe v. Wade,* pushes the Court forward in time.

The second is for the American people, the president, and Congress to understand the horror of the consequences of such a decision and break with the Court.

Arguably, this happened with the *Dred Scott v. Sanford* decision in 1857, which ruled that black *persons* were actually *property* and thus led us directly into the Civil War. That Supreme Court decision led to Abraham Lincoln's Emancipation Proclamation and the passage of legislation clarifying the rights of African Americans, although it ultimately took a war and the passage of the Thirteenth, Fourteenth, and Fifteenth Amendments to purge slavery from our laws and our Constitution.

Ironically, the *Citizens United* case is the mirror of *Dred Scott* in that it ruled that a *property*—a corporation—is now a *person.*

The third way to undo—or supersede—a Supreme Court decision is to amend the Constitution itself so that the Court can no longer play with the semantics of ambiguous or broadly worded language. We did this, for example, to both institute and then repeal the prohibition, manufacture, and sale of alcohol.

The constitutional amendment route seems the most practical and long lasting, even though it may be the most challenging.

More than 29,000 amendments to our Constitution have been put forth in Congress since the founding of our republic, and only 27 have passed the hurdle of approval by two-thirds of the members of Congress and three-fourths of the states. Nonetheless, successful amendments are driven by a widespread sense that the change is absolutely essential for the good of the nation.

An example of this is the Twenty-Sixth Amendment to drop the voting age from 21 to 18. It was largely brought about by the rage and the impotence that young people felt in America during the Vietnam War era. The need for young people to participate in a political process that could lead them to war was so clear that the Twenty-Sixth Amendment passed the Senate in March 1971 and was completely ratified by the states on July 1, 1971.

As Americans see our politicians repeatedly being corrupted by corporate influence—from health care to banking to labor standards to the environment—and the middle class continues to collapse as a result, this may well be one of those moments in time when an amendment can make it through the Congress and the states in relatively short order.

Several proposals are on the table, but I particularly recommend the models put forth by Jeff Milchen and David Cobb. Milchen, who founded ReclaimDemocracy.org, is one of the leading resources on the issue of corporate personhood; and Cobb's website, www.MoveTo Amend.org, incorporates Jeff's proposed constitutional amendment as well as other options. Milchen's proposed amendment, more explicit than simply inserting the word *natural* before the word *person* in the Fourteenth Amendment, could seriously begin the process of returning the United States to a democratic republic that is once again responsive and responsible to its citizens instead of its most powerful corporations. The proposed amendment reads as follows:

Section 1. The US Constitution protects only the rights of living human beings.

Section 2. Corporations and other institutions granted the privilege to exist shall be subordinate to any and all laws enacted by citizens and their elected governments.

Section 3. Corporations and other for-profit institutions are prohibited from attempting to influence the outcome of elections, legislation or government policy through the use of aggregate resources or by rewarding or repaying employees or directors to exert such influence.

Section 4. Congress shall have power to implement this article by appropriate legislation.

The elegance of explicitly denying constitutional rights to anything except "living human beings" is that it will not only roll back _Citizens United_ but also allow future legislatures to challenge corporate claims to "rights" of privacy (Fourth Amendment), protection from self-incrimination (Fifth Amendment), and the power to force themselves on communities that don't want them because to do otherwise is "discrimination" (Fourteenth Amendment).

We must be very careful that any amendment put forth isn't just limited to giving Congress the power to regulate campaign spending; to do so would leave a wide swath of other Bill of Rights powers in the hands of corporations. Instead, an amendment must explicitly overturn the headnote to the 1886 _Santa Clara_ decision that asserted that corporations are the same as natural persons in terms of constitutional protections.

By doing this we can begin the transition back from a corporate oligarchic state to the constitutionally limited representative democratic republic our Founders envisioned.

From _Rebooting the American Dream: 11 Ways to Rebuild Our Country_
by Thom Hartmann, © 2010, published by Berrett-Koehler.

Medicine for Health, Not for Profit

From *Screwed: The Undeclared War against the Middle Class*

Andy Stephenson was an activist, a vigilant worker on behalf of clean voting in America. He worked tirelessly to help uncover details of electronic voting fraud in the 2000, 2002, and 2004 elections. He devoted years of his life to making America a more democratic nation.

But in 2005 his friends had to pass the hat to help pay for surgery to save him from pancreatic cancer. The surgery cost about $50,000, but the hospital wanted $25,000 upfront, and Andy was uninsured.

We are the only developed democracy in the world where such a spectacle could take place.

Dickens wrote about such horrors in Victorian England—Bob Cratchit's son, Tiny Tim, in need of medical care that was unavailable without a wealthy patron like Ebenezer Scrooge—but the United Kingdom has since awakened and become civilized.

Even the tyrants of communist China provide health care to their people, a bitter irony for the unemployed American factory workers they've displaced and for the poorly insured Wal-Mart workers who sell their goods.

Through some serious online fundraising, we pulled together enough money to pay for Andy's surgery. Unfortunately, the delays in raising that much money meant that his cancer had advanced to the point where it killed him soon after the surgery. Andy Stephenson's story is something that could happen only in an oligarchic banana republic—or in the USA.

Rights versus Privileges

To understand what happened to Andy, we first have to look at the big picture. Is health care a right or a privilege? If it's a right, it's part of the commons. By being born into a society, you are entitled to health care. If it's a privilege, it makes sense that only the rich have full access to it and that poor and uninsured working people may die from lack of coverage.

If you go back over the thousands of years of human history, you will discover that health care has always been considered a right. The village shaman was always available. People helped each other.

In this country, in the Golden Age of the middle class—from 1940 to 1980—most states had laws requiring that hospitals be nonprofit organizations and take in anybody who showed up on their doorstep. Most states had laws that required health insurance companies to be nonprofit. Blue Cross and Blue Shield, for example, began as nonprofit companies.

The thinking behind this was that we don't want someone making a profit off our health care—we want them making decisions based on what's best for our health.

All that changed starting in the 1980s, when Reagan, followed by Bush Sr., Clinton, and Bush Jr., began defining health care as a privilege, not a right. Public hospitals started being replaced by private hospitals. Nonprofit insurance was gradually replaced by for-profit insurance— now even many of the Blue Cross/Blue Shield programs are for-profit. People like former Senate Majority Leader Bill Frist's father were able to acquire tremendous wealth—literally billions of dollars of personal riches—by privatizing the commons of health care and squeezing all the cash they could out of previously public hospitals.

Of the other 36 fully industrialized democracies in the world, every single one of them has concluded that health care is a right. The United States is the only country in which this debate, thanks to the cons, is still going on.

Private Health Care Has Failed the Middle Class

Although we now have the most expensive health-care system in the world, it has not succeeded in making the American people healthy.

- The United States ranks twenty-seventh in the world for the quality of its citizens' health.

- The United States has 45 million uninsured people.

- The United States ranks twenty-fifth in the world in life expectancy, infant mortality, and immunization rates.

Even our health insurance is often tragically deficient—about a quarter of all bankruptcies last year in this nation were among insured people who were wiped out by co-pays, deductibles, and not-covered hospital and health-care expenses. (And with the 2005 bankruptcy law, such bankruptcies will be infinitely more difficult in the future for anybody who's not a millionaire.)

The cons say there are enough protections in place to help those who fall through the gaping holes in the health-care system. That's simply not true.

Fully insured people have died because their insurance companies refused to cover their treatment, calling it "experimental." Others couldn't get care because their insurance companies claimed their illnesses were "pre-existing conditions" and thus were not covered.

Increasingly, hospitals are turning away people or moving into a for-profit status that lets them avoid the obligation to serve people who can't pay. The bottom line is that health care is rationed in the United States, as the *Wall Street Journal* noted in a front-page article by Geeta Anand titled "The Big Secret in Health Care: Rationing Is Here."[1]

The article tells the story of Lorraine Micheletti, an intensive-care unit (ICU) nurse. "As her hospital faces a cost crunch," notes Anand, "she's under pressure to get patients out of the glass-walled unit quickly."

Laying it out in unsparing tones, the *Wall Street Journal* article notes: "The word for what Ms. Micheletti does every day in this 173-bed hospital is one of the big secrets of American health care: Rationing."

The article adds: "Sometimes, rationing causes Ms. Micheletti to take on her own hospital." But, overall, rationing at Northeastern Hospital has worked out well for its owners. "In 2002, it posted a profit of $2.6 million, on an operating budget of around $85 million." Still, it's tough. "While Ms. Micheletti has worked hard to decrease the average patient stay this year, one person can throw off her numbers. 'You can eat up all of your profits if one or two patients linger in the ICU,' she says."

And it's not limited to public hospitals. "Nursing homes also ration care," notes Anand's article. "They have little incentive to take very sick patients, because in many cases they receive a fixed reimbursement rate from insurance which doesn't cover the full cost of care. As a result, nursing homes often try to limit the number of severely ill patients they take, to make sure they can cover costs."

With our largely privatized health-care system, the rich get very good health care. But if you are uninsured and you are not in a crisis—if you have an early-stage symptom, say, of cancer, that could be diagnosed and treated—and you show up at a public hospital, odds are that you will not be diagnosed and not be treated. You will be turned away.

The cons say the solution is more competition. This is nonsense. Right now hospitals compete against each other, insurance companies compete against each other, doctors compete against each other, and we all get screwed. What we need is cooperation.

When hospitals went private, they came under tremendous pressure to cut costs, and they did that by rationing and by laying off experienced nurses and replacing them with nurses' aides. Now nurses take care of eight or nine patients each. A ratio of 1 nurse to 4 patients in a medical/surgical clinic would provide better health care (and a ratio of 1:1 in the ICU). Cutting the nursing staff made a lot of money for the insurance companies and the private hospitals, made Bill Frist's father a billionaire, and made a lot of trouble for the rest of us.

When insurance companies went private, they too came under tremendous pressure to cut costs. They quickly noted that there's an easy way to do that: don't insure people who are likely to get sick. Insurance companies protect their profits by either refusing to insure people with "pre-existing conditions" or by charging them very high rates.

And they set the bar low. If you're self-employed and have tried to get private health insurance recently, you'll know that the companies send an adjustor to your house to screen you. They draw your blood and take your weight. If you weigh a few pounds over their "ideal," or they find any of your blood work a bit off, watch out—you may actually need health care, and therefore you'll pay higher rates, assuming they deign to cover you.

Meanwhile, because most of the system is private, We the People have no way to put a brake on costs. Pharmaceutical companies, for example, can charge as much as they want for their drugs because they know that cost is just passed on to the health insurance companies, who pass the cost on to us. That's why, even though Americans make up just 4 percent of the world's population, in 2004 we spent $4 trillion on health care. That's 40 percent of the money spent on health care on the entire planet for 4 percent of the world's population.

The problem isn't that American health care needs to be more competitive. The problem is that health care in America is treated as a privilege, and only the privileged have unfettered access to it.

How Much of a Right?

The solution to America's health-care problem is to join the rest of the developed world and make health care a right for all citizens. The only question then becomes: *How much of a right?*

There are two ways to deliver health care in a society that considers health care a right.

One way is to create "socialized medicine" whereby the government provides all of the health care itself, largely through facilities that it owns and doctors and nurses whom it hires as federal employees.

There may still be private hospitals or doctors for the very rich, but most of the hospitals in the country would be owned and run by the government, and the vast majority of health-care workers—from technicians to nurses to doctors—would be employees of the government. This is, by and large, the British system.

Another way is the "single-payer system," like they have in Germany. In this system the government is basically the insurance company. The very rich could still pay their own way if they wanted to be in separate high-end private hospitals (much like they fly in private jets instead of use the airlines), but most people would get their health insurance directly from the government. Hospitals and doctors would still be private—they would manage their own business and even compete with each other—but they would be paid, by and large, by the government's insurance program.

We already have both of these systems in the United States.

The Veterans Administration (VA) is socialized medicine. The US government owns all the VA hospitals and employs all the VA health-care workers. Veterans, just by showing their identification card, which proves they are veterans, can walk into any VA hospital or VA medical clinic and get care free of charge.

Our single-payer system is Medicare. Those Americans eligible for Medicare can mostly choose their own doctors and their own hospitals. They show their Medicare card to their health-care provider, who then bills the government.

Veterans tell me that they like the VA system, but there are also problems with it. When the government gets in a squeeze, it starts cutting back funding—until people get politically active. The problem is that veterans, while being a significant political group, aren't "all of us," so when they yell it's easier for politicians to ignore them than if everybody were yelling. Thus VA doctors, nurses, and other staff often feel underpaid and underequipped.

I experienced the single-payer system when I lived in Germany. What I liked most about it was that I was able to pick my doctor. I found a doctor who specialized in homeopathy as well as conventional medicine, and another one who specialized in herbology and conventional medicine. I could choose anybody anywhere, and all I had to do was show my health-care card—the equivalent of everyone's having fully funded Medicare.

The cons say that the only way to create a competitive market is privatization, but experience demonstrates that that's not true. Unregulated privatization tends to lead to monopoly because it is simply cheaper for a company to monopolize supply and then ration health care.

The best system is the one that allows We the People the most choice and still rewards diversity and innovation. The single-payer system does that by regulating the market but not regulating our choices within that market.

We Have National Health Care Already: Medicare

Ever since democratic president Harry S. Truman proposed a national, single-payer health insurance system, Republicans and "conservative" Democrats have fought it. Nonetheless, Lyndon Johnson did manage to slip a single-payer system through Congress in the form of Medicare.

Medicare terrifies the corporate cons because it has the potential—with a single stroke of legislation—to overnight become a program that covers every American, a national single-payer health insurance system.

This is one reason why Republicans inserted a poisoned pill into Medicare in 2005, creating a drug benefit but mandating that Medicare cannot negotiate wholesale prices with drug companies but must always pay full retail. The increased cost of this "benefit" will create a Medicare crisis.

The cons knew that if they allowed Medicare to negotiate for pharmaceuticals the way the Veterans Administration does, Medicare and the Americans who depend on it would benefit, rather than the system's being weakened, which was their objective. Instead of creating a benefit that would actually make health care cheaper for millions of Americans and for the government, the cons created a "benefit" that's going to destroy Medicare.

Like the proposed privatization of Social Security, it's another attempt by the cons to further dismantle the safety net—and it's not 40 years down the road but will come in this decade.

Medicare today is almost running in the red, and the "nonnegotiable" drug benefit will probably push it over that edge. Cons in the right-wing think tanks and in Congress are hoping that the upcoming Medicare crisis will provide a good excuse to then privatize it and kill it off.

We need to not only save Medicare but expand it to cover every man, woman, and child in America.

According to a study published in the *New England Journal of Medicine,* if all of America's health insurance companies, HMOs, and other middlemen were eliminated, and the government simply paid your medical costs directly to whomever you chose to provide you with health care, the savings would be so great that without increasing the health-care budget we could provide cradle-to-grave health care for every American.[2]

That's because for every $100 that passes through the hands of the government-administered Medicare programs, between $2 and $3 is spent on administration, leaving $97 to $98 to pay for medical services and drugs.

But of every $100 that flows through corporate insurance programs and HMOs, $10 to $34 sticks to corporate fingers along the way. After all, Medicare doesn't have lavish corporate headquarters, doesn't use corporate jets, and doesn't pay expensive lobbying firms in Washington to work on its behalf. It doesn't "donate" millions of dollars to politicians and their parties. It doesn't pay profits in the form of dividends to its shareholders. And it doesn't compensate its top executive with more than $1 million a year, as do each of the largest of the American insurance companies.

Medicare has one primary mandate: serve the public. Private corporations also have one primary mandate: generate profit.

There are some things that government does do better than private for-profit industry, and providing affordable health care is a classic example, proven by the experience of every other nation in the industrialized world.

From *Screwed: The Undeclared War against the Middle Class*
by Thom Hartmann, © 2006, published by Berrett-Koehler.

Privatizing the Commons

From *Unequal Protection: How Corporations Became "People"—and How You Can Fight Back*

fas-cism (fâsh'iz'em) n. A system of government that exercises a dictatorship of the extreme right, typically through the merging of state and business leadership, together with belligerent nationalism. [Ital. *fascio,* group.] -fas'cist n. -fas-cis'tic (fa-shis'tik) adj.

—*AMERICAN HERITAGE DICTIONARY* (1983)

PRIVATIZATION IS THE IDEA OF TAKING COMMONS FUNCTIONS OR resources out of the hands of elected governments responsible to their voters and handing their management or ownership over to private enterprise answerable to shareholders. Many arguments have been advanced about privatization; those in favor argue that corporations run for a profit can be more efficient than government, and those opposed usually argue that the resources of the commons should always be held in the hands of institutions that are answerable only to the people who use them—the citizens—and thus must be managed by elected and responsive governments.

Opponents of privatization of the commons also usually point out that whatever increases in efficiency a corporation may bring to a utility, the savings produced by those increases in efficiency rarely make their way to the consumer but instead are raked off the top by the corporation and distributed to shareholders. One of the more high-profile examples is Enron and its role in the privatization of electricity worldwide, with particular focus on how Enron's privatization of electricity in California worked to the detriment of California's citizens but produced millions in profits for a small group of Texas stockholders; another example is an Enron subsidiary's meetings in 1999 with Governor Jeb Bush of Florida in which it proposed to privatize and take over much of the state's water supply.[1]

Supporters of privatization point to the creative ways corporations can extract profits from things governments previously just supervised in a boring and methodical fashion. For example, an article in the *Houston Chronicle* in January 2001 titled "Enron Is Blazing New Business Trail" noted the "extraordinary year" the Houston-based company was having, with most of the company's revenues coming "from buying and selling contracts in natural gas and electricity."

The article quoted Kenneth Lay, who, the newspaper said, "has a doctorate in economics," as extolling the virtues of profiting from trading in previously regulated or government-run commodities. "The company's emphasis on trading to hedge against risk has been emulated by other firms in energy," the article said, including "Duke Energy, Dynegy, Williams Energy—and increasingly in other industries."[2]

Who Owns the World's Water?

While Enron started the discussion in Florida in 1999 about privatizing that state's water supplies and the Everglades, the process was already a done deal in Bolivia. In 1998 the Bolivian government requested a $25 million loan guarantee to refinance its water services in the community of Cochabamba. The World Bank told the Bolivian government that it would guarantee the loan only if Bolivia privatized the water supply, so it was handed over to Aguas del Tunari, a subsidiary of several large transnationals, including an American corporation that is one of the world's largest private construction companies.

The next year Aguas del Tunari, in an effort to squeeze profits out of Bolivia's water, announced that water prices were doubling. For minimum wage or unemployed Bolivians, this meant water would now take half their monthly income, costing more than food. The Bolivian government, acting on suggestions from the World Bank and Aguas del Tunari, declared all water corporate property, so even to draw water from community wells or to gather rainwater on their own properties, peasants and small farmers had to first pay for and obtain permits from the corporation.

The price of water was pegged to the US dollar to protect the corporation, and the Bolivian government announced that none of the World Bank loan could go to poor people to help with their water bills.

With more than 90 percent of the Bolivian people opposing this move, a people's rebellion rose up to deprivatize the water system. A former machinist and union activist, Oscar Olivera, built a broad-based coalition of peasants, workers, and farmers to create La Coordinadora de Defensa del Agua y de la Vida, or La Coordinadora. Hundreds of thousands of Bolivians went on a general strike, brought transportation in Cochabamba to a standstill, and evoked violent police response in defense of the Aguas del Tunari corporation's "right" to continue to control the local water supply and sell it for a profit. Victor Hugo Danza, one of the marchers, was shot through the face and killed: he was 17.

The government declared martial law, and members of La Coordinadora were arrested and beaten in the middle of an early-April night. The government seized control of the radio and television stations to prevent anti-corporate messages from being broadcast. But the uprising continued and grew.

The situation became so tense that the directors of the American corporation and Aguas del Tunari abandoned Bolivia on April 10, 2000. They took with them key files, documents, computers, and the assets of the company—leaving a legal shell with tremendous debt.

The Bolivian government handed the debts and the water company, SEMAPA, to La Coordinadora. The new company is now run by the activist group—essentially a local government itself now—and its first action was to restore water to the poorest southern neighborhoods, more than 400 communities, which had been cut off by the for-profit company because the residents didn't have the money to pay profitable rates for water. Throughout the summer of 2000, La Coordinadora held hearings through the hundreds of neighborhoods it now served.

In the meantime the American corporation moved its holding company for Aguas del Tunari from the Cayman Islands to Holland so that it could legally sue the government of Bolivia (South America's poorest country) under World Trade Organization and Bilateral Investment Treaty rules that Bolivia had signed with Holland.

On January 19, 2006, a settlement was reached between the government of Bolivia and Aguas del Tunari, and it was agreed that "the concession was terminated only because of the civil unrest and the state of emergency in Cochabamba and not because of any act done or not done by the international shareholders of Aguas del Tunari." With this statement both parties agreed to drop any financial claims against the other.[3]

Why take such extraordinary steps against such a poor country? There's more at stake than the immediate situation. If this citizens' group is successful in turning a water supply back from private to government hands, and thus improving water service and making it more egalitarian and less expensive in this poverty-stricken country, it could threaten water-privatizing plans of huge corporations around the world.

The stakes are high, even as cities across India, Africa, and other South American countries hand their local water systems to for-profit corporations. Nonetheless politicians around the world are stepping up the rate at which they're pushing for a transfer of the commons to the hands of for-profit corporations. Checking voting records and lists of corporate contributors, it's hard not to conclude that there is a relationship between this political activity and the generous contributions these corporations give to pro-privatization politicians.

"Private Equity" Can Erase a Firm's Values

In today's business environment, when corporations are run in ways that benefit the environment or their workers as much as their stockholders, they're at risk. When good salaries and pension plans are cut, it's referred to as "unnecessary fat" that can be trimmed. (Note that such cuts are made much more feasible when wages are forced down by exporting jobs from the local economy.) Similarly, behaving in a more expensive but environmentally friendly way is "not efficient."

In an article in *Yes!* magazine, economist and author David C. Korten pointed out that for many years the Pacific Lumber Company was, in many regards, a model corporate citizen. It paid good salaries, fully funded its pension fund, offered an excellent benefit package to employees, and even had an explicit no-layoffs policy during soft times in the lumber economy. Perhaps most important to local residents who weren't employed by the company, Pacific Lumber "for years pioneered the development of sustainable logging practices on its substantial holdings of ancient redwood timber stands in California."[4]

In a nation where such employee- and nature-friendly values were both valued and defended, Pacific Lumber Company would have a bright future. But in a world where profit is the prime value, and humans and ancient trees are merely excess fat, Pacific Lumber was a sitting duck.

As Korten documents in his article, a corporate raider

> gained control in a hostile takeover. He immediately doubled the cutting rate of the company's holding of thousand-year-old trees, reaming a mile-and-a-half corridor into the middle of the forest that he jeeringly named "Our wildlife-biologist study trail." He then drained $55 million from the company's $93 million pension fund and invested the remaining $38 million in annuities of the Executive Life Insurance Company—which had financed the junk bonds used to make the purchase and subsequently failed.

> The remaining redwoods were the subject of a last-ditch effort by environmentalists to save them from clear-cutting.[5]

In the end the government stepped in to save some of the old-growth forests, but the business and its employees were already screwed, and the private equity artist had already taken his cut.

Once upon a time, America had laws that corporations couldn't own other corporations. If that were still true, situations like that chronicled by Korten would become illegal rather than the norm. (And people who become multimillionaires by employing such predatory leveraged-buyout and private equity techniques, from Mitt Romney to T. Boone Pickens, would actually have to work for a living.)

The reason James Madison and Thomas Jefferson—and even Alexander Hamilton and John Adams—worried so loudly about "associations and monopolies" growing too large and powerful is that they would begin to usurp the very lives and liberties of the humans who created them. It becomes particularly problematic when companies are bought and stripped of their assets by other companies that aren't even in their industry but are simply asset hunting.

In the realm of government, the Founders kept power close to the people with the Tenth Amendment and other constitutional references to the powers of states over the federal government. A similar principle could apply to corporations.

The breakup of AT&T between 1974 and 1984 led to vigorous growth in the telecommunications industry, although that industry is once again reconsolidating in the absence of Sherman Antitrust Act enforcement.

Seizing Other Nations' Commons via Patent

Because international courts have recently held that life forms and their by-products are patentable, multinational corporations in wealthy nations have been busily patenting the living products of poorer nations.

For example, people in India have been using the oil of the neem tree as a medicine for millennia: but now more than 70 patents have been granted on the tree and its by-products in various nations. One European patent on its use as a fungicide was recently thrown out, but others stand.[6]

In similar fashion, Maggie McDonald notes in the British magazine *New Scientist* that "a botanical cure for hepatitis traditionally used in India can be patented in the US." She notes that Vandana Shiva documents how this is not a process that is driving innovation or competition, as multinationals often claim, but instead, "a survey in the US showed that 80 percent of patents are taken out to block competitors."[7]

Ironically, that same issue of *New Scientist* has a feature on recruit-ment news that extols the wonders of becoming a patent agent. In the new world of international biotechnology, the article says, "Wealth is measured not in gold mines, but in the new currency of 'intellectual property.'" Eerily echoing Shiva's claim, the very upbeat article on get-ting a job in the patent business says, "The aim is to lock away these prize assets [for your company] so they can't be plundered by com-mercial rivals."[8]

And the business of locking up these assets pays very well. Ted Blake of Britain's Chartered Institute of Patent Agents is quoted as say-ing, "You're looking at six-figure salaries for those who make it as part-ners in an agents' firm." Not only is the pay good but the work is also very chic. Reiner Osterwalder of the European Patent Office told the magazine, "Patents are no longer stuck in a dusty corner. They're sexy, and touch questions of world order."[9]

The British Broadcasting Corporation (BBC) notes that not only can plants and their uses be patented but the very genetics of the plants can be nailed down. An article about the patenting of the neem tree published in 2000 on the BBC website says, "Genes from nut-meg and camphor have also been patented with the aim of producing their oils artificially—a move which would hit producers in develop-ing countries."[10]

And it's in developing countries where the race to patent indig-enous life forms is most rapid, particularly by American-based com-panies, because US patent law doesn't recognize indigenous use of a product as "prior art," meaning once a use for a plant is "discovered" by an American company—even if that plant has been used in that way for 10,000 years by local tribes, it's considered new and thus patentable. The website www.globalissues.org notes, "In Brazil, which probably has the richest biodiversity in the world, large multinational corpora-tions have already patented more than half the known plant species."[11]

The consequences of this behavior are profitable for corpora-tions but can be devastating to the humans who find that their food or medicinal plants are now the property of a multinational corporation.

Corporations say that this is necessary to ensure profits, but the thriving herbal products industry—made up mostly of domestic plants that cannot be patented—testifies to the untruthfulness of this assertion. Selling plants may not be as profitable as selling tightly controlled and patented plants, but it can be profitable nonetheless.

This is not to say that plants should or should not be patentable. In a democracy the benefits or liabilities of corporations' patenting life forms would be discussed and decided by popular vote. Because of the *Santa Clara* "decision" and its consequences, however, corporations have exercised their "right" to get patent laws changed and exemptions established that would be difficult to impossible for an ordinary human to accomplish.

Changing Your Citizenship in a Day

For a human to change his or her citizenship from one country to another is a process that can take years, sometimes even decades, and, for most of the world's humans, it is practically impossible. Corporations, however, can change their citizenship in a day. And many do.

The New Hampshire firm Tyco International moved its legal citizenship from the United States to Bermuda and, according to a 2002 report in the *New York Times,* saved "more than $40 million last year alone" because Bermuda does not charge income tax to corporations while the United States does. Stanley Works, which manufactures in Connecticut, will avoid paying US taxes of $30 million. Ingersoll-Rand "saves" $40 million a year.[12]

Offshore tax havens figured big in the Enron debacle, as that corporation spun off almost 900 separate companies based in tax-free countries to shelter income and hide transactions. Through this device the company paid no income taxes whatsoever in four of its last five years and received $382 million in tax rebates from Uncle Sam.[13]

Generally, when a human person changes citizenship, he is also required to change his residence—he has to move to and participate in the country where he is a citizen. But Bermuda and most other tax havens have no such requirement. All you need do is be a corporate person instead of a human person, pay some fees (it cost Ingersoll-Rand $27,653), and, as Ingersoll-Rand's chief financial officer told the *New York Times,* "We just pay a service organization" to be a mail drop for the company.[14]

Similarly, if you or I were to open a post office box in Bermuda and then claim that we no longer had to pay US income taxes, we could go to jail. Corporate persons, however, keep their rights intact when they decide to change citizenship—and save a pile in taxes.

Corporations are taxed because they use public services and are therefore expected to help pay for them.

Corporations make use of a workforce educated in public schools paid for with tax dollars. They use roads and highways paid for with tax dollars. They use water, sewer, power, and communications rights-of-way paid for and maintained with taxes. They demand the same protection from fire and police departments as everybody else, and they enjoy the benefits of national sovereignty and the stability provided by the military and institutions like the North Atlantic Treaty Organization and the United Nations, the same as all residents of democratic nations.

In fact, corporations are *heavier* users of taxpayer-provided services and institutions than are average citizens. Taxes pay for our court systems—the biggest users of which are corporations, to enforce contracts. Taxes pay for the maintenance of our transportation infrastructure—our roads, bridges, and ports—used heavily by corporations to move their goods. Taxes pay for our Treasury Department and other government institutions that maintain a stable currency essential to corporate activity. Taxes pay for our regulation of corporate activity, from ensuring safety in the workplace, to a pure food and drug supply, to limiting toxic emissions.

Taxes also pay (hugely) for our military, which is far more involved in keeping shipping lanes open and trade routes safe for our corporations than protecting you and me from an invasion by Canada or Mexico (our closest neighbors, with whom we've fought wars in the past). It's very difficult to calculate because government doesn't keep track of it, but it's not hard to see that corporate use of our commons—what is funded with our taxes—is well over half of worker use.

Yet, as professor of political economics Gar Alperovitz points out, "In the Eisenhower era, corporations paid an average 25 percent of the federal tax bill; they paid only 10 percent in 2000 and [following the first Bush tax cuts only] 7 percent in 2001."[15]

One of the foundational principles of democracy is that all people are treated equally in regard to issues of the law, citizenship, and their access to the commons. As Lawrence E. Mitchell, a John Theodore Fey research professor of law at the George Washington Law School and author of *Corporate Irresponsibility: America's Newest Export,* said, "The function of corporations in light of their constitutional personhood is effectively to foreclose access to the commons for most citizens. The entire proposition that a corporation is a person is ridiculous."[16]

From *Unequal Protection: How Corporations Became "People"—and How You Can Fight Back* by Thom Hartmann, © 2010, published by Berrett-Koehler.

Sociopathic Paychecks

From *Threshold: The Crisis of Western Culture*

I know a planet where there is a certain red-faced gentleman.
He has never smelled a flower. He has never looked at a star. . . .
And all day he says over and over, just like you: "I am busy
with matters of consequence!" And that makes him swell
up with pride. But he is not a man—he is a mushroom.

—Antoine de Saint-Exupéry,
The Little Prince (1943)

Americans have long understood how socially, politically, and economically destabilizing are huge disparities in wealth. For this reason, the US military and the US civil service have built into them systems that ensure that the highest-paid federal official (including the president) will never earn more than 20 times the salary of the lowest-paid janitor or army private. Most colleges have similar programs in place, with ratios ranging from 10-to-1 to 20-to-1 between the president of the university and the guy who mows the grass. From the 1940s through the 1980s, this was also a general rule of thumb in most of corporate America; when CEOs took more than their "fair share," they were restrained by their boards so that the money could instead be used by the company for growth and to open new areas of opportunity. The robber baron J. P. Morgan himself suggested that nobody in a company should earn more than 20 times the lowest-paid employee (although he exempted stock ownership from that equation).

But during the "greed is good" era of the 1980s, something changed. CEO salaries began to explode at the same time that the behavior of multinational corporations began to change. When Reagan stopped enforcing the Sherman Antitrust Act of 1890, a mergers-and-acquisitions mania filled the air, and as big companies merged to become bigger, they shed off "redundant" parts. The result was a series of waves of layoffs, as entire communities were decimated, divorce and suicide rates exploded, and America was introduced to the specter of the armed "disgruntled employee."

Accompanying the consolidation of wealth and power of these corporations was the very clear redefinition of employment from "providing a living wage to people in the community" to "a variable expense on the profit and loss sheet." Companies that manufactured everything from clothing to television sets discovered that there was a world full of people willing to work for 50 cents an hour or less: throughout America factories closed and a building boom commenced among the "Asian Tigers" of Taiwan, South Korea, and Thailand. The process has become so complete that of the millions of American flags bought and waved after the World Trade Center disaster, most were manufactured in China. Very, very, very few things are still manufactured in America.

And it wasn't unthinking, unfeeling "corporations" that took advantage of the changes in the ways the Sherman Antitrust Act and other laws were enforced by the Reagan, Bush Sr., Clinton, and Bush Jr. administrations. It took a special type of *human* person.

In his manuscript "Toys, War, and Faith: Democracy in Jeopardy," Maj. William C. Gladish suggests that this special breed of person is actually a rare commodity and thus highly valued. He notes that corporate executives make so much money because of simple supply and demand. There are, of course, many people out there with the best education from the best schools, raised in upper-class families, who know how to play the games of status, corporate intrigue, and power. The labor pool would seem to be quite large. But, Gladish points out, "There's another and more demanding requirement to meet. They must be willing to operate in a runaway economic and financial system that demands the exploitation of humanity and the environment for short-term gain. This is a disturbing contradiction to their children's interests and their own intelligence, education, cultural appreciation, and religious beliefs.

"It's this second requirement," Gladish notes, "that drastically reduces the number of quality candidates [for corporations] to pick from. Most people in this group are not willing to forsake God, family, and humanity to further corporate interest in a predatory financial system. For the small percentage of people left, the system continues to increase salaries and benefit packages to entice the most qualified and ruthless to detach themselves from humanity and become corporate executives and their hired guns."

One of the questions often asked when the subject of CEO pay comes up is, "What could a person like William W. McGuire or Rex W. Tillerson [the CEOs of UnitedHealth and Exxon Mobil, respectively] possibly do to justify a $1.7 billion paycheck or a $400 million retirement bonus?"

It's an interesting question. If there is a "free market" of labor for CEOs, you'd think there would be a lot of competition for the jobs. And a lot of people competing for the positions would drive down the pay. All that UnitedHealth's stockholders would have to do to avoid paying more than $1 billion to McGuire is find somebody to do the same CEO job for $0.5 billion. And all they'd have to do to save even more is find somebody to do the job for a mere $100 million. Or maybe even somebody who'd work the necessary 60-hour weeks for only $1 million.

So why is executive pay so high?

I've examined this question with both my psychotherapist hat on and my amateur economist hat on, and only one rational answer presents itself: CEOs in America make as much money as they do because there really is a shortage of people with their skill set—such a serious shortage that some companies have to pay as much as $1 million per week or per day to have somebody successfully do the job.

But what part of being a CEO could be so difficult—so impossible for mere mortals—that it would mean that there are only a few hundred individuals in the United States capable of performing it?

In my humble opinion, it's the sociopath part.

CEOs of community-based businesses are typically responsive to their communities and are decent people. But the CEOs of the world's largest corporations daily make decisions that destroy the lives of many other human beings. Only about 1 to 3 percent of us are sociopaths—people who don't have normal human feelings and can easily go to sleep at night after having done horrific things. And of that 1 to 3 percent of sociopaths, there's probably only a fraction of a percent with a college education. And of that tiny fraction, there's an even tinier fraction that understands how business works, particularly within any specific industry.

Thus there is such a shortage of people who can run modern monopolistic, destructive corporations that stockholders have to pay millions to get them to work. And, being sociopaths, they gladly take the money without any thought to its social consequences.

Today's modern transnational corporate CEOs—who live in a private-jet-and-limousine world entirely apart from the rest of us—are remnants from the times of kings, queens, and lords. They reflect the dysfunctional cultural (and Calvinist/Darwinian) belief that wealth is proof of goodness and that goodness then justifies taking more of the wealth.

In the nineteenth century in the United States, entire books were written speculating about the "crime gene" associated with Irish, and later Italian, immigrants because they lived in such poor slums in the East Coast's biggest cities. It had to be something in their genes, right? It couldn't be just a matter of simple segregation and discrimination!

The obverse of this is the CEO culture and, in the larger world, the idea that the ultimate CEO—the president of the world's super-power—should shove democracy or anything else down the throats of people around the world at the barrel of a gun.

Democracy in the workplace is known as a union. The most democratic (i.e., "unionized") workplaces are the least exploitative because labor has a power to balance capital and management. And looking around the world, we can clearly see that those cultures that most embrace the largest number of their people in an egalitarian and democratic way (in and out of the workplace) are the ones that have the highest quality of life. Those that are the most despotic, from the workplace to the government, are those with the poorest quality of life.

Thus a repudiation of the sociopathic corporate norms that led to a business culture that is cancerous to our planet is a vital first step toward reinventing our culture in a way that is healthy and sustainable.

From *Threshold: The Crisis of Western Culture* by Thom Hartmann, © 2009, published by Viking Penguin, a division of Penguin Group (USA) Inc.

Acknowledgments

Tai Moses is one of the most brilliant, insightful, thought-ful, and talented writers and editors I've ever had the pleasure to work with. Thank you, Tai, for turning about a million words of my jumble into a coherent and readable whole!

Johanna Vondeling, who had the idea for this book, is equally incredible—I've never before so mourned the loss of an editor/publisher as when she moved to Australia.

And Neal Maillet of Berrett-Koehler has done an absolutely wonderful job of shepherding this book along from concept to completion. It's been our first time working together, and I'm so impressed by his ability to "get things done," as they say in the Dale Carnegie course.

Many thanks and much gratitude to a couple of real pros—Gary Palmatier and Elizabeth von Radics of Ideas to Images—for the book's design and copyediting.

And thanks so much to Louise Hartmann, who has been first-draft editor, idea-bouncer, inspiration, and nudge for *all* of these books and who has been my best friend, wisest adviser, and beloved wife for well over three decades.

Notes

PART I: WE THE PEOPLE

The Story of Carl

1. *Business Week,* April 21, 2003. *Business Week,* April 18, 2005. US Bureau of the Census, H-6 Table, 2004.

2. "Controversy Continues over Outsourcing Report: Commerce Department 'Disses' Congressional Democrats," *Manufacturing and Technology News,* January 19, 2006; and "Jobs Picture: Payrolls Up Moderately, but Slack Persists Despite Low Unemployment," Economic Policy Institute, September 2, 2005, http://www.epi.org/publications/entry/web features_econindicators_jobspict_20050902/.

3. Kathy Chu, "For More Companies, 401(k) Becomes Automatic: Employers Freeze Pensions, Push Saving onto Workers," *USA Today,* January 10, 2006.

4. Editorial, "The Pension Deep Freeze," *New York Times,* January 14, 2006.

5. Allstate, October 4, 2005.

6. L. Conradt and T. J. Roper, "Group Decision-Making in Animals," *Nature* 421 (January 9, 2003): 155–58.

7. James Randerson, "Democracy Beats Despotism in the Animal World," *New Scientist,* January 8, 2003.

8. Paul Craig Roberts, "The True State of the Union: More Deception from the Bush White House," *Counterpunch,* February 1, 2006, http://lists.fahamu.org/pipermail/debate-list/2006-February/000048.html.

9. Gary Wolfram, "Econ 101: How Do Tax Cuts Work?" January 11, 2006, http://www.mrc.org/bmi/commentary/2006/Econ__How_do_Tax_Cuts_Work_.html.

10. Ravi Batra lays this out brilliantly in his book *The Greenspan Fraud* (New York: Palgrave Macmillan, 2005).

11. US Census as reported in The Century Foundation report, "New American Economy: A Rising Tide That Lifts Only Yachts," http://tcf.org/publications/2008/7/pb467.

Democracy Is Inevitable

1. Per Ahlmark, "How Democracy Prevents Civic Catastrophes," address to European Parliament, April 8, 1999.

2. http://www.hawaii.edu/powerkills/DP.CLOCK.HTM.

3. R. J. Rummel, *Death by Government* (Somerset, NJ: Transaction, 1997).

4. Mark Palmer, *Breaking the Real Axis of Evil: How to Oust the World's Last Dictators by 2025* (New York: Rowman & Littlefield, 2005).

5. http://www.freedomhouse.org.

An Informed and Educated Electorate

1. "Ted Koppel Assesses the Media Landscape," BBC World News, April 12, 2010, http://news.bbc.co.uk/2/hi/programmes/world_news_america/8616838.stm.

2. "Studio," Museum of Broadcast Communications, http://www.museum.tv/eotvsection.php?entrycode=studio.

3. Yochai Benkler, "Ending the Internet's Trench Warfare," *New York Times*, March 20, 2010, http://www.nytimes.com/2010/03/21/opinion/21Benkler.html.

4. Wallace Turner, "Gov. Reagan Proposes Cutback in U. of California Appropriation; Would Impose Tuition Charge on Students from State; Kerr Weighs New Post," *New York Times*, January 7, 1967, cited in Gary K. Clabaugh, "The Educational Legacy of Ronald Reagan," NewFoundations.com, January 24, 2009, http://www.newfoundations.com/Clabaugh/CuttingEdge/Reagan.html.

5. Steven V. Roberts, "Ronald Reagan Is Giving 'Em Heck, *New York Times*, October 25, 1970, cited in Clabaugh, "Educational Legacy" (see note 4).

6. Richard C. Paddock, "Less to Bank On at State Universities," *Los Angeles Times*, October 7, 2007, http://articles.latimes.com/2007/oct/07/local/me-newcompact7.

7. Gary K. Clabaugh, "The Educational Legacy of Ronald Reagan," NewFoundations.com, January 24, 2009, http://www.newfoundations.com/Clabaugh/CuttingEdge/Reagan.html.

8. James C. Carter, *The University of Virginia: Jefferson Its Father, and His Political Philosophy: An Address Delivered upon the Occasion of the Dedication of the New Buildings of the University, June 14, 1898* (Ann Arbor: University of Michigan Library, 1898).

9. Thomas Jefferson, *The Writings of Thomas Jefferson: Containing His Autobiography, Notes on Virginia, Parliamentary Manual, Official Papers, Messages and Addresses, and Other Writings, Official and Private,* eds. Andrew A. Lipscomb and Albert Ellery Bergh (Washington, DC: Thomas Jefferson Memorial Association, 1905), http://www.constitution.org/tj/jeff 02.txt.

PART II: BRAINSTORMS

The Edison Gene

1. "Hail to the Hyperactive Hunter," *Time,* July 18, 1994, http://www.time.com/time/magazine/article/0,9171,981099,00.html.

2. Razib Khan, "People, Not Pots, in Africa," *Discover,* August 29, 2010, http://blogs.discovermagazine.com/gnxp/2010/08/people-not-pots-in-africa.

3. John F. Shelley-Tremblay and Lee A. Rosen, "Attention Deficit Disorder: An Evolutionary Perspective," *Journal of Genetic Psychology* 157, no. 4 (1996): 443–53.

4. Peter S. Jensen, David Mrazek, Penelope K. Knapp, et al., "Evolution and Revolution in Child Psychiatry: ADHD as a Disorder of Adaptation," *Journal of the American Academy of Child and Adolescent Psychiatry* 36, no. 12 (1997): 1672–81.

5. Ibid.

6. J. M. Swanson, P. Flodman, J. Kennedy, et al., "Dopamine Genes and ADHD," *Neuroscience and Biobehavioral Reviews* 24, no. 1 (2000): 21–25.

7. Yuan-Chun Ding, Han-Chang Chi, Deborah L. Grady, et al., "Evidence of Positive Selection Acting at the Human Dopamine Receptor D4 Gene Locus," *Proceedings of the National Academy of Science* 99, no. 1 (2002): 309–14.

Framing

1. To give conservatives their due, they try to make a case that gun ownership lowers crime. Yet all the statistics they can marshal are indirect and may have other causes. For a good example, see this paper defending gun ownership by the very highly regarded conservative think tank the Cato Institute: David

Kopel, "Trust the People: The Case Against Gun Control," July 11, 1988, http://www.cato.org/pubs/pas/pa109.html.

2. "Youth Violence and Firearm Statistics," http://www.athealth.com/Consumer/issues/gunviolencestats.html.

3. Coalition for Gun Control, "More Guns = More Death," http://www.gun control.ca/English/Home/Facts/moregunsmoredeathsJan2011.pdf.

4. United for a Fair Economy, "New Poll Finds Americans Support Estate Tax 2 to 1: National Petition Shows Growing Support for Tax among Farmers, Businesspeople," August 31, 2005, http://faireconomy.org/press_room/2005/new_poll_finds_americans_support_estate_tax_2_to_1.

5. United for a Fair Economy, Estate Tax Campaign, http://faireconomy.org/news/estate_tax_campaign.

6. "Most Americans Support Some Form of an Estate Tax, Poll Finds," April 18, 2006; http://foundationcenter.org/pnd/news/story_print.jhtml;jsessionid=MHSCTVOIMV0AHLAQBQ4CGXD5AAAACI2F?id=140100009.

7. Luntz, Maslansky Strategic Research, "Iowa/New Hampshire Democrats Talk Inheritance Taxes," February 16, 2006, http://www.policyandtaxationgroup.com/pdf/LuntzSchoenNH-IAFeb06%20.pdf.

Walking the Blues Away

1. Emmy E. Werner and Ruth S. Smith, *Vulnerable but Invincible: A Longitudinal Study of Resilient Children and Youth* (New York: McGraw-Hill, 1982).

2. Charles Darwin, *The Descent of Man* (Princeton, NJ: Princeton University Press: 1871, 1981), 166.

3. Thomas Jefferson, *The Writings of Thomas Jefferson: Containing His Autobiography, Notes on Virginia, Parliamentary Manual, Official Papers, Messages and Addresses, and Other Writings, Official and Private,* eds. Andrew A. Lipscomb and Albert Ellery Bergh (Washington, DC: Thomas Jefferson Memorial Association, 1905), *Notes on Virginia,* 1784–85.

4. See note 2.

5. Daniel Quinn, *Ishmael* and *My Ishmael* (New York: Bantam Books, 1995 and 1998).

6. Peter Farb, *Man's Rise to Civilization, as Shown by the Indians of North America from Primeval Times to the Coming of the Industrial State* (New York: Avon Books, 1976).

PART III: VISIONS AND VISIONARIES

Life in a Tipi

1. This early interest later led me to study wild plant taxonomy at Wayne State University, and then to get CH, MH, and PhD degrees from Emerson College, Dominion Herbal College, and Brantridge Forest School (UK) in herbal and homeopathic medicine. In the mid-1970s, I started the Michigan Healing Arts Center, and in the 1980s I studied and practiced acupuncture in the world's largest acupuncture teaching hospital in Beijing, China.

How to Raise a Fully Human Child

1. Joseph Chilton Pearce, *The Biology of Transcendence: A Blueprint of the Human Spirit* (Rochester, VT: Park Street Press, 2002).

2. Allan N. Schore, *Affect Regulation and the Origin of the Self* (Hillsdale, NJ: Lawrence Erlbaum, 1999).

3. Walter J. Ong, *Orality and Literacy: The Technologizing of the Word* (London: Methuen, 1982).

4. Robert K. Logan, *The Alphabet Effect: The Impact of the Phonetic Alphabet on the Development of Western Civilization* (New York: St. Martin's Press, 1986).

5. Leonard Shlain, *The Alphabet versus the Goddess: The Conflict between Word and Image* (New York: Viking, 1998).

6. Erik Erikson, *The Erik Erikson Reader,* ed. Robert Coles (New York: W. W. Norton, 2000).

7. See note 2.

Starting Salem in New Hampshire

1. J. Tevere MacFadyen, "The Miracle of a 'Normal' Home," *Country Journal,* December 1981, http://www.thomhartmann.com/articles/2007/11/miracle-normal-home.

2. Robert Frost, "The Death of the Hired Man," lines 122–23, http://www.bartleby.com/118/3.html.

Younger-Culture Drugs of Control

1. Sigmund Freud, *Civilization and Its Discontents* (London: Penguin, 1941, 2010).

2. Theodore Roszak, *The Voice of the Earth: An Exploration of Ecopsychology* (Grand Rapids, MI: Phanes Press), 2002. Theodore Roszak, *Ecopsychology: Restoring the Earth, Healing the Mind* (New York: Sierra Club Books), 1995.

3. Julian Jaynes, *The Origin of Consciousness in the Breakdown of the Bicameral Mind* (New York: Houghton Mifflin, 2000).

4. Terence McKenna, *Food of the Gods: The Search for the Original Tree of Knowledge: A Radical History of Plants, Drugs, and Human Evolution* (New York: Bantam Books, 1993).

PART IV: EARTH AND EDGES

The Atmosphere

1. Jon Bowermaster, "Global Warming Changing Inuit Lands, Lives, Arctic Expedition Shows," National Geographic News website, May 15, 2007, http://news.nationalgeographic.com/news/2007/05/070515-inuit-arctic.html.

2. John Roach, "Ice Shelf Collapses Reveal New Species, Ecosystem Changes," National Geographic News website, February 27, 2007, http://news.national geographic.com/news/2007/02/070227-polar-species.html.

3. James Hansen, Larissa Nazarenko, Reto Ruedy, et al., "Earth's Energy Imbalance: Confirmation and Implications," *Science* 308, no. 5727 (June 3, 2005): 1431–35.

4. Ibid.

5. James Hansen, Makiko Sato, Pushker Kharecha, et al., "Target Atmospheric CO_2: Where Should Humanity Aim?," *Open Atmospheric Science Journal* 2 (2008): 217–31, http://arxiv.org/abs/0804.1126.

6. Ibid.

7. Brad Knickerbocker, "Humans' Beef with Livestock: A Warmer Planet," *Christian Science Monitor,* February 20, 2007, www.csmonitor.com/2007/0220/p03s01-ussc.html.

8. Ibid.

9. Daniel D. Chiras, *Environmental Science: A Systems Approach to Sustainable Development* (Boston: Jones & Bartlett, 2006), 230.

10. Ibid.

11. "Pathology of a Diseased Civilization," based on *Canticle to the Cosmos,* documentary series produced by mathematical cosmologist Dr. Brian Swimme, http://www.anoliscircle.com/Pathology.html.

The Death of the Trees

1. Consultative Group on International Agricultural Research, *Report of the Fourth External Programme and Management Review of the International Institute of Tropical Agriculture (IITA),* March 1996, http://www.fao.org/Wairdocs/TAC/X5806E/x5806e00.htm

2. John Robbins, *Diet for a New America* (Tiburon, CA: H. J. Kramer, 1987).

3. Dirk Beveridge, "More Madness over Cow Bones in English Water Filters," Associated Press, April 8, 1998.

Cool Our Fever

1. Jim Hansen, "State of the Wild: Perspective of a Climatologist," April 10, 2007, http://www.davidkabraham.com/Gaia/Hansen%20State%20of%20the%20Wild.pdf; also in Eva Fearn, ed., *State of the Wild 2008–2009: A Global Portrait of Wildlife, Wildlands, and Oceans* (Washington, DC: Island Press, 2008), 27.

2. Jad Mouawad and Andrew C. Revkin, "Saudis Seek Payments for Any Drop in Oil Revenues," *New York Times,* October 13, 2009, http://www.nytimes.com/2009/10/14/business/energy-environment/14oil.html.

3. Wallace S. Broecker, "CO_2 Arithmetic," *Science* 315 (2007): 1371; and comments in *Science* 316 (2007): 829; and Oliver Morton, "Is This What It Takes to Save the World?" *Nature* 447 (2007): 132.

4. Millennium Ecosystem Assessment, *Living Beyond Our Means: Natural Assets and Human Well-Being, Statement from the Board,* March 2005, 5; and Jonathan A. Foley et al., "Global Consequences of Land Use," *Science* 309 (2005): 570.

5. James Lovelock, *Gaia: A New Look at Life on Earth,* 3rd ed. (New York: Oxford University Press, 1979, 2000).

6. http://en.wikipedia.org/wiki/Standby_power.

7. http://en.wikipedia.org/wiki/Electric_power_transmission.

8. A concise description of the 100,000 Roofs Program can be found at http://www.professionalroofing.net/closeup.aspx?id=1838.

9. Preben Maegaard, "Sensational German Renewable Energy Law and Its Innovative Tariff Principles," Folkecenter for Renewable Energy, http://www.folkecenter.dk/en/articles/EUROSUN2000-speech-PM.htm.

10. http://en.wikipedia.org/wiki/Solar_power_in_Germany.

11. "US Nuclear Energy Plants," Nuclear Energy Institute, http://www.nei.org/resourcesandstats/nuclear_statistics/usnuclearpowerplants.

12. See note 10.

13. http://en.wikipedia.org/wiki/German_Renewable_Energy_Sources_Act.

14. Mark Landler, "Germany Debates Subsidies for Solar Industry," *New York Times,* May 16, 2008, http://www.nytimes.com/2008/05/16/business/worldbusiness/16solar.html.

15. Jim Tankersley and Don Lee, "China Takes Lead in Clean-Power Investment: US Falls to No. 2 in Funding for Such Alternative Sources as Wind and Solar," *Los Angeles Times,* March 25, 2010, http://articles.latimes.com/2010/mar/25/business/la-fi-energy-china25-2010mar25.

PART V: JOURNEYS

Caral, Peru: A Thousand Years of Peace

1. Worldwatch Institute, http://www.worldwatch.org/node/4109.

PART VI: AMERICA THE CORPORATOCRACY

The True Story of the Boston Tea Party

1. *A Retrospect of the Boston Tea-Party with a Memoir of George R. T. Hewes, a Survivor of the Little Band of Patriots Who Drowned the Tea in Boston Harbour in 1773* (New York: S. S. Bliss, 1834). All subsequent quotes from Hewes are from this volume.

2. Howard Jay Graham, *Everyman's Constitution: Historical Essays on the Fourteenth Amendment, the "Conspiracy Theory," and American Constitutionalism* (Madison: State Historical Society of Wisconsin, 1968).

Wal-Mart Is Not a Person

1. Robert Barnes, "Justices to Review Campaign Finance Law Constraints," *Washington Post,* June 30, 2009, http://www.washingtonpost.com/wp-dyn/content/article/2009/06/29/AR2009062903997.html.

2. *Citizens United v. Federal Election Commission,* 558 US 08-295 (2010), http://www.supremecourt.gov/opinions/09pdf/08-205.pdf.

3. David D. Kirkpatrick, "In a Message to Democrats, Wall St. Sends Cash to G.O.P.," *New York Times,* February 7, 2010, http://www.nytimes.com/2010/02/08/us/politics/08lobby.html.

4. Bill Moyers and Michael Winship, "What Are We Bid for American Justice?" *Huffington Post,* February 19, 2010, http://www.huffingtonpost.com/bill-moyers/what-are-webid-for-ameri_b_469335.html.

Medicine for Health, Not for Profit

1. Geeta Anand, "The Big Secret in Health Care: Rationing Is Here," *Wall Street Journal,* September 12, 2003, http://health.groups.yahoo.com/group/iatrogenic/message/1070.

2. David U. Himmelstein and Steffie Woolhandler, "A National Health Program for the United States: A Physicians' Proposal," *New England Journal of Medicine* 320 (January 12, 1989): 102–8, http://www.pnhp.org/publications/NEJM1_12_89.htm.

Privatizing the Commons

1. Michael Grunwald, "How Enron Sought to Tap the Everglades," *Washington Post,* February 8, 2002.

2. James Flanigan, "Enron Is Blazing New Business Trail," *Houston Chronicle,* January 26, 2001.

3. See http://www.ratical.com/ratville/CAH/BechtelBlood.pdf and http://en.wikipedia.org/wiki/2000_Cochabamba_protests.

4. David C. Korten, "Money versus Wealth," *Yes!,* Spring 1997, http://www.ratical.org/many_worlds/cc/Korten.html.

5. Ibid.

6. Maggie McDonald, "International Piracy Rights," review of *Protect or Plunder? Understanding Intellectual Property Rights* by Vandana Shiva, *New Scientist,* January 12, 2002, 23.

7. Ibid.

8. "Patently Rewarding Work," *New Scientist,* January 12, 2002, 50.

9. Ibid, 51.

10. Karen Hoggan, "Neem Tree Patent Revoked," *BBC News,* May 11, 2000, http://news.bbc.co.uk/2/hi/science/nature/745028.stm.

11. Anup Shah, "Food Patents—Stealing Indigenous Knowledge?" (September 26, 2002), http://www.globalissues.org/article/191/food-patents-stealing-indigenous-knowledge.

12. David Cay Johnston, "US Companies File in Bermuda to Slash Tax Bills," *New York Times,* February 18, 2002, http://www.nytimes.com/2002/02/18/business/18TAX.html?pagewanted=all.

13. David Cay Johnston, "Enron's Collapse: The Havens; Enron Avoided Income Taxes in 4 of 5 Years," *New York Times,* January 17, 2002, http://www.nytimes.com/2002/01/17/business/enron-s-collapse-the-havens-enron-avoided-income-taxes-in-4-of-5-years.html?pagewanted=1.

14. See note 12.

15. Gar Alperovitz, "Tax the Plutocrats!" *The Nation* 276, no. 3 (January 27, 2003), http://www.bsos.umd.edu/gvpt/alperovitz/taxplutocrats.html.

16. Lawrence Mitchell, in a discussion with the author, February 2002.

Index

About the Author

THOM HARTMANN IS THE FOUR-TIME PROJECT CENSORED Award–winning, best-selling author of more than 20 books in print in 17 languages on five continents. He is the number one progressive radio and TV talk-show host in the United States, also carried on radio stations in Europe and Africa, syndicated by Pacifica, Dial-Global, and RT; and he has the number one program on the Free Speech TV Network. He does a three-hour daily radio show and a one-hour evening TV show.

His work has inspired several movies, including *The 11th Hour,* produced and narrated by Leonardo DiCaprio, and *I Am,* by Tom Shadyac. He has met in personal audiences with, at the invitation of, both Pope John Paul II and the Dalai Lama. He's built several successful businesses and for more than 30 years did international relief work in almost a dozen countries for the international Salem organization based in Germany.

Thom and his wife, Louise, founded a community for abused children and a school for learning-disabled children in New Hampshire. The couple now lives in Washington, DC, where Thom spends what's probably an unhealthy amount of time sitting in the Jefferson Memorial and the National Archives.

About the Editor

T AI MOSES IS THE FORMER MANAGING EDITOR OF ALTERNET.ORG, a progressive news and opinion daily. During her tenure AlterNet won two Webby Awards for Best Print and Zines and an Independent Press Award for Best Online Political Coverage. Previously, she edited alternative newsweeklies in the Monterey and San Francisco Bay Areas and was on the staff of *Esquire* magazine. Her writing has been widely published in the independent press, and she has been a panelist and a speaker on progressive media issues in the United States and abroad. She lives in Oakland, California, where she edits nonfiction books and writes the blog Aerophant.com.

Also by Thom Hartmann from Berrett-Koehler Publishers

Rebooting the American Dream
11 Ways to Rebuild Our Country

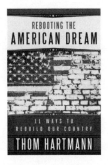

For years the Right has been tampering with one of the best political operating systems ever designed. The result has been economic and environmental disaster. Here Thom Hartmann outlines eleven common-sense proposals, deeply rooted in America's history, which will once again make America strong and all Americans—not corporations and billion-aires—prosperous. Some of these ideas are controversial, but the litmus test for each is not political correctness but whether or not it serves to revitalize this country we all love and make life better for its citizens.

Hardcover, 240 pages, ISBN 978-1-60509-706-0
Paperback, ISBN 978-1-60994-029-4
PDF ebook, ISBN 978-1-60509-909-5

Unequal Protection
How Corporations Became "People"—and How You Can Fight Back

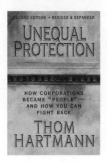

Unequal Protection tells the astonishing story of how an offhand comment by a Supreme Court justice in the mid-nineteenth century led to corporations being given the same rights as human beings. Hartmann outlines the destructive consequences and proposes specific legal remedies that will finally put an end to the bizarre farce of corporate personhood. This thoroughly updated edition features his analysis of recent landmark Supreme Court cases, including *Citizens United*.

Paperback, 384 pages, ISBN 978-1-60509-559-2
PDF ebook, ISBN 978-1-60509-560-8

BK Berrett–Koehler Publishers, Inc.
www.bkconnection.com

800.929.2929

Cracking the Code

How to Win Hearts, Change Minds, and Restore America's Original Vision

How can we connect with the millions of Americans who have bought into the right-wing line? Drawing on his background as a psychotherapist, advertising executive, and radio host, Hartmann applies what science has learned about how people actually perceive information to give you the tools you need to make the progressive message even more compelling and persuasive.

Hardcover, 240 pages, ISBN 978-1-57675-458-0
Paperback, ISBN 978-1-57675-627-0
PDF ebook, ISBN 978-1-57675-533-4

Screwed

The Undeclared War Against the Middle Class—and What We Can Do About It

Starting with Ronald Reagan and accelerating under George W. Bush, American policy makers have waged an assault on the middle class, the very foundation of American democracy, as seen by the Founding Fathers. Hartmann chronicles this assault and recommends actions people can take to restore a prosperous middle class and keep America strong.

Paperback, 264 pages, ISBN 978-1-57675-463-4
PDF ebook, ISBN 978-1-57675-529-7

BK Berrett–Koehler Publishers, Inc.
www.bkconnection.com   800.929.2929

Berrett–Koehler
Publishers

Berrett-Koehler is an independent publisher dedicated to an ambitious mission: *Creating a World That Works for All*.

We believe that to truly create a better world, action is needed at all levels—individual, organizational, and societal. At the individual level, our publications help people align their lives with their values and with their aspirations for a better world. At the organizational level, our publications promote progressive leadership and management practices, socially responsible approaches to business, and humane and effective organizations. At the societal level, our publications advance social and economic justice, shared prosperity, sustainability, and new solutions to national and global issues.

A major theme of our publications is "Opening Up New Space." Berrett-Koehler titles challenge conventional thinking, introduce new ideas, and foster positive change. Their common quest is changing the underlying beliefs, mindsets, institutions, and structures that keep generating the same cycles of problems, no matter who our leaders are or what improvement programs we adopt.

We strive to practice what we preach—to operate our publishing company in line with the ideas in our books. At the core of our approach is stewardship, which we define as a deep sense of responsibility to administer the company for the benefit of all of our "stakeholder" groups: authors, customers, employees, investors, service providers, and the communities and environment around us.

We are grateful to the thousands of readers, authors, and other friends of the company who consider themselves to be part of the "BK Community." We hope that you, too, will join us in our mission.

A BK Currents Book

This book is part of our BK Currents series. BK Currents books advance social and economic justice by exploring the critical intersections between business and society. Offering a unique combination of thoughtful analysis and progressive alternatives, BK Currents books promote positive change at the national and global levels. To find out more, visit **www.bkconnection.com**.

Berrett–Koehler
Publishers

A community dedicated to creating
a world that works for all

Visit Our Website: www.bkconnection.com

Read book excerpts, see author videos and Internet movies, read our authors'
blogs, join discussion groups, download book apps, find out about the BK
Affiliate Network, browse subject-area libraries of books, get special discounts, and more!

Subscribe to Our Free E-Newsletter, the *BK Communiqué*

Be the first to hear about new publications, special discount offers, exclusive articles, news about bestsellers, and more! Get on the list for our free
e-newsletter by going to **www.bkconnection.com**.

Get Quantity Discounts

Berrett-Koehler books are available at quantity discounts for orders of ten or
more copies. Please call us toll-free at (800) 929-2929 or email us at **bkp
.orders@aidcvt.com**.

Join the BK Community

BKcommunity.com is a virtual meeting place where people from around the
world can engage with kindred spirits to create a world that works for all.
BKcommunity.com members may create their own profiles, blog, start and
participate in forums and discussion groups, post photos and videos, answer
surveys, announce and register for upcoming events, and chat with others
online in real time. Please join the conversation!

MIX
Paper from
responsible sources
FSC® C012752